C.S. Lewis
The Art
of Enchantment

C.S. Lewis
The Art
of Enchantment

Donald E. Glover

Ohio University Press, Athens, Ohio

Library of Congress Cataloging in Publication Data

Glover, Donald E. 1933-
C.S. Lewis: the art of enchantment.

Includes bibliographical references and index.
1. Lewis, Clive Staples, 1898-1963—Criticism
and interpretation. I. Title.
PR6023. E926Z664   823'. 912   80-21421
ISBN 0-8214-0566-7
ISBN 0-8214-0609-4 pbk.

Dedicated to
ALICE, CATHY, BILL, CHRIS, & MERRI

Contents

Acknowledgments

I would like to express my gratitude to Mary Washington College for granting me study leave which permitted the time and opportunity to take my family to live in Headington near The Kilns for a year while I did the research for this book. To Father Walter Hooper, I extend special thanks for permission to work with and quote extensively from the unpublished material in the Lewis Collection housed in the Bodleian Library, Oxford University, and for his encouragement in the completion of this study.

To my family, to whom this book is dedicated, I give my heartfelt appreciation for their patience, their support, and their thoughts which have colored my view of Lewis. To my students, I extend thanks because over the years they have taught me much I could not otherwise have learned about Lewis and his works. I thank my colleagues for their support and encouragement. To Una Crist, my friend and typist, I give thanks for her assistance.

To the following publishing houses who have graciously permitted the reprinting in this book of copyrighted material, I extend thanks:

Cambridge University Press—C.S. Lewis,
> *An Experiment in Criticism*
> *Selected Literary Essays*

Wm. B. Eerdmans Publishing Co., Grand Rapids, Mich.—C.S. Lewis,
> *The Pilgrim's Regress*
> *Till We Have Faces*
> (Used by permission.)

Harcourt Brace Jovanovich, Inc., New York, N.Y.—C.S. Lewis,
> *The Dark Tower*

The Letters of C.S. Lewis, copyright 1966 by W.H. Lewis and
> Executors of C.S. Lewis. Reprinted by permission of Harcourt,
> Brace, Jovanovitch, Inc., and in England, permission granted
> by Collins Publishers.
Of Other Worlds
Surprised by Joy

Preface

Many critics have attempted to define the particular achievement of C. S. Lewis as a writer. Responses to his work have been nearly as varied as the works themselves, and critics have tended to be narrowly selective in analyzing these responses. For some critics, Lewis is a Christian writer, and the sum of his achievement rests upon his facility in phrasing the doctrine for common men. For others, Lewis is a modern allegorist whose moral preaching is nicely coated in imaginative fictions but with a central didactic motive of proselytizing. Still others see his work as the runoff of a scholarly and academic mind, drawing together myths and fables which are then retold with considerable artistic skill, mainly for the display of that learning and skill. Most often the method of critical examination is that of classification (e.g., adult fantasy, children's stories, allegory, science fiction) and then dissection.

Little attention has been given to the unity of the work except to suggest that it is basically Christian, even though surely that view subdues the medium within the message. A few critics have attempted to define the nature of Lewis's particular view of romance or his use of it as a literary technique. Interest has centered on his commitment to romantic emotion, the often mentioned "northernness" and longing which played so strong and undeniable a role in Lewis's life and in his fiction but which cannot singly be said to account for the impact of his work on modern readers. It was in anticipation of arriving at a more comprehensive answer than we have yet had to the question of why Lewis has caught the modern imagination with his fiction that I undertook this study. Although I am a Christian and thus admittedly biased in Lewis's favor, my study will, I hope, range over the broad field of meaning and craftsmanship which constitutes Lewis's particular approach to fiction.

Lewis left clear statements on his "theory" of literature. They appear in his earliest letters, his lectures and essays, in the creative work, both prose and poetry, and in his extensive *An Experiment in Criticism*. His views of the task of the artist and the function of art are neither esoteric nor purely academic. I begin by discussing these views and move on to an examination of the fiction in the light shed by Lewis's own critical theory and practice. Since the details of his life [1898–1963] are available in *Surprised by Joy* and *C. S. Lewis: A Biography*, I do not give them again, assuming that the reader can pursue them as he wishes.

I also assume that my readers are familiar with Lewis's fiction, so I do not provide plot summaries and hope the reader will find time and encouragement to read those works still unfamiliar to him. The first fourth of the book covers Lewis's approach to literature and his critical theory. The method in these two chapters is to trace Lewis's development as a reader and writer through his letters and then his lectures and essays touching on subjects like literary criticism and matters of style and content. The movement of Chapter I is chronologically through Lewis's life. The endnotes indicate the location of letters, published and unpublished, and other material directly related to this study. The remaining three fourths of the book applies that theory to Lewis's fiction in a series of sections devoted to each of the major works.

Donald E. Glover
Mary Washington College
1979

Introduction

The beginning of this book was a simple question that kept coming back to me as I read and reread the works of fiction which make up the body of C. S. Lewis's contribution to literature. Why do so many people continue to read Lewis? The answer seemed obvious and simple: they enjoyed what they found in Lewis. The books were engaging and always logical in the way they built up a story. They were just good.

I could not, as an English professor, really stop there. So I began to investigate what other readers had to say in books and articles on Lewis. What I found them saying went much deeper than my initial response. Many found Lewis an exciting writer because he was able to say religious things in an essentially nonreligious way, or, in more scholarly jargon, Lewis was a Christian allegorist and apologist. These critics saw Lewis as a Christian convert turned from his early interest in secular subjects like medieval chivalric romance and northern myth to the great subjects of Christian belief: the Incarnation, the Sacrifice, the Resurrection, and the Redemption.

I agreed wholeheartedly with this view of Lewis, but I was troubled by the feeling or suspicion that in my case at least this reasonable view of Lewis's importance did not really cover all I saw and responded to in his fiction. The further I went, the less satisfied I felt with the explanations offered by friend and foe alike. Lewis, some said, was a contemporary phenomenon, the answer to a felt need in a society where the gap between the church and the people had widened to nearly unbridgeable proportions. Others claimed him to be a cult figurehead for a small and rather elite group of academic, intellectual critics. One of his former students thought he was silly and his works juvenile. Those who admired Lewis most extravagantly were impressed by his logic and practicality, as well as his irony, wit, and creativity. Some critics found him timely; others

1

found him timeless. Lewis was a realist, an idealist, a utopian, a mythmaker, a myth-borrower.

As I went further, I found critics squabbling over whether Lewis was better on the imaginative or the informational side of his works. Few seemed to find that he made both the form and the content work in harness. Only a few critics found the books compellingly readable, as I did, offering me more meaning than that found in the explicit content. To my dismay, I began to find some of these critics, reputable critics, did not share my enthusiasm. They spoke of Lewis's metallic tone, his smugness, his carelessness.

When I went back to the classroom, where I had begun to teach Lewis's work, I encountered a different sort of response. My students are not uncritical, and over the years they have taught me not to trust all published critics or even my own cherished literary opinions too rigidly. They reinforced my original feeling that Lewis is read and reread because he is a supremely good writer of fiction. They consistently replied, when asked why they ranked *The Lion, The Witch and the Wardrobe* so high on their list of favored fantasies, that it was "one of the best." However, when we together tried to analyze what they meant, we came back to items like good plot, believable characters, fast action, and that still undefined and seemingly undefinable feeling Lewis left with them and that they returned to recapture, time after time.

This book is an attempt to define the origin of that feeling and to explain how Lewis's fiction creates such a response in his rapidly growing audience. I began by looking at what Lewis himself had to say about his own works and found that he was not as helpful as I had hoped. In his letters about his own writing, he more often than not is deprecatory or depressed when he is troubled by a problem in moving a story ahead. I had to turn back to his earliest comments about how he perceived other writers and their works before I found any material that offered clues about his attitudes or critical standards in literary matters.

I found, as I read Lewis's letters to Arthur Greeves, begun in youth and continued until Lewis's death, just the sort of material which might lay the foundation for an analysis of Lewis's theory of literature. The letters were quite explicit about what Lewis admired and disliked in his wide and sometimes unorthodox reading. Talk about style, characterization, and literary techniques formed the basis of letter after letter, stretching up to the point where Lewis himself became the author of *The Pilgrim's Regress*. There were other correspondents too, Sister Penelope and Joan Lancaster, Ruth Pitter and Katherine Farrer, to name only a few. Lewis began to show me, through his delightful and voluminous correspondence, that he had thought, analyzed, and responded to fiction from an early age and had provided a quarry for a study of this sort.

The next step was to look beyond the letters in order to find out what Lewis had to say about the subject of writing or reading fiction in his lectures and essays. Since he did not often review other writers' work in a formal way, most of his comments on the subject were general, and they were widely scattered through time and in essays and lectures on such diverse subjects as psychoanalysis, anthropology, and children's stories. What emerged as I pursued this side of Lewis's approach to literature was a consistent set of principles which form his literary theory. I learned that he valued his readers' accessibility to new ideas, that he felt his readers were better judges of the value of a literary work than critics, and that his chief delight as a reader himself and then as an author was the compelling suggestiveness of a finely crafted story.

Lewis makes us feel good to be readers. For him, the reader is the most important element next to what is read. His readers, ideally, are individuals with individual needs and diverse backgrounds. Their one common denominator is a willingness to open themselves to new feelings and ideas. He lays considerable importance on a reader's feeling for a book, his receptivity, and his acceptance of what he reads regardless of how the book might be assumed to be of use.

The further in I went toward what Lewis himself found valuable in the experience of reading, the more I became aware that he insisted upon a message which would bring the reader closer to the truth. He even seemed to suggest that an author's indirect approach to the message might work best because it would slide past the reader's inhibitions and prejudices and catch him unaware. At the time I first encountered this idea, it seemed a bit subversive for a Christian writer but not for a novelist. Lewis almost never explained what techniques he used in order to project his message, so I was left to look at the novels themselves in order to examine in detail how Lewis operated in his own practice of the craft.

As I moved into an examination of the books, what I had learned from the letters and the lectures came into play as I judged what Lewis was attempting to do and was accomplishing. His works showed a conscious sense of craftsmanship which was manipulated to provide a vehicle for messages which were myth-like in their intent and scope. Lewis merged theme and form in an organic unity which would have made Whitman and Coleridge proud. He called the elements of his creation by two terms which may be foreign to many of his readers. Let me define these terms as follows:

Poiema: (something made) The words themselves, stacked upon each other and shaped by careful attention to techniques ranging from allegory and symbolism to the use of humor, sentiment, and irony.

Logos: (something said) The meaning of those words which awakens the reader's sense of a longing or feeling never so clearly understood before.

There is a skill required to link the form and content (*Poiema* and *Logos*) and make them so support and reinforce each other that readers scarcely realize that Lewis is consciously manipulating each to produce an effect. Lewis obscures what he is doing by saying that he picks a particular form, say for example, the children's fantasy tale, because it best suits what he wants to say. A closer look shows that he consciously chooses and selects, molds and develops both the forms and the messages to produce a final effect upon his readers which is satisfying and deceptively simple.

So now I knew what I wanted to do in this book. I wanted to clear a way for readers of Lewis through the tangle of an increasing body of criticism, to satisfy their curiosity about why we read Lewis in the first place and why we return to him again and again. There is no mystery involved. It is not just a matter of popular appeal or relevance. Quite simply, it is a matter of skill, the craftsman shaping a body of work, learning by practice and experiment what techniques are useful and rejecting those which are not. Lewis grows as a writer as well as growing on the reader.

It is fascinating to watch Lewis develop from a young aesthete who worries over his own sensuousness into a reborn Christian who recognizes the place those feelings have in his new life. For us, that early shift in vision is only the beginning of Lewis's story as a writer of fiction because he makes that new understanding the basis of his theory of literature and the keystone of his literary edifice. Thus a good book invites us to experience its depths by making us feel and absorb its message. It invites us to indulge our senses, recalling to our memories joys or sorrows out of the past. Building on these remembrances, the story, carefully structured and developed, opens for us a new way of seeing because it draws us out of our shells, and we transcend our littleness and become something more than we were. The fusion of feeling and thought produces an "other worldly" experience in which we are open to a message, receptive to what the author will tell us. When we leave the book and return, our shell should be a little bigger, a bit less confining. That is the feeling Lewis gives us; it is the feeling he sought when he read; it is the answer to my initial question of why people continue to read Lewis. How he produces that kind of reading in us and for us is the subject of what follows.

1

The Letters

We are fortunate in having a long and varied correspondence on which to draw for the basic characteristics of Lewis's thought about art. The longest, most intimate, and detailed correspondence is that with J. A. Greeves, which began in 1914 and ended with Lewis's death in 1963. In the early years of this correspondence, when Lewis was away from Belfast at schools in England and then at Oxford and serving in World War I, he had many experiences of an intellectual or emotional nature to share with his closest boyhood friend. He catalogues his reading, the works and particular bindings he has bought; discusses his romantic attachments; and expands on his reactions to music, a passion he shared with Greeves. Often he outlines his evolving aesthetic theory and its effect upon his creative work in poetry. There is a strain of adolescent emotionalism and sentimentality running through these early letters; we should expect that of a professed romantic, devotee of Wagner's *Ring* cycle, writer of childhood fantasy and apostle of *Sehnsucht* (longing). What is remarkable in even the earliest of his comments is his deeply felt response to nature, his dedication to the craftsmanship implicit in the production of an imaginative work of art, and his insistence on a meaningful transformation of emotion through structured language into art.

Early in 1915, happy at last as a private student of Kirkpatrick's at Great Bookham, he ordered a book, Malory's *Morte d'Arthur*, which had an intense effect on his imaginative life. He was poised and ready for a plunge into the world of romantic legend.

How I long to break away into a world where such things [a march of dwarfs across the snow] were true: this real, hard, dirty, Monday morning modern world stifles one.[1]

Lewis had sufficient reason in the early loss of his mother, his disastrous school experiences, and his poor rapport with his father, all recounted in *Surprised by Joy*, to account for such a longing to be transported to a happier realm. Many an embryonic Keats felt the same pull even after a completely happy and unblemished childhood. Analyzing his own sentimentality, he wrote:

By the way, I am perhaps more sentimental than you, but I don't blow a trumpet about it. Indeed, I am rather ashamed of it. Feelings ought to be kept for literature and art, where they are delightful and not intruded into life where they are merely a nuisance.[2]

This passage is central to Lewis's early distinction between unfocused emotion and its transformation by discipline into art. Though a lifelong professed "romantic," he here clearly distinguishes what at the outset is a guiding principle in his criticism and art: art transmutes feeling into delight giving it meaning and purpose, legitimizing it. Thus the suspect and irrational longing found an early outlet in art. Long before Lewis, as a serious student, had encountered the history of either literature or aesthetic theory, he acknowledged an allegiance which he held to the end of his artistic career. To the rational man, feelings are at best an embarrassment, a "nuisance." That Lewis was a rational man, at least from the time of his indoctrination by Kirkpatrick, no one will deny. That he was also a passionate lover of feeling cannot be denied when one reads his letters with their references to "faerie," to George MacDonald, Malory, William Morris, John Keats and the Brontës, to *Sehnsucht* and "northernness." His discerning rejection of Ainsworth, Sassoon, and Housman's *A Shropshire Lad*, ("what a terrible little book")[3] are perhaps counterbalanced by his hasty rejection of Laurence Sterne, Robert Browning, and George Meredith. Of *Tristram Shandy* he said at this time,

The absolute disconnection or scrappiness, the abundant coarseness of an utterly vulgar, nonvoluptuous sort and the general smoking-room atmosphere of the book were too much for me.[4]

His bent was toward all that stimulated the imagination artfully: Dürer, Rackham, the "romantic" Morris, the "voluptuous" Keats, the "grand" Wagner, the "weird" Poe. He wrote to Greeves saying that he found Trollope, Goldsmith, and Austen too stolid and wondered if Greeves would accuse him of being unbalanced in his almost exclusive reading of fairy tales and lyrics.[5]

Lewis was by the time he was eighteen years old deeply committed to writing. Although the Boxen stories, written by Lewis and his brother, Warren, as children, are not mature works, he had in addition written a considerable number of poems, begun an opera, *Loki Bound*, for which Greeves was to do the music, a prose romance called *The Quest of Bleheris*, and a narrative poem, "The Childhood of Medea."

His early letters to Greeves show his dedication to the craft of writing as he understood it, to the practice which he felt was essential in mastering a style, to the cultivation of a romantic charm.[6] Tediousness, too much "brasting and fighting," may overwhelm the main feeling generated by an imaginative plot.[7]

If anything concrete can be put down as a definition of Lewis's adolescent aesthetics, it would have the following general outline. A literary work must contain emotion; it must move the senses and the imagination; it must be pictorial and evocative, resounding and elevated. It should smack of the past and subdue action to feeling. Viewed without the further qualification of a formal structure which he approved in the works of Spenser, Milton, Austen, and Samuel Johnson, his basic response to literature is an almost pure romanticism. Although at the outset he was moved most by highly colored and imaginative literature, he also demanded a high degree of professionalism in his own poetry and in the works of poets he admired. His insistence on practice, clarity, and conciseness, all are basic in his response to literature.

Beyond his many expressions of interest in the craft of writing as he experienced it in his broad and avid reading, we begin to find Lewis discussing with Greeves his concern over the subject matter of his admired writers. At the center of his interest lies the issue of how beauty as it is perceived by sense experience acts to communicate some meaning to the reader, and what the nature of that communication might be. Lewis was torn between feeling that beauty might only be a sensuous cheat, or at best an end in itself, and reasoning that it might convey some spiritual meaning of significance.

By working backward from *Surprised by Joy* and through hints in the letters, we see that Lewis conceived of spiritual meaning as operating through beauty, expressing itself in objects of beauty and communicating with human intelligence through an elevation of the senses.

You see the conviction is gaining ground on me that after all Spirit does exist; and that we come in contact with the spiritual element by means of these "thrills." I fancy that there is Something right outside time & place, which did not create matter, as the Christians say, but is matter's great enemy: and that Beauty is the call of the spirit in that something to the spirit in us.[8]

Lewis's acknowledged spiritualism at this period took a decidedly artistic bent, though not like that of Yeats whom he was to visit in Oxford soon, but more aligned with that of Poe, Coleridge, and the Neoplatonists. Lewis was quick to distinguish between sheer emotionalism or sentimentality and the heightened consciousness provoked by intensely imaginative art. In *Surprised by Joy*, he records how the contrast of his mother's happy and cheerful disposition and his father's moody and changeable emotional approach to life led him at any early age to hold emotions as something to be distrusted because they were unsettling and even dangerously disruptive.[9]

It is in the early pages of his autobiography that in retrospect Lewis links his perception of nature and the memory of such perceptions as the toy garden made by his brother or the recalled view of the Castlereagh Hills from their nursery window with *Sehnsucht* and indicates a distinction between the formal aesthetic experiences of beauty and those of romantic feeling. More significant for us, he indicates that these feelings of longing replace religious experiences and were only later perceived by him as the beginning of Joy in the Christian sense. Lewis sees the progress of his imaginative life as linked to a growing perception of spirit in nature, misunderstood in childhood and youth as a desire to repeat a particular experience and understood fully only after his conversion, as a longing for union with God. However clear in hindsight all this may seem, the fact remains that as he began to compose the poems published in *Spirits in Bondage* and moved into the stimulating and rarefied academic atmosphere of Oxford, his recorded impressions and attitudes reflect a philosophic objectivity toward his own subjectivity.

I *can* feel otherwise about lusts of the flesh: is not desire merely a kind of sugarplum that nature gives us to make us breed, as she does the beetles and toads so that we and they may beget more creatures to struggle in the same net: Nature, or the common order of things, has really produced in man a sort of Frankenstein who is learning to shake her off. For man alone of all things can master his instincts....I am true to the old cannons [sic]...but I do believe that I have in me a spirit, a chip, shall we say, of universal spirit; and that, since all good & joyful things are spiritual & nonmaterial, I must be careful not to let matter (=nature=Satan, remember) get too great a hold on me, & dull the one spark I have.[10]

The image of transformation so central in Lewis's life and work surfaces here. Man the monster is perfectible; Eustace as the dragon,

Edmund as the betrayer, and Orual the possessive sister are all examples. By the mastery of his baser feelings, his instincts, man can rise to the universal Spirit. Lewis emphasized the process of self-perfection in his early discussions of man and Spirit, but later he found that the transformation would be made by Grace. His interest in distinguishing between nature and instinct on the one hand and Spirit on the other is reflected in a shift away from the high, impersonal drama of Loki and mythological subjects to the narrower and more personal examination of inner states as seen in *Spirits in Bondage*. After the war and his return to Oxford, he wrote poems on Ask, King Mark and Tristram, Merlin and Nimue, Venus, and Medea.[11] Greeves was the correspondent above all others during this period with whom he shared his literary discoveries. The reading he particularly drew to Greeve's attention was: Shakespeare's comedies; Browning's *Paracelsus*;[12] Yeats' *Countess Cathleen*;[13] Gilbert Murray's translation of the *Bacchae*;[14] Marco Polo; Walter Scott's *The Talisman*;[15] and Charles Doughty's *Mansoul* and Borrow's *Lavengro*.[16] Although not drawn by current enthusiasm for *vers libre*, in fact distinctly averse to all its appeals, Lewis was experimenting with poetry and using many traditional themes, always in extended poetic forms. By 1920 he had distinguished his preference for the "northernness" or Saxonism which he felt in Wagner, the Norse myths and Eddas, as against the "southernness" of the Latin or Mediterranean view.

In a letter to his friend Leo Kingsley Baker written probably during the Easter vacation of 1920, he discoursed on the theme of originality in contemporary English literature.

All poetry is one, and I love to see the great notes repeated.... A plague on these moderns scrambling for what they call originality—like men trying to lift themselves off the earth by pulling at their own braces: as if by shutting their eyes to the work of the masters they were likely to create new things themselves.[17]

Steeped as he was by early reading in the classics, it is understandable that he would take a conservative attitude toward the current literary avant-garde. His often professed love for the remote, romantic, and archaic made him an anachronism from the beginning of his career.

It was in a letter to Baker that he gave one of his earliest definitions of poetry: "Poetry is the art of utilizing the informal or irrational values of words to express that which can only by symbolized by their formal or conventional meanings."[18]

In an expanded version, found in a letter to Baker ten months later, Lewis describes in detail his attitudes about beauty and the role of memory.

To me it seems that a great many different emotions are united in the perception of beauty: it may turn out to be not a simple thing but a result of unions. For one thing nearly all beautiful sights are to me chiefly important as *reminders* of other beautiful sights: without memory t'would be a poor affair. The process presumably has a beginning but once going it grows like a snowball. Could it be that joy remembered ("Which now is sad because it has been sweet") is a necessary element in Beauty? There is too, I think, a purely sensuous element: that such and such notes or tints (*in themselves*—not in their combinations) just happen to satisfy our nerves of hearing & sight—as certain foods satisfy those of tastes. This wd. be rather a condition of beauty, perhaps, than an element in it. One thing is plain, that the statements continually made about Beauty's being pure contemplation, stirring no impulse, being the antithesis of the practical or energizing side of us, are wrong. On the contrary, beauty seems to me to be always an invitation of some sort: usually an invitation to we don't know what. A wood seen as "picturesque" by a fool (who'd like a frame round it) may be purely contemplated: seen as "beautiful" it seems rather to say "come unto me."[19]

"Joy remembered" strikes the keynote of his theory of beauty. The sensuous perception of beauty triggers a reaction in which the feeling of joy from perceived beauty is linked with remembered beauty, accumulating in intensity as it increases in scope through time. Lewis is not originating a new aesthetic theory here. There are reminders of the classical theory of mimesis, of Aristotle's theory of art as a representation of nature, and of Longinian sublimity. Also we recall the creative imagination of Coleridge, Keats' belief in the power of the imagined to snatch us away from care, and Poe's theory that earthly beauty is the visible spectrum drawing us back to the unified white light of supernal or universal Beauty.

In Lewis's creative work, the power of description always ranks as one of the most important aspects, one on which he would lavish much time and attention. In giving advice to young authors, as we will see later, he insisted that a description always make us feel what is being described. His stories and novels are full of instances in which attention focuses on the scene as in the dying world of Charn, the creation and the destruction of Narnia, or the sea world of Perelandra, always evoking, much more than the dialogue or narrative, a sense of the quality of the experience being presented. It is "further in and higher up" as we see at the end of *The Chronicles of Narnia*. This movement up and in, penetrating into the ultimate truth, approaching the central and universal reality, returning to simple values out of a perplexing multiplicity of choices, characterizes the descriptive movement and the thematic structure of his fiction.

Interestingly enough, it was not his desire to make an allegorical application of Christian monism that brought him to this aesthetic position, though undoubtedly this feature cannot be discounted as a later influence and addition. It was his earliest commitment to an almost pagan love of sensuous beauty, the wild and eerie, the rhapsodic and emotive seen in his admiration for the sagas, the *Ring* cycle, Keats, MacDonald, the Brontës, and Dürer, which brought him to recognize spirit in beauty.

To reinforce his conviction that our response and remembrance of the sensuous experience of the beautiful is the basis of art, he dismisses the claims of pure contemplation, of cold aesthetics, as invalid. Beauty becomes an "invitation" to further mystery, a "come unto me." Again his work gives ample evidence that he practiced his own theory. Though the earliest fiction was written some twelve years later (*The Pilgrim's Regress*, 1933), after Lewis's return to Christianity, it reflects most strongly his adherence to this central idea: that the impulse to create beauty stems from a desire to reproduce "notes and tints," sensuous experiences which through memory and association have taken on particular meaning for the artist and which have drawn him toward a central mystery, a beauty, which cannot perhaps be fathomed.

While his skill as a writer developed, his method remained the same. He consistently linked together, in an organic unity of form and content, feelings which lead to meanings. His themes may show considerable variety, but on occasion, e.g., in *The Pilgrim's Regress*, *The Screwtape Letters*, and *The Great Divorce*, the meaning becomes so strong a message that it overshadows the feeling and unbalances this unity.

His letters give early evidence that he practices this form of descriptive writing even in casual correspondence. In a letter to A. K. Hamilton Jenkin, written after Lewis had become a Fellow at Magdalen, Oxford, he described the deer which grazed under his college window.

Have you ever lived among deer? The windows of my Northern room look into the grove. There is a flat stretch of grass receding into big forest trees (all day long at present the leaves are eddying up the sky from them and the wind among them at night is magnificent.) There is nothing in sight, not even a gable, to remind me that I am in a town: and over this grass the 'little dappled fools' come right up to my window. One morning there will be seven there chewing the cud in close squadron: next day not one in sight, till I go down to the bathroom. The window there is level with the ground and on these autumn mornings one gets a delicious earthy freshness and a horizontal view of dew and cobwebs along the turf: and perhaps one tiny solitary stag nibbling quite close to the sill as if he were the first animal in the world. But best of all is to hear them at night. They don't moo and they don't neigh, but they have two sounds. The one is a thin little hooting, rather like a faint cough, and most unearthly. The

other (mark the catholicity of these beasts) the other is absolutely indistin-
guishable from the grunting of old fat pigs. And this last being most unpoetical
and an anticlimax in the eyes of the unwise, is really the best. If only to hear this
you should come. You shd. come if only to enter Magdalen after dark across the
grove by my master key—on a moonlight night. With such a key at such an hour
of night under such massy archways, through the length of such blind walks,
that sudden [sic] opened out into the freckled moonshine of tall groves,
so secret and so wrapped Medea went by stealth to gather the enchanted herbs
that did renew old Aeson. In plain prose there are two or three moments in that
night entry by three successive posterns that I do it for the love of it when I
might just as well go in past the porter's lodge. And if there is no moon (dazzlingly
bright among the trees after a long dark cobbled passage) perhaps instead there
will be thick darkness and drumming rain and the hoofs of the deer (invisible)
scampering away—and ahead the long lighted line of the cloisters in New Build-
ings.[20]

His correspondence is full of such descriptions, particularly of
autumn mornings, which he held in special esteem and described
with unfailing enthusiasm. The evocation of scene, the descriptive
detail, and the loving attention to remembered experiences accumulated over a long period, these all characterize even his informal
writing. There is a notable absence of extensive literary allusion,
usually a common characteristic of an academic's prose. Here there is
only one reference, one to Medea, perhaps a reference from the
poem on that subject which had been under way for some time. His
perceptions and descriptions are fresh and vivid and although personal, are never quaint or eccentric.

By 1920, Lewis had settled into his life at Oxford, had published
Spirits in Bondage, and submitted work for an anthology of young
poets to be called *The Way's the Way*, a volume which was never
published.[21] His Medea poem he described as "stillborn," and the
poem on Merlin and Nimue had been changed from monologue to
narrative form, written in a stanza form for which he felt indebted
to Keats' "The Eve of St. Agnes" with touches of Coleridge's
"Christabel."[22] By autumn of 1920 he wrote to Greeves that he
needed a change from the philosophers and Wordsworth perhaps to
something purely imaginative, perhaps mystical.[23]

Unadulterated imagination formed the bulk of his early reading,
at least what he shared with Arthur Greeves. The letters recount the
conquest of Malory, Spenser, Charlotte Brontë, Scott's *Ivanhoe*,
Keats, MacDonald's *Phantastes*, Hawthorne, Morris, Yeats, and
James Stephen's *Crock of Gold* to name only a few. The possible
influences, sources, and inspirations both conscious and unconscious
could hardly be gleaned from a full list of Lewis's reading at any
given point in time. He was an omnivorous and indefatigable reader

and readily acknowledged on numerous occasions, upon the request of scholars, the sources, as nearly as he could determine them, of his fictional work. He believed in creative borrowing as in the Cupid and Psyche story of *Till We Have Faces* or Aslan's death and resurrection in *The Lion, the Witch and the Wardrobe*. However, he discounted attempts to define a writer by his reading, both in his criticism of others and in his analysis of the nature of criticism itself.

We can sketch in the outline of his reading, which ranges from the Greek and Latin classics to contemporary science fiction, and we can focus upon his tastes in literature with some clarity. He came to admire Shakespeare's sonnets, *The Tempest*, *A Midsummer Night's Dream*, and *The Winter's Tale* although he showed little early enthusiasm for the other works. He said that Chaucer and Dickens shared the bourgeois morality and revealed their incapacity for romance by their indulgence in low humor and what he called moral vulgarity and indecency.[24] He particularly admired the prose style of Malory, Bunyan, Ruskin, Samuel Johnson, and the authorized version of the Bible, but reserved for highest praise Catullus, Keats, and Morris. He tended, at this period in his development (1919-1926), to regard imaginative works, works of faerie in poetry or prose, as preferred reading. Among critics, he admired Johnson above all others, which seems a bit odd in view of Johnson's antipathy to faerieland. His view of Macaulay was that his real thought was not worth twopence.[25] His journal entries for July 4, 1926, and February 8, 1927, capture the recurrent call of the past as he now rereads Morris's *The Well at the World's End*, a book he admired to the last, and then reads the *Eddas* for the first time in the original. The "remembered joy," here the "old authenic thrill," returns to buoy him up.

By the late twenties, Lewis had established a familiar routine centering around his teaching at Magdalen College and his research on allegorical love poetry and his home life with his brother, Warren Lewis, Mrs. Moore, and her daughter, Maureen Moore, in Headington. At Magdalen he met with his students in tutorial sessions and demanded of them close reading and clear, rational analysis of their subject. According to those with whom I talked, he was either a stimulating tutor, if you argued your point, or a most fearsome critic, if you failed to do so. At the Kilns, he was a subject of Mrs. Moore's domestic tyranny and washed dishes and fed the chickens with an aplomb that worries many of his critics. He appears, however, not to have been unhappy in his chosen life style.

In a letter to A.K. Hamilton Jenkin he itemizes his status:

(4.)   I am not married nor like to be.
(5.)   I have given up trying to write poetry.

(6.) I no longer think myself a genius.
(7.) I am trying to write a book on the allegorical love poems—Romance of the Rose and its successors.
(8.) I subscribe to the League of Nations but don't & can't read Headway.
(9.) I am trying also to write a short story.[26]

We do not know the name or nature of this short story, only that Lewis had turned away from poetry to short fiction. At about this time Lewis's thoughts were drawn increasingly toward his father whose health was beginning to fail, and perhaps understandably enough, the literary theme of "homeliness" as a topic in letters begins to assume importance. Lewis never defined "homeliness," but the many references which follow its initial appearance in his thoughts at this time indicate that he meant initially by the word a sense of settled domesticity. Humphrey Carpenter's recent study of the Inklings and of Lewis in particular has made clear how little of that domestic comfort Lewis and his brother had after their mother's death. Going to Little Lea was not returning to find "homeliness." The explanation of why Lewis subjected himself to Mrs. Moore's authority in the matter of household chores may be simply that he found a home with her for the first time since he left childhood.

This period also coincides with his return to the Christian faith, or if you will, his conversion to an understanding of what religious belief entails. Although the letters do not by any means give a full record, the fullest account appears in *Surprised by Joy*, they are helpful in highlighting the impact of these events on Lewis's evolving attitudes about the nature of art and his particular theory of creativity.

In a 1929 letter to Greeves, he recounts a conversation with Owen Barfield which evidently crossed the line from faith to literature.

He [Barfield] said among other things that he thought the idea of the spiritual world as *home*—the discovery of homeliness in that wh. is otherwise so remote—the feeling that you are coming *back* tho' to a place you have never yet reached—was peculiar to the British, and thought that Macdonald, Chesterton, and I, had this more than anyone else. He doesn't know you of course—who, with Minto, [Mrs. Moore] have taught me so much in that way.[27]

It is easy enough to explain Lewis's emphasis on home, the "remembered joy," as the search conducted by all romantics for the ineffable child and for the holy and innocent place. A superficial examination of Lewis's life would explain why he felt this pull: the loss of his mother, his unhappy school experience, the difficulty of his relationship with his father. Psychological stress or plain adolescent nostalgia could account for such an interest.[28] It is not, however, for Lewis the traditional home you can never get back to, as in Thomas Wolfe's *You Can't Go Home Again*, but rather the homeliness which underlies all later sophistication and anchors it. Homeliness in this sense is physically unattainable in this world but nevertheless a potent, mysterious yet compelling force whose call constitutes at least a species of that Joy which Lewis was later to designate as the center of his life.

The term is used again in a January 1930 letter to Greeves when Lewis describes magic and homeliness as enhancing one another and then goes on to report that in reading Jacob Boehme, the German mystic [1575-1624], he has been shaken by the realization that the simple things in life must be gripped firmly to provide an anchor for further speculation about God and nature.[29]

In a June 22, 1930, letter, he records remarks of J.R.R. Tolkien on the subject.

Tolkien once remarked to me that the feeling about home must have been quite different in the days when a family had fed on the produce of the same few miles of country for six generations, and that perhaps this was why they saw nymphs in the fountains and dryads in the wood—they were not mistaken for there was in a sense a *real* (not metaphorical) connection between them and the countryside. What had been earth and air & later corn, and later still bread, really was *in* them. We of course who live on a standardised international diet...are really artificial beings and have no connection (save in sentiment) with any place on earth. We are synthetic men, uprooted. The strength of the hills is not ours.[30]

Tolkien's hobbits and their diet come immediately to mind, but so too come the Pevensie's meal at the Beaver's, Lucy's with Tumnus and by contrast Edmund's Turkish Delight and Eustace's diet while a dragon. For whatever reason, personal or artistic, Lewis was being drawn away from the highly ornamental and elaborate vision of *Dymer* to value the simplicity which he felt to be at the core of William Morris's work. After reading Morris's play *Love is Enough*, he felt that he perceived a new holiness which revealed the essential reality behind the surface of romantic sensuousness.

For the first (and last?) time the light of *holiness* shines through Morris' romanticism, not destroying but perfecting it. Reading this has been a great experience to me: and coming on top of the *Angel in the House* has shown me that in my fear of the sensual cheat wh. lurked at the back of my old romantic days (*see* Dymer VII) I have aimed at too much austerity and even dishonoured love altogether. I have become a dry prig. I do hope I am not being mocked—that this is not merely the masked vanguard of a new sensuality. But I verily believe not.[31]

How much and in what ways Lewis's evolving attitudes toward faith affected his perception of literature is difficult to determine with any accuracy. That he mistrusted his early enthusiasm for the sensuous, emotional, and imaginative experiences is clear from a letter to Greeves written in July 1930.

I never meant for a moment that I was beginning to doubt whether absolute chastity was the true goal—of that I am certain. What I meant was that I began to think that I was mistaken in aiming at this goal by the means of a stern repression and even a contemptuous distrust of all that emotional & imaginative experience wh. seems to border on the voluptuous: whether it was well to see in certain romances and certain music nothing but one more wile of the enemy: whether perhaps the right way was not to keep always alive in ones [sic] soul a certain tenderness & luxuriousness always reaching out to *that of which* (on my view) sex must be the copy. In other words, whether, while I was right in seeing that a copy must be different from an original, I ought not to have remembered that it must also be *like* it—else how wd it be a copy? In the second place, what I feared was *not* lest this mood should be temporary but lest it should turn out to be another wile. What I also ought to have said in my last letter but didn't is that the whole thing has made me feel that I have never given half enough importance to love in the sense of *affection*.[32]

These three letters indicate a reevaluation expressed in new terms of Lewis's basic response to works of the creative imagination. The earliest appeal of such works was a sensuous one, the call of *faerie*. That he should come to doubt and mistrust the validity of sensuous responses at this turning in his emotional and intellectual development is not difficult to accept, but the fact remains that after careful consideration he did not discard them in favor of more mature and "spiritual" insights. He came finally to perceive them in an altered light, a vision which was to allow him to retain their most basic form and force.

One of the most fascinating aspects of Lewis's conversion is often lost in the critic's hurry to get on to what Lewis became, forgetting what he was before. Up to this point, Lewis had been the typical intellectual student and then tutor of his day. He was articulate, brilliant, witty, and dedicated to his teaching career. He was happily settled with Mrs. Moore and Warren, and his life seemed in every aspect normal and satisfactory. There were few overt signs of uneasiness which indicated that he stood on the verge of a decision which promised to change his whole life, academic and spiritual. Yet the letters show a gradual shift toward the thoughtful analysis of the role played by emotion and sensuous response in an otherwise rational man's life.

Lewis was never one to dismiss the old way merely because progress or growth indicated a new one. So he mulled over the meaning of the sensuous delight which had so strongly drawn him to the novels and poems we have seen him refer to. The result of his quite rational consideration of the meaning and role of the imagination as it created images of beauty in the reader's mind was the realization that he had stopped short of understanding the aim of this delight, mistaking it for an end in itself.

We might pause here on the verge of Lewis's reentry into the established church and prior to the publication of his fictional works to examine the basic elements of his early responses to art. At the outset, Lewis distinguishes between the almost subconscious instinctual response which is placed under rigid control and always regarded as suspect, and the less restricted and conscious emotional or sensuous response to beauty. The emotional response is directly to nature in the Wordsworthian and Emersonian manner, exposing the naked nerves to every natural experience. The thrill of this encounter with nature originates not in matter but with spirit expressing itself through matter, infusing it with meaning. The authentic thrill is always noted by an elevation of the senses which Lewis felt was proof of the communication of a spirit outside of and antagonistic to matter, contacting the bit of spirit in each perceiver. Thus we seem to have many elements of traditional aesthetic theory: the elevation of nature by the infusion of spirit, the link of nature through beauty with the ideal or spiritual; the heightened response which signals the operation of spirit.

The sensuous response to beauty in nature to which Lewis repeatedly refers in his letters, especially to Greeves, their responses to firsthand experience in nature rambles, and their admiration for the music of Wagner, Chopin, and Beethoven, are not valued in themselves. Although these heightened states are valued for the momentary thrill and exaltation, their value is other and twofold. They prove by their intensity the power and value of beauty as it operates in nature, and they signal the meaning implicit in the experience and the route which leads men to the source of beauty.

Beauty leads back and in, back to a central, primal reality which serves as a symbol of primal or ideal meaning. This meaning is the source from which beauty emanates. Without the attraction of beauty, meaning would be difficult to communicate to man. Again, strong reminders of the theories of Coleridge, Poe, and the organic theorists suggest themselves as parallels.

The meaning which passes through the sensuous experience of natural beauty to the perceiver remains a mystery, for all the fact of its primal and central quality; and it appears essential that it remain so. It may be compelling to the limits of distraction, but it remains undecipherable; it is always that which we cannot know. Much of its force apparently rests in its impenetrableness and indivisibility. All this sounds like a description of high romance: the holy mystery is shrouded in elaborate and gorgeous ornamentation which lifts the soul ever heavenward but never close enough to the mystery to tarnish it with reality.

For Lewis, however, the most attractive quality of this experience is, unromantically, its homeliness or homeyness. It is centered within, in warmth at the heart's core, in Joy and personal satisfaction, not out there, drawing the perceiver into a cold world of external abstract verities seen in cold contemplation. The words "nostalgia" and "remembrance" come into play here. The reader or listener is attracted by beauty and brought back to memories which are reinforced and strengthened by this experience. Each time we feel a pang of Joy in a highly imaginative description of, say, a landscape, that event triggers earlier memories to which the current one is added to build the nostalgia which remains, a vague longing for something we can grasp but never hold for long.

The process is an organic one, circular and internalized, not spiraling outward. We are seduced by the voluptuous beauty of a perception in nature which brings with it the remembrance of similar previous experiences. Memory operates to correlate and integrate these experiences, adding weight to the continued mystery of the call of what we do not know, and though our longing is not assuaged, the very anticipation of renewed delight leads us on in the search. The theory appears ego-centered and to a degree hedonistic. These features were thorny ones for the post-adolescent academic but were ultimately absorbed in the conversion of his essentially pagan aesthetics into a Christian theory of art.

It might be helpful at this point to look at the stylistic features of literary works which excited these responses in Lewis. He pointed out in *Surprised by Joy* that he was sympathetically drawn to works like *Phantastes* and *Lilith* whose religious meaning he did not at all appreciate until after his conversion. He felt in retrospect that what had attracted him was their hidden Joy. But it should be clear from what has already been said of his early reading (pre-Oxford) that he consistently admired narrative skill, descriptive power, elevation of style, and grandeur of scope over facile and flashy romance. Homer, Milton, Bunyan, and Dr. Johnson, rank with Scott, Keats, MacDonald, and Morris. He appears to have been most at home with native English writers, finding little elevation or stimulation for his own imagination in foreign and exotic materials or styles. Though he mentions an interest in Eastern art and literature as a phase, he basically shows the orthodox and insular taste of a highly educated Englishman of his time. It is the very homey, almost patriotically insular material and style which he seems most to admire, e.g., George MacDonald's *Diary of An Old Soul*. Later in examining his fiction, we see that this preference for native beauty and place will feature prominently in his creation of Narnia and will function significantly in the other works as well.

Turning back to the letters of the period of his conversion, we find reflected there many of the doubts concerning his role as a writer which are not recorded in *Surprised by Joy*. The shift in his spiritual alignment caused second thoughts about many matters, and although we cannot say that he was basically a different man after his conversion, we can say that he was a new man. The brag and swagger of the Kirkpatrick and early Oxford years, the *literati* tone which one feels when he writes to Coghill of *Dymer* or to Greeves of *Spirits in Bondage* now shifts to self-effacement. He tells Greeves in an August 18, 1930, letter that his one ambition from age sixteen onward was to be a poet. Acknowledging his failure, Lewis consoles himself by suggesting that the humbling process which he has gone through and the loss of his contentment is at least over. Better now, he says, than at age sixty and after a life of achievement to begin seeing worldly success fade to ashes.[33]

For all the fact that he had apparently forsaken the hope of success as an author—more likely he had foregone the egoism of enjoying the anticipated praise—he was clearly assembling material which was to appear in fictional form later in the decade. While working on *Perelandra*, he had a particularly distressing dream about his dead father which reveals his fear of ghosts and corpses.[34] The very horror of speculation on Weston's probable status, which draws heavily on this dream, adds immeasurably to the mounting suspense of *Perelandra*.

The change in his vision of life was reflected in some readjustments of his view of writers he had previously admired, like H. G. Wells. Indicating that Wells' planetary novels were almost his earliest favorites, Lewis writes to Greeves that he now finds he is much less interested because the probable explanations of the real universe are much less interesting than conjecture and speculation. Lewis compares looking for excitement, the curiosity of a planetary story, in Wells being rather like looking at the edge of a curtain when you really want to look at what is behind the curtain and beyond.[35]

The letters of 1931 give many indications that Lewis was rethinking his other earlier assessments of individual writers and of fiction in general. On rereading *War and Peace* in March 1931, he wrote of his restored faith in the novel, suggesting that one danger for the novelist is "narrative lust," the tendency to lead the reader to find out what happens at the expense of all other considerations.[36] For Lewis, Tolstoy's greatness as a novelist rests on his sublime indifference to life and death, his variety, his admirable war descriptions, his humor (Austenian, according to Lewis), his homely pictures of village life and his profound conception of religion underlying it all.[37] It is significant that his emphasis has shifted now to the underlying meaning, the inner life of the work. Lewis's view of literature from his own perspective, his use of it, becomes in these years noticeably directed toward literature as a spiritual aid or tool. Reading George MacDonald is like being bathed or healed spiritually, he wrote to Greeves.[38] Perhaps it is unfair to be so selective since Lewis probably mentions only those works which are applicable to his situation at the time of writing a particular letter. However, the weight does shift from approval of works on the general principles of the qualities outlined earlier, to emphasize a new and shifting center of meaning Lewis now perceives in works he long admired for other reasons. His revised attitude to William Morris is a prime example.

I feel more and more that Morris has taught me things he did not understand himself. These hauntingly beautiful lands which somehow never satisfy,—this passion to escape from death *plus* the certainty that life owes all its charm to mortality—these push you on to the real thing because they fill you with desire and yet prove absolutely clearly that in Morris's world that desire cannot be satisfied....If ever you feel inclined to relapse into the mundane point of view—to feel that your book and pipe and chair are enough for happiness—it only needs a page or two of Morris to sting you wide awake into uncontrollable longing and to make you feel that everything is worthless except the hope of finding one of his countries. But if you read any of his romances through you will find the country dull before the end. All he has done is to rouse the desire: but so strongly, that you *must* find the real satisfaction. And then you realize that *death* is at the root of the whole matter, and why he chose the subject of the Earthly Paradise, and how the true solution is one he never saw.[39]

Here appears the first of many statements indicating that the role of art is that of Christian propaganda, an idea Lewis expands on later in describing the literature he admires the most and his own fiction. Lewis maintains that the values of literature come to rest on its ability, by whatever means of art, to express what he termed the "great myths." The greatest of these myths Lewis now acknowledges is the story of Christ.

Now the story of Christ is simply a true myth: a myth working on us in the same way as the others, but with this tremendous difference that *it really happened*:

and one must be content to accept it in the same way, remembering that it is God's myth where the others are men's myths: i.e. the Pagan stories are God expressing Himself through the minds of poets, using such images as He found there, while Christianity is God expressing Himself through what we call 'real things.' Therefore it is *true*, not in the sense of a 'description' of God (that no finite mind could take in) but in the sense of being the way in which God chooses to (or can) appear to our faculties.[40]

It is another twenty-four years before Lewis writes in *Surprised by Joy* the conclusive statement to this train of thought.

The inherent dialectic of desire itself had in a way already shown me this; for all images and sensations, if idolatrously mistaken for Joy itself, soon honestly confessed themselves inadequate.... All the value lay in that of which Joy was the desiring.[41]

The unsatisfied desire, the "uncontrollable longing" which was the center of pleasure, promising all and only propagating further longing in an egocentric cycle, proved now in the light of Christian faith to be the prelude to heavenly fulfillment. Where Lewis had felt drawn toward an inner meaning, tantalized by hints of *faerie* in the realms of the imagination, he now saw that for him, at least, the impulse had been toward a spiritual reality, the absolute truth. The desire proved an acceptable tool, a bait to draw the reluctant or ignorant on to salvation. This realization conveniently dispatched earlier worries of egoism, self-indulgent daydreaming, and hedonistic thrill-seeking for its own sake.

It is the convert who defends his faith most ardently, and critics have implied that Lewis in his confusion of faith with literature wrote works of moral strength and insight but of little lasting literary value. Because of the pronounced Christian bias of his fictional work, especially prominent in *The Pilgrim's Regress*, 1933, and muted in the later novels, there has been at least the implied categorization of Lewis as a merely "Christian writer." Lewis became a Christian prior to writing these fictional works for which he has become internationally known. The influences of Christian belief and the accumulated influences of Christian literature and art upon Lewis and his fiction are clear. Lewis acknowledges such influences, though he does not overrate their force in his work. There is the question, however, of whether the discussion ends here and tells us all we would like to know about why people read Lewis. We want to know why readers of the *Chronicles of Narnia*, reading after reading, experience a pleasurable jolt akin to Lewis's repeated reactions to *Phantastes*. Out of a host of "Christian" writers of fiction, Lewis remains after a generation, one of the few to find high favor with the intellectual and common reader alike. We want to examine why.

I hope by looking at the remaining thirty years of Lewis's life, the period of his productive career as a writer of fiction, and by examining his casual comments in letters, his academic writing on the subject of literature and literary criticism, and later the fiction in a separate section of analysis, to show that his evolution as a writer is just that and not a sudden conversion. His work is significant as literature which happens also to be written by a Christian—no one now calls Eliot the Christian Poet. The gaps in our appreciation of Lewis's achievement may be appropriately filled by a standard literary critical treatment of his work, using a method which Lewis himself proposed in *An Experiment in Criticism*.

One of Lewis's favorite comments on the subject of choice between alternatives of any sort uses the following distinction.

... the subordination of Nature is demanded if only in the interest of Nature herself. All the beauty withers when we try to make it an absolute. Put first things first and we get second things thrown in: put second things first and we lose *both* first and second things. We never get, say, even the sensual pleasure of food at its best when we are being greedy.[42]

This distinction serves to illustrate the dichotomizing influence of Lewis's renewed Christian belief. Before he accepted Christianity, he accorded first place to the heightened state of longing and expectation aroused by highly imaginative music, tales of the mysterious, antique and romantic, or the natural beauty of scenic views. The pleasure of repeating experiences like reading or walking which had produced the thrill initially came to be almost an end in itself, although literature was never for Lewis reduced to its effect without regard for meaning and intellectual response. Still, he might be said to have been at least tempted by the pleasures of the aesthete. Even after the realization that he was mistaking the secondary pleasure for the primary, the desire in place of the object desired, he continued to enjoy the pleasure of rereading, especially when sick or depressed, works like the romances of Morris or MacDonald which had given him an original thrill.[43]

But the thrill begins, in his thinking of the mid-thirties, to take secondary position and to become the herald of deeper meanings.

I think the thrill of the Pagan stories and of romance may be due to the fact that they are mere beginnings—the first, faint whisper of the wind from beyond the world—while Christianity is the thing itself: and no thing, when you have really started on it, can have for you then and there just the same thrill as the first hint.[44]

It is a mistake to presume that upon conversion Lewis suddenly saw all literature as somehow nascently Christian in the way our psychoanalytically committed critics have applied their theories wholesale. He was an academic, a student of literature, a pupil of Kirkpatrick, the "Great Knock," and was as tough a rationalist as his teacher. He was as shrewd an evaluator of literature and its history, traditions, and meaning as one would expect in a man of his brilliance and training. The shift in his viewpoint is subtle and slow to develop. He was, during the thirties, working on *The Allegory of Love*, writing *Out of the Silent Planet*, meeting with the Inklings and the Socratic Club, and if we can judge accurately from his letters, spending considerable time on the analysis of fiction.

...I personally enjoy a novel only in so far as it fails to be a novel pure and simple and escapes from the eternal love business into some philosophical, religious, fantastic, or farcical region.[45]

Since term began I have had a delightful time reading a children's story which Tolkien has just written. I have told of him before: the one man absolutely fitted, if fate had allowed, to be a third in our friendship in the old days, for he also grew up on W. Morris and George Macdonald. Reading his fairy tale has been uncanny—it is so exactly like what we wd. both have longed to write (or read) in 1916: so that one feels he is not making it up but merely describing the same world into which all three of us have the entry. Whether it is really *good* (I think it is until the end) is of course another question: still more, whether it will succeed with modern children.[46]

We [Tolkien and Lewis] remarked how odd it was that the word *romance* should be used to cover things so different as Morris on the one hand and Dumas or Rafael Sabatini on the other—things not only different but so different that it is hard to imagine the same person liking both. We agreed that for what *we* meant by romance there must be at least the hint of another world—one must 'hear the horns of elfland.'[47]

His interests and concerns center around the word "romance," the definition of it as otherworldly, and his insistence on clarity in language, his preference for native words over literary ones. The best example of his interests and thoughts on the subject of literature at this time, and most helpful to students of Lewis's and George MacDonald's works is an extended analysis of MacDonald's *Lilith*.[48] His analysis is a remarkably detailed reaction to a work that had fascinated him for years, from his earliest reading of it.

Lewis was among the first to see in *Lilith* both the Will to Power and the spoiled ideal. He saw MacDonald using exciting and imaginative symbolism and characterization to present new and important Christian truths. He reveals MacDonald's use of religion as in a sense providing temptations of a new sort. The analysis centers wholly on meaning, and the interpretation is couched in Christian terms, but MacDonald is after all a Christian. Lewis makes no judgment of the value of such a philosophically oriented piece of fiction, but he approves of works of this sort, and as we shall see later, MacDonald has a profound influence on his understanding of the role fiction has when presented in a Christian context.

Another major influence which continued through this period was the romantic fiction of William Morris. In a letter to Owen Barfield on September 2, 1937, Lewis discussed the romancer's use of other worlds and Morris's formula for using such worlds.

Retiring to what seems an ideal world to find yourself all the more face to face with gravest reality without ever drawing a pessimistic conclusion but fully maintaining that heroic action in, or amelioration of, a temporal life is an absolute duty though the disease of temporality is incurable.... [49]

Rather than decreasing in importance as he underwent the changes which are part of his evolving spiritual conversion, his interest in and dedication to his earliest love for *faerie* remained strong. In fact, if anything, this interest moved to the center of Lewis's belief that an apparently simple fairytale or romance could convey, better than a complex novel, the physical attraction of nature and the deeper meaning of spirit combined in one aesthetically satisfying and spiritually provoking unity. His love and delight in nature and in descriptions of nature in literature is the first basic component of this theory, springing as it does from his earliest reaction and responses to physical nature and to the artistic representations of it. This element is the strongest, the one which appears to govern the course of his own fiction as he began to write. From his response to nature, he created the descriptions of Perelandra and later Narnia that for many of his readers remain a higher achievement than his "message." As we will see later, it is the critic's tendency to separate the message out from its integral and organic connection with these sensuous descriptions which does a disservice to readers of Lewis's work who are naturally drawn to these very descriptions.

To his friend Dom Bede Griffiths he wrote about the love he felt for nature,

I think this is one of the causes of our love of inanimate nature, that in it we see we see [sic] things which unswervingly carry out the will of their creator, and are therefore wholly beautiful: and though their *kind* of obedience is infinitely lower than ours, yet the degree is so much more perfect that a Christian can see the reason that the Romantics had in feeling a certain holiness in the wood and water. The Pantheistic conclusions they sometimes draw are false: but their *feeling* was just and we can safely allow it in ourselves now that we know the real reason.[50]

"Now that we know the real reason," we can safely follow our inclination to sensuous beauty, to simple tales, to romance and the horns of elfland, because they are sanctified with meaning and purpose. Now Lewis saw first things first, as he would say. He recognized that the joy he felt in his early sensuousness was the first inkling of the "come unto me," drawing him further in and higher up through literary and cultural myth to the ultimate truth of God. Literature, his own and others, now became a legitimate tool to use for saying what needed to be said, and fairy tales, fantasies, science fiction all became useful tools sanctified by their organic connection to their purpose and message. He saw a natural and holy connection between what we feel when we read a powerfully imaginative story and what that story teaches us. He wrote to Greeves in 1935 expressing his sadness over the unsettled prospects for the present generation who were indulged by science but had so little real affection or common sense; for example, they were never exposed to fairy tales or nursery rhymes.[51]

Lewis was beginning his career as a writer of fiction during the mid-thirties; *The Pilgrim's Regress* appeared in 1933 and *Out of the Silent Planet* in 1938. Although there are scattered references to these works and hints of his progress, they shed little light on the process of composition or on Lewis's thoughts while he was writing. His correspondence with Arthur Greeves ceases to afford many insights into Lewis as a writer and flattens out into desultory comments of a personal nature. There are now other correspondents who came into his life: Sister Penelope of the Community of Saint Mary the Virgin at Wantage; E. R. Eddison, the author of *The Worm Ouroboros*; Ruth Pitter, a writer, and others with whom Lewis corresponded at some length on literary matters, often giving advice, but as frequently offering observations of a theoretical sort or comments on his own growing body of fiction. Though these comments lack the consistency of those from the Greeves correspondence, they serve to broaden our understanding of Lewis's development as he came to the actual task of writing fiction.

In 1939 he noted to A.K. Hamilton Jenkin that the reaction of readers to his story, "a journey to Mars," revealed that division among readers occurred more on the basis of the sharp frontiers of taste than from other formal divisions:

These sharp *frontiers* of taste are a very interesting literary fact which I've never seen discussed by any critic, and which are far more important in dividing readers than any of the *formal* divisions, even that of verse and prose.... but Aristotle, Johnson, and Coleridge have nothing to say about them.[52]

It was with perhaps a cavalier disregard for the formal divisions, e.g., romance, detective fiction, space fantasy, fairy tale, etc., that Lewis embarked on the writing of his first two novels. His concern was to say what needed saying in the most appropriate and affecting manner, and he must have hoped that the natural inclination of interested readers would take care of the rest. His own *An Experiment in Criticism* indicates his approval of a direct and uncluttered response to literature rather than the sterility of New Critical dissection by type.

What brought him to write fiction in the first place was certainly not primarily the anticipated fame. He had been burned at that fire before. Nor was it initially to use fiction as a mouthpiece for his newly discovered belief however much critics may be tempted in all good will to assign this cause as a prime factor. From what he has told us, mainly in letters, he felt moved to discuss certain matters of concern to him by using this medium. His partially published letter to Sister Penelope at the outset of their correspondence in mid-1939 (*see Letters*, pp. 166-7) gives his purpose in writing *Out of the Silent Planet* as a serious answer to the Westonian or scientific view with its hope of defeating death. He goes on to suggest somewhat playfully that a writer with more talent and leisure might profitably engage in smuggling good news to people through romance.[53] In a later letter recommending *Phantastes* to her, he indicates that part of the attraction of this novel for him is George MacDonald's capacity to entice the reader beyond his understanding, a method Lewis would firmly subscribe to in the *Chronicles of Narnia*.

Isn't *Phantastes* good! It did a lot for me years before I became a Christian, when I had no idea what was behind it. This has already made it easier for me to understand how the better elements in mythology can be real *praeparatio evangelica* for peoples who do not yet know whither they are being led.[54]

His published letter to Griffiths (April 16, 1940) makes a clear stand for the commitment of art and literature to moral truth. Art for art's sake is unhealthy balderdash.[55] Art and literature, says Lewis, can only work satisfactorily when they are clearly moral in their intent or else merely providing innocent recreation.[56] Designating art as a handmaid to religion, Lewis indicates that art is secondary to truth, moral or religious, and reveals how far he has come from his euphoric adolescent response to MacDonald and Malory. The operation of religion in and through fiction must be subtle, for by drawing attention to itself it blunts its message. Lewis comes increasingly to prefer imaginative works with an underlying theme of spiritual significance to those of outright theology. In a letter to a Miss Jacob, he discusses his reaction to short stories of this kind, especially those of George MacDonald.

What I was really liking in the stories was just the Xtianity tho I didn't know it. I think it worked this way. In the stories I got their theology as it really was: in their explicitly religious works I brought all my own conceptions of Xtianity ready made and read those into them.[57]

Lewis's preference for this sort of fiction and his belief that fiction could serve as an evangelical tool prepares us for his later descriptions of his own fiction in this perspective.

It is in letters to Sister Penelope of this period, many published in part in *Letters*, that Lewis has most to say about his work on *Out of the Silent Planet*, *The Screwtape Letters*, and *Perelandra* and on the role of the writer who is a Christian. In October 1941, he sent her the manuscript of *The Screwtape Letters*, which she later asked his permission to sell in order to further some project of the Sisterhood; Lewis graciously granted his permission.[58] On several occasions he gave advice on her writing and praised her achievements. He discussed with her the problems of presenting the green Lady of *Perelandra* as both a pagan goddess (Eve) and the Blessed Virgin (Ave).[59] In August 1942, having finished *Perelandra* in May, except for the revision of the first two chapters, he discussed the nature of mythology with her.

No. I *don't* believe people sat down and "made up" mythology. There are both divine and diabolical elements in it. And anyway what *is* the process we describe as "making up." I am willing to believe, with Henry More (the Cambridge Platonist) that some, at least, of the "gods" were good spirits "as innocent of the worship idolatrously offered them as Peter and Mary are of that offered them by the Papists." (The simile is his.) But of course we know nothing. It's a view good enough to base a romance on—not part of mythology.[60]

About the process of creativity as it operates in human terms, he wrote extensively in 1943. In a letter of February 20, he commented significantly that man was incapable of creating anything *de novo*:

Try to imagine a new primary colour, a third sex, a fourth dimension, or even a monster which does not consist of bits of existing animals stuck together. Nothing happens. And that surely is why our works (as you said) never mean to others quite what we intended; because we are re-combining elements made by Him and already containing *His* meanings. Because of those divine meanings in our materials it is impossible we shd. ever know the whole meaning of our works, and the meaning we never intended may be the best and truest one. Writing a book is much less like creation than it is like planting a garden or begetting a child; in all three cases we are only entering as *one* cause into a causal stream which works, so to speak, in its own way.[61]

Lewis would probably not have been so baldly "religious" in his interpretation of the creative act had he been writing one of his academic colleagues rather than a Sister. But his feelings about the secondary role of human imagination and genius, of human "originality," are clearly stated and remind us of his admiration for Tolkien's theory of sub-creation outlined in Tolkien's 1938 lecture, "On Fairy Tales." Human art according to this theory is an act, within the microcosm, which exercises the God-like power of creativity and which aspires to the discovery of universal truths; but the human insight revealed in art can only be a weak reflection of that truth.

The purpose of art, of fiction in particular, by Lewis's definition and use at this period, appears to find its center in the imaginative revelation of truth—moral and spiritual.

On the imaginative level I think the deepest truths enter the mind much better as arbitrary marvels than as universal theorems. Cinderella has to be back at midnight—Psyche must not see Cupid's face—Adam and Eve must not eat the fruit: how much better these statements are than any philosophical generalities about obedience.[62]

Imaginative writing fills two functions: it provides an outlet for the human's desire to mimic his creator, using materials ready to hand, and it assists in drawing home to readers the inner truths which have greater force when absorbed through an imaginative medium than when given in philosophical or historical form.

A rather different view of Lewis's attitudes toward the writing of fiction appears in a series of unpublished letters to the novelist E.R. Eddison. Eddison's replies to Lewis and most of Lewis's letters are laboriously composed in pseudo-Middle English. Lewis here is dealing with a brother writer whose first novel, *The Worm Ouroboros*, he greatly admired, and who as a professional admired Lewis's fiction. The subject matter and tone of the letters is in marked contrast to those to Sister Penelope. Although some of the letters are undated, they can be approximately dated by reference to the publication of the respective men's novels.

In one of the earliest letters, Lewis lists as sources of *Out of the Silent Planet*: Morris, Snorri, Homer, and Sir Thomas Browne, commenting that they outstrip "the clam jamfrey and whymperinges of the rakehellie auctors in these latter daies, as the Eliots, Pounds, Lawrences, Audens, and the like."[63] The letter praises the achievement of *The Worm* and chastises Eddison for failing to include a map and appendix. In a letter received by Eddison on December 30, 1942, Lewis questions Eddison on his knowledge of the nuptial practices of bears, evidently in hopes of receiving information to use in the description of Mr. Bultitude's nuptials at the end of *That Hideous Strength*.[64] Eddison proved of little help. A letter of January 10, 1943, questions as possible influences on *The Worm*: Homer, Morris, Snorri and on Eddison's second book, *The Mistress of Mistresses* of Swinburne, Beckford, and to a lesser extent Flaubert, Baudelaire, and Poe.[65] Eddison's reply indicates that his sources for *The Worm* were Aristotle, Homer, the classic sagas, Sir Thomas Browne, *A Thousand and One Nights*, and Milton. He disclaimed any influence from Beckford and Morris (he had not read them) and acknowledged Swinburne, Baudelaire, and Poe to be superficial influences.[66]

Eddison had read *Perelandra* first and thus came to Lewis's work in the middle of the trilogy. His reactions were favorable; he approved of the description of the planet, the animals, and the vegetation but disliked the "eldila" because they were "unsexual" and found that the wound in Ransom's heel lacked adequate explanation. He criticized the portrait of Weston as unrealistic. He wrote:

And how may we be content to all eternity to do without them, [evil persons] unless we subsist for ever upon pasteurized poppy-cocke in a world nicely ordered for olde virgins & theyr prudently gelded lappe-dogges?[67]

Four days later, Lewis laments the fact that Eddison had not been able to read the two first novels of the trilogy in sequence.

...but it means your reading back from the greater to the less—the first book ending on a merely satiric note. But Lanes [the publisher] *are* fools. Note how they blab out my whole theme in the blurb, wh. was meant to come over the reader by stealth. Idiots![68]

In the same letter he bemoans the slow progress of *That Hideous Strength*.

...I have just read through what is already written (about 300 sheets) and come to the uncomfortable conclusion that it is all rubbish. Has this ever happened to you? A nauseous moment—when the thought of trying to mend it, and of abandoning it, seem equally unbearable.[69]

When Eddison had read *Out of the Silent Planet*, he sent his analysis:

What everlastingly delights me in your books is, first, your technique of narrative together with your power of presenting ideal worlds which have both outward and inward reality, a most rare quality in a writer. And secondly—& what I value most of all—a kind of comfortable warmth in your imagination. This I find in the whole treatment of your "furry people," who have traits in them to touch the heart, & whose outward aspect, be it strange, is by no means displeasing.... [70]

Eddison has caught here the quality which distinguishes the best of Lewis's work, that comfortable warmth of his imagination. There is no record of Lewis's response to this praise, but his feelings about Eddison's work are clearly stated.[71] He was drawn by the virtuosity of imagination displayed in *The Worm*, the sheer creative inventiveness of the story, setting, and language. But by the time he had finished *Mistress of Mistresses*, he had begun a running argument over Eddison's portrayal of cruel rulers, tyrants, and autocratic highborns, whose purpose in the novel seemed to Lewis that of elevating the level of excitement but offering no deeper meaning. The quality of warmth which Eddison admired in Lewis's work, Lewis found lacking in Eddison's.

We assume that what Eddison meant more specifically when he wrote of Lewis's warmth was the persistent focus on human qualities, particularly those of compassion, friendship, and loyalty, even in nonhuman relationships, e.g., Ransom and the hross, Hyoi, in *Out of the Silent Planet*. An examination of his work shows that it is this quality of warmth which characterizes Lewis's earliest response to beauty in nature, in music, art, and literature, and which comes to characterize his own fiction.

In rather marked contrast to the warmth and hope of his writing during this time is a note in a letter to Griffiths.

I think that though I am emotionally a fairly cheerful person my actual judgment of the world has always been what yours now is and so I have not been disappointed. The early loss of my mother, great unhappiness at school, and the shadow of the last war and presently the experience of it, had given me a very pessimistic view of existence. My atheism was based on it: and it still seems to me that *far* the strongest card in our enemies' hand is the actual course of the world: and that, quite apart from particular events like wars and revolutions. The inherent "vanity" of the "creature," the fact that life preys on life, that all beauty and happiness is produced only to be destroyed—this was what stuck in my gullet.[72]

Conveniently for scholars, Lewis discussed in a 1944 letter to Charles Brady, who had recently completed a study of the sources of Lewis's work, the influences of various writers on his fiction. Lewis named Morris, MacDonald, the early Yeats, James Stephens, Chesterton, Rackham in art, Wagner in music, and David Lindsay in *A Voyage to Arcturus*, which Lewis called the source of his space trilogy.[73] This last work had a profound influence on Lewis's writing as he indicated by repeated references to it always accompanied by high praise and increasingly with the warning that it was a dangerous, a Manichaean book, unfit for young readers. A letter to Greeves in 1934 indicated that Greeves had read it and mentioned it to Lewis earlier, but Lewis had not yet read the book.[74] In a 1947 letter to Ruth Pitter, the poet, Lewis revealed his debt to Lindsay and his feelings about the influence of *A Voyage to Arcturus* on his own work.

Can you bear the truth—*Voyage to Arcturus* is not the parody of *Perelandra* but its father. It was published, a dead failure, about 25 years ago. Now that the author is dead it is suddenly leaping into fame; but I'm one of the old guard who had a treasured second hand copy before anyone had heard of it. From Lyndsay [sic] I first learned what other planets in fiction are really good for; for *spiritual* adventures. Only they can satisfy the craving which sends our imagination off the earth or hurtling it another way. In him I first saw the terrific results produced by the union of two kinds of fiction hitherto kept apart: the Novalis, G. Macdonald, James Stephens sort and the H. G. Wells, Jules Verne sort. My debt to him is very great: tho' I'm a little alarmed to find it so obvious that the affinity came through to you even from a talk about Lyndsay [sic]. For the rest, *Voyage to A* is on the borderline of the diabolical: i.e. the philosophy expressed is so Manichaean as to be almost Satanic. Secondly, the style is often laughably crude. Thirdly, the proper names (Polecrab, Blodsombre, Wombflash, Tydomin, Sullenbode) are superb and perhaps Screwtape owes something to them. Fourthly, you must read it. You will have a disquieting but not-to-be-missed experience.[75]

His correspondence with Ruth Pitter, covering the last seventeen years of his life, touches frequently, because of their shared literary interests, on matters related to literary theory and practice, mainly poetry. One of his earliest letters advises against the use of sheer size or number to sway readers.

But as a rule, the bigger a thing is physically, the less it works in literature. One ghost is always more disquieting than ten; no good fight in a story can have more than a dozen or so combatants; the death of a million men is less tragic than that of one.[76]

In the same letter he cautioned her against thinking of poetry as immortal and included several of his poems for her comments.

Poetry is as mortal as man. One's favorite lyrics can wear out. A change of language can make the best line first ridiculous, then (ugh!) "so quaint," then meaningless. A change in education can blot out a whole dead language and Virgil ceases to be.[77]

He distinguishes between two sorts of poetry: the apparently spontaneous and unwilled, giving Blake and Donne as poets of this type, and the ritualistic, with Milton as an example.[78] Of the poet, he said,

He is not the creator, only the mother, of something whose father is the Universe or Time; and the child will grow up in its own way & make its own friends long after he is dead.

He admitted in the same letter that in his own poetry, making the meter produce the desired effect might come above all other considerations.

The "tension" you speak of is real. It means that in most of these poems I am enamored of metrical subtleties—not as a game; the truth is I often lust after a meter as a man might lust after a woman. The effect I want, even if attained wd. not be of the elusive kind—more like heraldry on enamel—a blaze.[79]

In a note accompanying her gift of Lewis's letters to the Bodleian Library, Miss Pitter explained that Lewis's reaction to life, as she saw it, reflected "an almost uniquely persisting *child's* sense of glory and nightmare."[80] She feels that Lewis wanted to succeed as a poet but that his learning and scholarship militated against such a career. His success as a prose writer she attributes to his unique combination of openness with deep sensitivity and his unusual felicity in expression.[81]

Though he wrote to Miss Pitter about poetry and sent poems to her for criticism, his mind, judging from the bulk of his references to literary matters, was firmly centered on prose writing. He was entering the most productive period of his own career as a novelist, and his letters are sprinkled with comments and observations on general literary problems and questions relating directly to his own work. Discussing dialogue with Sister Penelope, he emphasized the need for the sound of reality: "It must always *sound* like real conversation but must be in reality clearer and more economical than that. Literature is an art of *illusion*."[82] To I.O. Evans, author of *Gadget City*, 1944, he expressed his belief that "art can teach (and much great art deliberately sets out to do so) without at all ceasing to be art."[83]

Engaged by now in writing the *Chronicles of Narnia*, he wrote to Owen Barfield after receiving what must have been an objection to the fur coats which appeared at the back of the wardrobe, in *The Lion, the Witch and the Wardrobe*.

The fur coats can be altered easily. The danger of getting shut in cupboards is much more serious and less easily altered. I don't know why Morrel shd. feel let down: fur *is* nice, otherwise there wd. be no temptation to trapping and one *does* find it in wardrobes. But that will be altered. The Beavers weren't there to prevent you taking it too seriously, but to supply the snug & homely and to give information. I'd have liked that chapter as a child.[84]

Snug and homely, the remembrances of childhood and happy days explain to us part of Lewis's attraction to the fairy tale. He offered in his later essays on the subject of fairy tales the explanation that they were appropriate to what he had in mind to express. He had read and appreciated Tolkien's *Hobbit* and his essay on fairy tales, and he had been an advocate of the great and little known writers of this genre from childhood. In a comment on the demonstrable proof of Christianity in answer to Sheldon Van Auken's query, he replied that even fairy tales can embody the truth.[85] In a letter to W. L. Kinter, part of a correspondence which centers on the space trilogy and Narnia books, Lewis responded to Kinter's suggestion that his works can be laid out as a cathedral. He calls *Miracles* and the other "treatises" the cathedral school. The children's fantasies are side chapels, and each one has its own altar.[86] To Miss Rhona Bodle, he wrote of his feelings, toward the end of the writing of the Narnia stories, about Hans Andersen.

I have come to like Hans Andersen better since I grew up than I did in childhood, I think both the pathos and the satire—both v. delicate, penetrating and ever-present in his work—disquieted me then.... He was, you know, a friend of Kirkegaard's and a v. disappointed novelist, for it was by his novels not his fairy tales that he wished to be known. I wonder if the story of the *Shadow* is connected with that—the shadow outgrowing the man as the fairy-tale writer outgrew the novelist. But I'm glad he did![87]

Though Lewis admired fairy stories, he was late in coming to write them himself. The initial impulse, he records, for the creation of

Narnia arose from nightmares about lions.[88] "All I can tell you is that pictures come into my head and I write stories about them. I don't know how or why the pictures come."[89]

There is little question that the books contain thinly veiled theology. Many comments in the letters refer specifically to this point.

I get lovely, and often most moving, letters from my child readers. I had expected that they wd. get the theology more or less unconsciously, but the truth is that they all see it perfectly clearly, bless 'em, and much more clearly than some grown-ups.[90]

He explained to one reader that his method in fiction and using symbols was that of catching the reader off guard or unaware.[91] More specifically, the method used in the Narnia stories he described as follows:

The fairy-tale version of the Passion in *The Lion* etc. works in the way you describe because—tho' this sounds odd— it bye-passes one's reverence and piety. We approach the real story in the Gospels with the knowledge that we *ought* to feel certain things about it. And this, by a familiar psychological law, can hinder us from doing so. The dutiful effort prevents the spontaneous feeling; just as if you say to an old friend during a brief reunion "Now let's have a good talk" both suddenly find themselves with nothing to say. Make it a fairy-tale and the reader is taken off his guard (unless ye become as little children...).[92]

He connects the Witch with classical prototypes in another letter to Kinter, suggesting a variety of sources and meanings beyond the Christian ones.

The Witch is of course Circe, Alcina etc. because she is (or they are) the same Archtype we find in so many fairy tales. No good asking where an individual author got that. We are born knowing the Witch aren't we? The stone has a glance at the stone tables of the Mosaic Law and its breaking to our liberation from the curse of the law at the crucifixion.[93]

On April 15, 1954, Lewis announced in a letter to one of his many young admirers and correspondents, Joan Lancaster, that he had come to the end of the *Chronicles of Narnia*.[94] Thus he rounded out the series of tales which brought him greater fame and popularity than any of his other works. He seems not to have regarded them as highly as his readers. His preference among the fictional work was for *Perelandra* or *Till We Have Faces*.[95] He was delighted by the response of his readers, particularly that of children who often wrote to him asking for more Narnian adventures. With some, he corresponded, giving advice on their writing. He was amused by the perceptiveness of the children and the density of their elders in finding the meaning of the fairy tales, and he held out some hope that his message might be subtly conveyed into young minds. In a letter to Harry Blamires, the author of *The Devil's Hunting Ground*, he wrote:

I am so glad you 'all' liked *The Silver Chair*. I am often surprised by the extreme youth of some of my child readers. I get lovely letters, and sometimes dare to hope that the Narnian infiltration may bear a little fruit when those who understand in childhood grow up and begin to do things.[96]

The professed purpose of writing these books is never that of allegorizing or moralizing on a Christian theme. The books grew out of pictures seen by Lewis. He was a close friend of Tolkien as Humphrey Carpenter has so carefully outlined in *The Inklings*. The influence which Tolkien exerted directly on Lewis's conversion and indirectly by his expressed reaction that the original version of *The Lion, the Witch and the Wardrobe* would not work as a story, suggest that their views of literature, allegory, and myth were similar.[97] That is not the case. In a published letter to Father Peter Milward, Lewis suggested what both his and Tolkien's view of allegory and myth might be.

Tolkien's book [*The Fellowship of the Ring*] is not an allegory—a form he dislikes. You'll get nearest to his mind on such subjects by studying his essay on Fairy Tales in the *Essays presented to Charles Williams*. His root idea of narrative art is "sub-creation"—the making of a secondary world. What you wd. call "a pleasant story for the children" wd. be to him *more serious* than allegory. But for *his* views read the essay, wh. is indispensible. *My* view wd. be that a good myth (i.e. a story out of which ever varying meanings will grow for different readers and in different ages) is a higher thing than an allegory (into which one meaning has been put). Into an allegory a man can put only what he already knows; in a myth he puts what he does not yet know and cd. not come by [to know] in any other way.[98]
I too have got *The Fellowship of the Ring* and have gluttonously read two chapters instead of saving it all for the week-end. Wouldn't it be wonderful if it really succeeded (in selling, I mean)! It would inaugurate a new age. Dare we hope?[99]

He was, however, by mid-1953 deeply immersed in another project, the *Oxford History of English Literature*, described in a letter to Dr. Warfield Firor as "a big and (to tell the truth) dull, academic work."[100] He had met his future wife, Joy Davidman Gresham; she and her sons had spent some time with the Lewis brothers at the Kilns in December 1953.

Warnie...and I are dazed: we have had an American lady staying in the house with her two sons aged 9½ and 6. I never knew what we celibates are shielded from. I will never laugh at parents again. Not that the boys weren't a delight: but a delight like surf-bathing which leaves one breathless and aching. The energy, the *tempo*, is what tires. I have now perceived (what I always suspected from memories of my own childhood) that the way to a child's heart is quite simple: treat them with seriousness & ordinary civility—they ask no more. What they can't stand (quite rightly) is the common adult assumption that everything they say shd. be twisted into a kind of jocularity. The mother (Mrs. Gresham) had rather a boom in USA in the *entre guerre* as the poetess Joy Davidman: do you know her work?[101]

The next day, Lewis wrote to Joy Gresham concerning a book by A. C. Clarke, *Childhood's End*, which she had mentioned to him. This letter and others directed to Clarke indicate Lewis's continued interest in space fiction, although it was not a genre and method he would return to in his later writing.

It [*Childhood's End*] is quite out of range of the common space-and-time writers; away up near Lindsay's *Voyage to Arcturus* and Wells' *First Men in the Moon*. It is better than any of Stapledon's. It hasn't got Ray Bradbury's delicacy, but then it has ten times his emotional power, and far more mythopoeia.[102]

In a 1956 letter to Clarke, Lewis insisted on the need for craftsmanship in science fiction writing. He emphasized throughout his correspondence with Clarke the need to subdue technology to narrative and to give attention to the commonly accepted literary demands of fiction.

Surely in a work of art all the material should be *used*. If a theme is introduced into a symphony, something must be made of that theme. If a poem is written in a certain metre, the particular qualities of that metre must be exploited.... For whatever in art is not doing good is doing harm: no room for passengers. (In a good black and white drawing the areas of white paper are essential to the whole design, just as much as the lines. It is only in a child's drawing that they're *merely* blank paper.)[103]

His insistence on economy, craftsmanship, and art in any literary endeavor, coupled with his fertile imagination and clear purpose, set Lewis apart from the other science fiction writers of the 1950s.

In 1954, Lewis was invited by the Milton Society of America to attend a testimonial dinner in New York honoring Lewis and Douglas Bush. Lewis was unable to attend, and he sent his regrets including in the letter a succinct summary of his development as a writer and critic up to this point in his career. It is worth quoting as it indicates

Lewis's assessment of both the direction and success of his various literary endeavors.

> The imaginative man in me is older, more continuously operative and in that sense more basic than either the religious writer or the critic. It was he who made me first attempt (with little success) to be a poet. It was he who, in response to the poetry of others, made me a critic, and, in defence of that response, sometimes a critical controversialist. It was he who, after my conversion led me to embody my religious beliefs in symbolical and mythopoeic forms, ranging from *Screwtape* to a kind of theologized science-fiction. And it was of course he who brought me, in the last few years, to write the series of Narnian stories for children; not asking what children want and then endeavouring to adapt myself (this was not needed) but because the fairy tale was the genre best fitted for what I wanted to say....[104]

It is the imaginative man to whom Lewis points as the moving force, and the focus of this study of his aesthetic theory and work is centered on determining what sort of imaginative man he was and the influence which his tastes and beliefs had on his work. The boundaries which he sets here are those of poetry, criticism, and symbolic and mythopoeic fiction, ranging over the formal structures from satire to science fiction and incorporating fairy tales at the end. The subject of his work he treats obliquely, indicating that it was after his conversion that he turned to symbolic and mythopoeic forms and fairy tales to express what he wanted to say. The important thing to note here is that he had made peace with his early desires for fame as a poet, and though not discounting his academic publications, he now places the focus of his statement on the operation of imagination in fiction and criticism. As he said in a letter, stories are really imagining out loud.[105]

One last work, *Till We Have Faces*, was already under way when Lewis wrote to the Milton Society. There are references in the correspondence that place its composition in mid-1955.[106] Letters to Kathleen Raine and to Anne and Martin Kilmer after the publication of *Till We have Faces* give some insight into Lewis's conception of the central character as do statements in the *Biography* which link the character of Orual with Joy Gresham.[107] It is premature at this point to speculate on Lewis's achievement in this last work, the one which some critics and perhaps Lewis himself at the end of his career came to regard as the best of his fiction. "I am glad you liked *Till We Have Faces*, because so few people do. It is my biggest flop for years, and so of course I think it is my best book."[108] We need, however, to know more of the principles upon which he formed critical judgments of his own and of other literary works. These basic statements are found in his academic studies and especially in the series of lectures which became *An Experiment in Criticism*. An investigation of what they afford by way of aid in studying the fiction will be the focus of the next section of this study.

Lewis wrote no major piece of fiction after the completion of *Till We Have Faces* in 1956. He married Joy Davidman Gresham, took up the Chair of Medieval Literature at Magdalene College, Cambridge, suffered from increasing debility through his own failing health, and then lost his wife. Yet through these last seven years, he remained a perceptive critic of fiction, adviser to young writers, and student of new trends in modern fiction. His letters are sprinkled with comments on the nature of fantasy, the uses of allegory and myth, and the place of imagination in contemporary literature.

To young writers like Jane Gaskell (age 15), he suggested that the demands of fantasy writing are: elevation of action and description and the necessity of not letting the earthly intrude so far as to break the spell.[109] The descriptive language must work to make the reader *feel*, and he emphasizes the need for testing the sound before being satisfied with a particular descriptive word. To Joan Lancaster, another young admirer, he wrote:

If you become a writer you'll be trying to describe the *thing* all your life: and lucky if, out of dozens of books, one or two sentences, just for a moment, come near to getting it across.[110]

Later responding to a story she had written and sent him, he wrote:

...You don't mix the reality and the fantasy quite in the right way. One way is Beatrix Potter's or Brer Rabbit's. By fantasy the animals are allowed to talk and behave in many ways like humans. But their *relations* to one another and to us remain the real ones. Rabbits are in danger from foxes and men. The other way is mine: you go right out of this world into a different creation, where there are a different sort of animals.[111]

For Martin Kilmer, he listed the writers he considered to be the most boring: Cicero, Ben Jonson, Launcelot Andrews, and Mrs. Humphrey Ward.[112] He questioned Ruth Pitter on whether her reading included Mary Norton's *The Borrowers*, *The Borrowers Afield*, K. M. Briggs' *Mobberly Dick*, and Margaret Kennedy's *The Feast*.[113] He shared with her in a later letter his reaction to drug visions, his experience originating most probably in the treatment of his illness.

The drug visions are a curious phenomenon. I can't say with you that *while they last* they aren't a "patch on the natural kind." To me, the difference is that they leave nothing behind, whereas the real ones, though equally transitory, "are yet the future light." etc.[114]

In a letter to a Mr. Masson, he explained the function of the imagination as he saw it in 1956. "The true exercise of imagination, in my view, is (a) To help us to understand other people (b) To respond to, and, some of us, to produce, art."[115]

These last years produced much from Lewis's pen which endears him to Christian readers: *Surprised by Joy*, 1955; *The Four Loves*, 1960; and *A Grief Observed*, 1961. They were trying years, and yet Lewis was able to put them in perspective, using the same amused detachment he had earlier outlined to Dr. Warfield Firor, when at the age of fifty Lewis commented on his contemplation of mortality.

One ought not to need the gloomy moments of life for beginning detachment, nor be re-entangled by the bright ones. One ought to be able to enjoy the bright ones to the full and at that very same moment live in perfect readiness to leave them, confident that what calls one away is better.[116]

It was this same humorous detachment which brought him to suggest two months before his death to Sister Penelope, that death is solemn fun and asking her to come down and visit him if prison visitation is permitted in Purgatory.[117]

His literary epitaph might well be found in a comment to a casual correspondent, written in 1952.

It is not settled comfort and heart's ease but momentary joy that transfigures the past and lets the eternal quality show through. (I sometimes eat parsnips because their taste, which I dislike, reminds me of my prep. school, which I disliked: but these two dislikes don't in the least impair the strange joy of "being reminded.")[118]

Before we look at Lewis's theory of literary criticism as he expressed it in his essays and lectures, we might review where we have been. As a young man, Lewis was strongly attracted by imaginative literature. At first, he responded to the sensuous beauty he felt when he came in contact with romantic poems and novels. Later, when a developing intellectual curiosity brought him to consider the craft of writing, he studied the methods by which writers achieve that special effect. He began to experiment with poetic forms and then the novel and became a practitioner of the art he admired.

His concern at the beginning of his own career as a writer was with the role played by meaning and form. He had come to meaning first, drawn almost against his will by the pull of longing and desire, the qualities which first attracted him to reading. Only later did he consider the role of structure and how the author crafts his meaning. Then he studied the tools of descriptive narration, characterization, and structure in order to apply them to his growing technical development.

These artistic questions are part of a larger concern which Lewis was working his way through at the same time: the question of how spirit and matter interact in life. As Lewis came to see that everything in life reflected some spark of spirit, and then to accept life as the reflection of God, his view of art and the artist also evolved. He came to see art as a reflection of spirit just as life itself is. His novels show that he consciously intended to move his readers to feelings of joy and delight in order to bring them to a better understanding of the real truth of life. That is why he placed such a premium on myth, which he saw as the ultimate achievement of an author who through the force of his skillful control of form could move the reader to the highest truth.

From looking at what Lewis understood as the purpose of writing as he expressed it in casual comments in letters to friends and other writers, we come now to his examination of what the act of reading such works involves. This first chapter looked at what for Lewis made the act of writing an important and worthwhile vocation. The next chapter helps us to understand how we are supposed to receive and evaluate the product of that vocation. We begin by looking with Lewis at what the role of the reader is and then consider what function the critic has in assisting in the act of reading. Here we have a more systematic analysis by Lewis in a series of essays and lectures which cover his attitudes toward the receipt of writing.

II

Critical Theory

SELF-TRANSCENDENCE

The key to Lewis's approach to literature appears in the epilogue to *An Experiment in Criticism*, the published (1961) lectures on the subject of literature and criticism:

But in reading great literature I become a thousand men and yet remain myself. Like the night sky in the Greek poem, I see with a myriad eyes, but it is still I who see. Here, as in worship, in love, in moral action, in knowing, I transcend myself; and am never more myself than when I do.[1]

It is important that what may be Lewis's final statement on this subject links the self-transcendence discovered through reading literature with the same experience in the realms of religion, love, moral action, and the intellect. Lewis did not see the function of art, or more particularly, that of reading or writing fiction, as separated from the total experience of life. If anything, he stressed its organic integration into the total life of his literary reader. He also implied its central position in the life of the writer of fiction, if we judge from his own example and his scattered references to the role of art in life.

Art, or more particularly fiction since that is the focus of this study, is the fulfillment of potential. Through reading we should seek "an enlargement of our being. We want to be more than ourselves."[2] Lewis cautions against egocentric castle-building, the "use" as opposed to the "receipt" of what a work has to give. By the "right" sort of reading, that is the type which opens new pleasures to the imagination, new ideas, stimulation from whatever the book may have to offer, the reader grows and expands. He becomes enlarged by the experiences both within the book—those the author is offering to be shared—and those generated in himself by his response to the story and the structure.[3]

In one of the few negative reactions to Lewis written in recent years, W. W. Robson, "C. S. Lewis," *Cambridge Quarterly* (Summer, 1966), 252-272, a former student of Lewis, designates *An Experiment in Criticism* as Lewis's critical testament, a work which Lewis wanted taken seriously.[4] Robson goes on to indicate that as a critic Lewis was superficial, simplistic, and overbearing. Lewis placed too much emphasis on saying what we think and not enough on knowing what we really feel.[5]

Because Lewis equates seriousness with religion, Robson feels he reduces literature to the level of rhetoric. Another of Lewis's many faults as a critic, writer, and man, according to Robson, is that of first making critical dicta from his hobbies, such as his nostalgia for romantic boyhood reading, and then dragooning his readers—pupils—into accepting his way as the only way to discuss literature rationally.[6] The worst offenses seem to center on Lewis's externalness and his silliness which result from a persistence in what Robson considers boyish romanticism. Robson has more to offer relating to Lewis's failure as a moralist, as a Christian, and as a writer of novels, verse, and fairy tales, as well as criticism, which I mention later in discussing the works. He leaves us with the final judgment that Lewis will prove more memorable as a person than as a writer.[7]

Lewis would have laughed the attack off, I suppose. If he took it seriously, he might have taken exception to the charge of his lacking self-knowledge. Lewis would not have disputed Robson's designation of him as a frustrated minor poet. He says as much in his letters to Greeves.[8] He would probably not have disputed the truth of Robson's statement about the impulse behind his critical work as resting at least partially on his need to express in general terms a desire for self-transcendence which he was unable to express in his other writing.[9] Robson's failure is in understanding the nature of this self-transcendence and in his confusion of spiritual certainty with critical dogmatism.

Against this background of complaints about Lewis's lack of inwardness, lack of seriousness, philistinism (Lewis's defense of the plain reader), critical moralizing, and clever silliness, let us turn to see what Lewis offers in theory, if not in practice, by way of response to the posthumous criticism.[10]

A reading of Lewis's more theoretical statements on art and literature, such as those found in *An Experiment in Criticism*, in the essays in *Of Other Worlds* and *Selected Literary Essays*, gives both a clear outline of Lewis's critical principles and some practical examples of their application.

The chief function of art, of literature, is what Lewis calls the primary literary experience. This is an experience we have in reading literature of any kind and under ideal circumstances; it is what Lewis defines as "good reading." It is an experience in which we are permitted, invited, or compelled to participate by the work itself.[11] We are told by Lewis to empty our minds and make ourselves receptive.[12] What we are invited to open ourselves to is

...an enlargement of our being. We want to be more than ourselves. Each of us by nature sees the whole world from one point of view with a perspective and a selectiveness peculiar to himself. And even when we build disinterested fantasies, they are saturated with, and limited by, our own psychology.... But we want to escape the illusions of perspective on higher levels too. We want to see with other eyes, to imagine with other imaginations, to feel with other hearts, as well as with our own. We are not content to be Leibnitzian monads. We demand windows. Literature as Logos is a series of windows, even of doors. One of the things we feel after reading a great work is "I have got out". Or from another point of view, "I have got in"; pierced the shell of some other monad and discovered what it is like inside.[13]

Further in and higher up, the phrase from *The Last Battle* recurs throughout Lewis's writing like a leitmotif. We read what others have to tell us, not in order to know them (*connaître*), but to know about or understand what they know (*savoir*).

Not only nor chiefly in order to see what they are like but in order to see what they see, to occupy, for a while, their seat in the great theatre, to use their spectacles and be made free of whatever insights, joys, terrors, wonders, or merriment those spectacles reveal.[14]

But one of the chief operations of art is to remove our gaze from that mirrored face [our own], to deliver us from that solitude. When we read the "literature of knowledge" we hope, as a result, to think more correctly and clearly. In reading imaginative work, I suggest we should be much less concerned with altering our own opinions—though this of course is sometimes their effect—than with entering fully into the opinions, and therefore also the attitudes, feelings and total experience, of other men.[15]

The basic elements of this experience lie in our receptiveness to the *Logos*—the meaning—and the *Poiema*—the thing itself—shaped as Lewis says to give "great satisfaction."[16] "We must look, and go on

looking till we have certainly seen exactly what is there....The first
demand any work of art makes upon us is surrender. Look. Listen.
Receive."[17] What we receive is conveyed to us, in literature at least,
partly by the object: its design, the adjustment of chronological and
causal order, its images, contrasts and language.[18] We are partly
drawn on by excitement and curiosity though these usually function
to draw us further in and not necessarily further up.[19] We are not,
however, to mistake art for life or attempt to use art for selfish
ends, as Lewis's unliterary readers do.

Good writing elicits the good reading described above. The abstract and idealist terminology covers a simpler meaning: good
writing liberates the spirit and expands both the intellect and the
soul. In *An Experiment in Criticism*, good writing is defined rather
more negatively than positively. We are told more about what it
does than what it is, and the exasperated reader wants to say, perhaps along with Lewis's students who were not invited to stop him
in mid-lecture and frequently shrank from his powerful and dialectical replies, "but what *is* good writing and good reading?"

Good writing is not pointed toward stereotyped reactions, the sort
which please bad readers; it is selective in the material it presents,
and it is generally not simple narrative.[20] Beyond these few comments, Lewis has little to say directly on this subject in *An Experiment in Criticism*. Good reading is a surrender to what the work can
offer, a receiving of the work which allows us to cross the border
into a new place which constitutes its domain.[21] Thus for Lewis,
the function of literature is to be found in the act of reading and
its consequences for the reader much more than in judgments of
value or historical placement. For him the manner of reading is a
far better criterion of judgment than the standard criticism of
literary evaluation which fluctuates with changing fashion. He
dismisses the categorizers, exposers, and debunkers, and simply
gives us the common sense dictum that what readers find good,
if they truly read, is probably good.[22] If Robson had *An Experiment
in Criticism* in mind when criticizing Lewis as an authoritarian critic,
we feel that he perhaps protests too much because he subscribes to
the literary principles which Lewis has particularly brought under
attack.[23] In fact, when Robson discusses *An Experiment in Criticism* and states that the level of discussion is low and the matter
oversimplified, that the imaginary opponents are straw men, one
suspects him of practicing upon Lewis what he attacks Lewis for
doing as a critic.

Certainly the role of the critic is greatly reduced by Lewis. The
process he outlines is one in which we receive the effect first and

then evaluate it. We know this process best as children when, like the young Lewis fired by the excitement and curiosity which good reading invites, we are drawn into a work, "knocked flat" by it, and only later come to judge it.[24] Before we have become jaded as older readers or perhaps as professional literary critics and academicians, we have that quality which Lewis prized most highly, "that inner silence, that emptying out of ourselves, by which we ought to make room for the total reception of the work."[25] Again we see Robson's allegations of a lack of inwardness and of superficiality in Lewis's character as stemming perhaps more from his objection to this idealistically simple theory of literature than from faults in the man. Clearly his objections to Lewis's "silliness" both as a writer and critic stem from Robson's critical opposition to all that Lewis approved.

Criticism and evaluation do become a habit, Lewis suggests, as we grow, but they must be subordinated to the main aim of reading, which is to allow the work to show itself to us. He subscribes to Matthew Arnold's view of the critic as one who assists us "to see the object as in itself it really is."[26] The critic stands aside or in Arnold's words, "The great art of criticism is to get oneself out of the way and to let humanity decide."[27] Lewis elaborates on this approach by suggesting that the critic attempts to show the reader what the character or definition of the work he admires or dislikes truly is and then lets the reader make a judgment on the basis of a better informed reception of the work.[28] Lewis places only secondary importance on the act of criticism, seeing it as an aid "to multiply, safeguard, or prolong those moments when a good reader is reading well a good book...."[29] He ranks in order the critics who in his opinion have been of some assistance when we see them in the role outlined in the preceding statement. First come the editors and textual critics, then the literary historians, the emotive critics and last the evaluative critics. The direction of Lewis's comments here suggests that he was not attracted by the F.R. "Leavisite" approach of close analysis and evaluation. Whether one reacts to his personal feeling as being projected as infallible dogma or not rests largely on the spirit in which one reads the book, remembering that it was drawn from a lecture series. That it sums up, at the end of his career, certain major points in his own thought on the subject of the nature and function of literature and criticism, can hardly be disputed. To recapitulate briefly: the reader is central to the experience of literature. If he is a "good" reader, he receives with a free mind and open and ready sensitivity, all that the work has to offer. He possesses what might be called a reader's "negative capability." The reader should be receptive to any and all experiences which the work may offer and should not approach the work with any prejudgments or special requirements. Children are the most receptive, if the least capable of knowing and using exactly what they have received. They respond to the excitement the work arouses, and their curiosity about language and narrative makes them nearly ideal readers.

The work read is central to the experience but of secondary importance. It has something to convey; it arouses, excites, compels attention at the deepest level. Thus it should have structure, artistry of presentation, unity and coherence, selectivity of material for an effect, and, by whatever magic of creativity, it offers the experience which draws us out of ourselves and enlarges our being; thus it, to an extent, is universal or at least broad in its appeal.

All else is peripheral. Criticism of the value of a work as social or moral statement, evaluation of the author's achievement judged against others, the psychological implications, the symbolic or allegoric structures, the "meaning" of the work, all these Lewis classifies as "uses" or abuses of literature. Under Lewis's ideal experimental conditions, we have in black and white the basic response of intelligent and perceptive readers to stimulating literature. What he has done, we might object with Robson, is to oversimplify. On the surface he seems to be advising us to do what we all as good readers have always done: enjoy most what really moves us despite official pronouncements on its value. He fails, however, to tell us how we are to distinguish between the varieties of experiences we may have as readers. Surely we are not to suppose that all that moves us to self-transcendence is equally good in itself or for us. We lack concrete examples, which Lewis avoids giving in order to keep his personal taste from intruding to limit the ideal experiment. Where we want more specific definition, we are given the vague outline of an abstraction, which we subscribe to but which requires more concrete material to give it a true claim to be called an experiment.

What we find in *An Experiment in Criticism* is not Lewis's final dogma on how and what we should read, nor even his definitive literary critical statement nor the summation of all he thought on the subject of literary criticism. There are many more specifically penetrating insights on literature in *A Preface to "Paradise Lost,"* *The Allegory of Love*, and his essays on Walter Scott or "Psychoanalysis and Literature." What we do find though is an outline of what Lewis considered basic to the understanding of the literary experience from the viewpoint of the reader, rather than of the writer. And since Lewis was above all things a "good reader," this outline is highly instructive in any examination of his works. It was written from the reader's point of view and exemplifies to a most astonishing degree, the principles which Lewis held dear. The theory outlined above explains why Lewis employed some of the formal structures he used for his message. Once we recognize the emphasis placed by Lewis on the "primary literary experience," the act of self-transcendence, then many of the questions which previous critics have dealt with separately fall into perspective. Whether or not Lewis made a lasting contribution to criticism in *An Experiment in Criticism* may depend on the use which the reader makes of it. I intend to study his literary work in the light of his professed concern for the reading experience and to examine the fiction in the context of this experience as Lewis defined it.

Before plunging into the works themselves, there are specific essays in which Lewis offers other material which is helpful in understanding both his method and aim in writing fiction. Although many of them were written earlier than *An Experiment in Criticism*, they should be seen within the context of Lewis's thinking expressed there since one of the characteristics of his literary development is the consistency of its aims and direction.

In the essay "On Stories," Lewis indicates that the pleasure of reading is twofold, arising from the lesser "excitement," and the more profound stirring of the "deeper imagination."[30] In fact, the first may to some extent inhibit the fullest development of the second and more desirable quality. It is the deeper imagination which catches our fancy. What exactly this deeper imagination is we know mainly by implication. It is the opposite of information or fact and of superficial excitement.

Deeper imagination is more suggestive than actual. Lewis feels that it is more a quality of surprisingness, a "quality of unexpectedness" than actual surprise or unexpected facts which delights us.[31] It is the "intrinsic surprisingness" which draws us in to catch the inner meaning.[32] In what is essentially a justification of the techniques of fantasy used by writers like E.R. Eddison, de la Mare, Lindsay, and Tolkien, Lewis focuses on methods by which art can show that side of experience normally excluded by the narrow, practical view of real life.[33] The method used by these writers of "other worlds" is a reciprocating one. The creation of an other world is drawn says Lewis from the world of the spirit which is the only real other world we know.[34] By stimulating the deeper imagination with stories set in other worldly surroundings, the author sends his readers back to the real world with a renewed pleasure. The value of highly imaginative stories like those written by the authors mentioned is that although they are unlike real life in a sense, they show the reader an acceptable image of reality at a more "central region."[35] Again we are confronted by the repeated inwardness of Lewis's vision of art. Art is the pursuit of the ideal, the never wholly attainable, the fleeting and evanescent. It heightens the very search for pleasure. Lewis uses the image of the bird to symbolize the quality sought, and the net used to capture it is for the author the plot.[36] The net may be imperfect, but it is the author's only tool to capture what would be otherwise lost. So far psychology and medicine have left these creative impulses unexplained, says Lewis. His inherent distrust of psychology led him to suggest that evolution or progress may bring us to a point where the net is no longer necessary, but until that time no doctor can teach us either how to find the bird or manipulate the net.[37] It was not a question Lewis felt could be answered as he made clear in his essays on the use of psychology and anthropology in literary criticism.

The success of the fiction writer in drawing us into the central region may depend on his use of dialogue or theme. David Lindsay used a passionate spiritual journey, Walter de la Mare a certain suggestiveness. Whatever device he may use, he will, if he is a writer of "pure story"—by which I take Lewis to mean works of pure creative imagination such as those referred to above—he will have succeeded if we feel compelled to return and reread the story not for its adventure, but for the "intrinsic surprisingness."[38]

Lewis appears on the defensive here, a natural pose for a writer of his dialectical propensities, but what he defends is the naturalness of an artist's use of the otherworldly, the nonnatural or supernatural. Art may excite us to thought in many ways, but it moves us through the creative imagination in ways quite unlike that of history or mathematics. Our imaginations are stimulated at their deeper levels. I do not say "deepest" because Lewis is careful to leave that possibility open to other stimuli. In defending the use of the otherworldly, he suggests that the methods used are simply an elevation to a higher creative level of what goes on in pedestrian life.

A similar defense occurs in his treatment of stories written for children. The central issue for Lewis, having established the purpose of literature as what I would call the elevation of the spirit, is utilitarian. An author uses a form because it offers the best art form to use for what he has to say.[39] Elevation of the spirit does not quite define Lewis's meaning. It is the imaginative tension which lifts the reader up and into deeper and higher or more sublime and central meaning—to the truth. For Lewis, truth equals spirit, and spirit is manifested in nature. Art heightens our perception of nature, clarifies it so that we see meaning more clearly and perceive beauty with greater clarity. We can never apprehend the ultimate truth, except in God, so that, taken in the largest context, art is only a tool, a rudder to steer the human skiff in the right direction. Like Poe, Lewis, when he speaks of art, is more interested in the beauty, the imaginative creativity, what he and Tolkien call the numinous [the Divine], than in reaching the goal at the end of the penetration into the beyond. Hence we never see the mystery revealed, partly because we cannot in this life and partly because the revelation would spoil our expectation, the relish of surprise, the possibility of further adventure, the possibility of possibilities which we could experience could we but go on just a bit further.

Among Lewis's most famous comments about the compelling nature of the deeper imagination are those which describe the pull of fairy tales. Fairy tales awaken a longing which the reader can neither identify nor satisfy. They enrich the reader by their disturbing enchantment which produces lifelong dividends in spiritual and artistic enrichment.[40]

Although Lewis was attracted by the discipline and economy of the fairy tale and its advantages in reaching readers, not necessarily always children, on whom other forms of novelistic presentation had little effect, his basic impulse was the satisfaction of that longing, the desire to communicate to others that sense of possibilities that he had felt so keenly as a child and throughout his adult life. He was to suggest in another essay, "Sometimes Fairy Stories May Say Best What's to be Said," that part of the impulse behind using such a form was its usefulness in breaking inhibitions and thawing frozen feelings. He speaks of the "real potency" of the fantastic and mythical, which rests not in their form or in formal devices but in their power to move and excite their readers. Their power he describes when he says that they can generalize and still be concrete and have the power to present in understandable form concepts which could be approached in no other direct fashion.[41] Lewis then may be uncharitably chastised for indulging in a self-satisfying exercise, writing the sort of thing which he enjoyed reading as a child. Many authors writing for a young audience have done just that. Lewis is, despite his defensive tone, making clear that the prospective audience claims only his secondary consideration. He wants to show the imagined world with its pictures and associations rather than just write moral tales for children.

Lewis's preference for the fairy tale or for fantasy has many facets. He enjoyed this type of literature more than any other as a

youth and wrote it as a child. Though he had little occasion to observe children firsthand until after the publication of his fairy tales,
he preserved enough of the childlike in his response to life and
beauty to sustain a sympathetic understanding both of what it is to
be a child and what it means to grow up. Children were clearly not a
class of readers to be written for as a group. Lewis may have believed
in a group of readers one could call childlike, but he dismissed as
rubbish the idea of writing for children, of giving them what they
want. His way was that of appealing to the childlike in his readers by
using forms that were familiar to them. Growth and progress do not
mean growing out of childhood; rather Lewis would stress in his
defense of fairy tales and fantasy that they could parallel or even
assist in the process of growth of the imagination and spirit. He
would agree with Tolkien's idea of sub-creation and accept the
Jungian concept of the collective unconscious as a type of built-in
self-knowledge.

His own method especially responded to two other aspects of
fantasy. First, its otherworldliness gave scope for the presentation of
that longing which forms the theme, as Lewis saw it, of much that
he admired in this genre. Second, the demands of a formal structure: brevity, severe descriptive restraint, flexible traditionalism, and
inflexible hostility to all analysis, digression, reflection, and "gas,"
lent themselves to his particular use of the genre.[42] The use which he
made of the genre was in part didactic. He admits that part of his
desire was to steal past the "watchful dragons" of traditional Christian symbology, the sort of inhibitions of stained glass and Sunday
school which paralyzed his own religious response when he was a
child. Once past these, he might give new meaning to uninhibited
readers.[43] Though Lewis was to discount the suggestion that he
began the Narnia stories with Christian doctrine as the starting point
and that the central meaning was a religious allegory, it is clear that
he hoped to put across a moral message by means of this form. But
weighed in the balance, the importance of stimulating the imagination of his readers overtops the message.

In his writing about science fiction, a form which had interested
him from his earliest reading and one he was to use in the trilogy,
we find repeated references to the imaginative enlargement which
this genre responds to and can, if well written, produce in its readers.
Lewis was rather critical of the trend of science fiction in the fifties,
preferring the sort written by David Lindsay, and even some of his
early favorite H.G. Wells books. Rejecting the technological
gimmickry of modern science fiction, Lewis placed emphasis on the
creativity of this form. He saw science fiction as adding to life: such

stories, says Lewis, operate like dreams which on rare occasions give, through an expansion of our consciousness, a range of experiences we never thought possible before.[44] The appeal in the imaginative presentation of other worlds lies in the possibilities open to the author. Science fiction offers a splendid opportunity by opening for the artist a new imaginative world with unlimited possibilities for wonder, beauty, and suggestiveness. For Lewis the proper study of man, as he said, is everything. The proper study of the artist is everything which assists him to broaden the imagination and the passions.[45] By actualizing what is imaginative, science fiction tales give form, in much the same way fairy tales do, to states of mind or sensations which are beyond the range of common experience. Although Lewis gave some attention to matters of technique, the burden of his defense of science fiction, like that of fairy tales, rests on his conviction that the form is a legitimate creative one which we judge on the merits or faults of individual works and not by giving a blanket condemnation of the type.

The emphasis in Lewis's published comments in defense of tales of fantasy or faerie and science fiction rests on his conviction that such forms of creative expression lead the reader into greater understanding and deeper perceptions of life. He makes no attempt to evaluate whether they are better or worse than other literary forms, staying within the bounds of his own critical tenets which prohibit such evaluations. Since these forms suit their purpose, they are satisfactory. The purpose which Lewis puts to work in these forms is the familiar one of stimulating the reader's imagination, suggesting new perceptions, jolting the reader into new perspectives, drawing him deeper in, further in and higher up. If there is a proselytizing motive on Lewis's part rather than the simple boyish romantic silliness projected by Robson, it is to win converts to the creative imagination as much as to any moral program. The test is to read any volume of the Narnia *Chronicles* as (a) fairy tale or (b) religious allegory and record the level of enjoyment rendered by each method. Any average reader of Lewis will say the pleasure of reading his work lies in the story or the descriptions; rarely is it in the message. If anything, it is the message which distracts or annoys the otherwise receptive reader who would prefer not to be bothered by the intrusion of what is either to him extraneous or intrusive and perhaps in some cases offensive matter.

Lewis has given us two examples of his response to other specific approaches to literary criticism, both modern. In essays treating psychoanalysis and anthropology and their use as literary critical devices, he has given us some specific insights into his conception of the critic's role and the function of literature. Lewis rejected outright what he designated as the psychoanalytic critic's desire to give the effective cause behind the production of a piece of literature. He would reverse this critic's emphasis, as we have seen before, suggesting that the critic's role is to answer the question of why and how a work should be read.[46] The critic's interest focuses on the work and not the psyche behind it. In his examination of psychoanalytic literary criticism, which for him in 1942 when the essay appeared was basically Freudian, he distinguished between two types of imagination which fuel the creative furnace; one he designated as the "interested," and the other the "disinterested" imagination.

The "interested imagination" has surface realism, a prosaic temper, and a nagging character. These traits are essentially for Lewis an enslavement of the creative response analogous to a self-serving use of literature which he designated as the quality of "bad" reading.[47] The "disinterested imagination," he describes in terms of approbation like "unpredictable ecstasy," or "otherness," and "externality."[48] The basic distinction is that of direction. The first moves inward upon the self, the second outward and upward toward higher and selfless goals, spiritual ones rather than egocentric ones.

There are two activities of the imagination, one free and the other enslaved to the wishes of its own for whom it has to provide imaginary gratifications. Both may be the starting point for works of art. The former or 'free' activity continues in the works it produces and passes from the status of dream to that of art by a process which may legitimately be called 'elaboration': incoherences are tidied up, banalities removed, private values and associations replaced, proportion, relief, and temperance are introduced. But the other, or servile kind is not 'elaborated' into a work of art: it is a motive power which starts the activity and is withdrawn when once the engine is running, or a scaffolding which is knocked away when the building is complete. Finally, the characteristic products of free imagination belong to what may be roughly called the fantastic, or mythical, or improbable type of literature: those of fantasy, of the wish-fulfilling imagination, to what may, in a very loose sense be called the realistic type. I say 'characteristic products' because the principle doubtless admits of innumerable exceptions.[49]

Though we may doubt Lewis's qualifications to speak authoritatively on the subject of Freudian psychoanalytical theory, we cannot dismiss his rational and dispassionate evaluation of the uses of such a theory when applied to literary criticism. His distinction between the two forms of imagination is very much in line with the basic outline of his own theory of creativity. For him, the direction of creative movement is always up and in rather than down and in.

The idealism of self-transcendence which marks his most carefully developed statements about the role of the artist could hardly be further from the psychoanalytic theory of literary creation and criticism which grew up around Freud. Lewis saw creativity, as did Eliot and Keats, as a liberator of the soul from personal concerns and base physical bonds. It is through the process of elaboration that art transforms the personal, instinctual drives, that art disciplines, tempers, and selects, that the creative imagination, the "deeper imagination" works to deliver the artist from his small round of ingrown daydreams. Art is not unconscious and it is not simply therapeutic. Lewis does not discount Freud's theories; he amends them to incorporate the possibility of other motive forces than the erotic. The Freudian and Jungian theories do not go far enough and are not inclusive of all the possible motives and meaning in the creative act or in the form created. There is more to the excitement of myth than Jungian theory accounts for, and for Lewis, the basis of literary criticism rests on grounds other than an interest in the erotic or the unconscious. He moves to the heart of objections voiced by many reasonable critics that psychoanalytic criticism deals with matters other than the literature or art it purports to be studying. It gives extraneous, though often enlightening, information which is supposed to explain all the reader could reasonably desire to know. But as Lewis points out, this form of criticism is narrow and restricted, offering a small part for the whole.

Much later in *An Experiment in Criticism*, Lewis explains in considerably more detail the nature of myth, the highest achievement of the disinterested imagination. Myth, as Lewis defines it in his chapter on the subject, has six characteristics: 1. it is extra-literary—that is it does not depend on its particular literary expression for its effect; 2. its ability to please rests upon its inevitability; 3. it calls forth no direct and personal identification; 4. it deals with "impossibilities and preternaturals"; 5. it is grave; 6. and the experience of it is numinous in quality.[50] Lewis's attention here is directed toward the reception of myth by the literary and nonliterary reader rather than toward an investigation of sources or meanings. The importance of this definition for our purposes lies in the distinction which he gives to myth and the relevance it has for his own literary creations. Of all forms, myths are the most compelling. They do not depend for their effect upon local or personal associations; they are not subject to the judgment of the form in which they take expression. The events which they narrate compel a response through their serious, inevitable and unearthly qualities. Myths are, then, ultimate stories which must be told and retold and which compel us despite the form (good or bad) by which they find expression. Lewis makes no attempt to trace their source or to direct our response as readers. He simply states that myth works in this manner upon what he has distinguished as the "literary reader."

We might challenge his definition of the process by which these ultimate stories operate: he is open to criticism on many fronts. The notion of primal fiction is Jungian, and Lewis appears to be simplifying and obscuring a clearly stated mythopoeic theory for his own purposes. He fails to define or analyze any part of the process, leaving us to guess or intuit how myth affects his literary readers, and to ponder who or what these readers are other than beings like himself with academic training and sensitively tuned literary perceptions. However we may respond, the significance of this definition of myth for Lewis lies in its application to his own work, more than in our scrutiny of it as a literary critical principle. Lewis was not a great literary critic. His theories are not fully developed in any extended and detailed work like those of Coleridge or Arnold. His significance, if judged from his current popularity, rests upon his fiction and his homiletic writing, not predominantly on his academic studies or his collected essays. The importance of his theory of the imagination in this study rests upon the help it gives in understanding his own literary work.

Lewis's emphasis on myth, stemming as it well might from his academic preoccupation with literature which was mythic or reflected mythic significance, indicates the essential conservatism of his literary outlook. For him, the preoccupation of the artist is with themes and events long established as central to the human experience. His earliest longings, springing from nature and from some of the classic works of the romantic creative spirit as well as the sterner northern myths, were transformed by Christian faith into what Lewis regards as the central myth or most primal of experiences. For Lewis the essential experience of literature depends upon the recipient's openness to the possibilities which the work offers. What the work may have to offer if it is myth or fantasy is a challenge to credibility, an invitation into other worlds, a compelling call to pass out of the realm of personal concerns, of egoistic castle-building, into a created world of numinous possibilities. The recipient is called away from personal cares and considerations, from the locked cell of the self, into self-transcendent events whose significance can have a soul–expanding impact upon him and from which he returns a changed being.

The type of literature which brings about this reaction originates from a similar process in its author. Although Lewis does not elaborate on the actual process of creation, we can by analogy discern the steps in the creative act. The writer of fiction responds to primal events, his imagination reaching beyond self-interested creation (daydreams, erotic fantasies, wish-fulfillments) and stretches toward the transcendent, the ecstatic, the unachievable, fantastic, mythic. This expansion of the self, the operation of a disinterested imagination, this elaboration on basic experiences, such as dreams, fantasies, and sensuous responses is art. Art tempers, restricts, selects, and passes in its operation beyond the initial motive power. For example, *The Lion, the Witch and the Wardrobe* began variously in nightmares about lions, pictures of fauns and little girls, both acknowledged as sources by Lewis, or in other sources suggested by critics: childish wish-fulfillment for a lost mother, erotic sublimation, religious evangelizing through fairy tales, etc. The end product, however, is not simply any of these. It contains them all, perhaps, but goes on to express certain primal and mythic events in a structure peculiar to Lewis, the artist and creator. The events: loss of innocence, disloyalty and rejection, sacrifice and redemption, evil confronting good, love prevailing over hate, are shown in a creation that is simple, but highly symbolic, fantastic yet real. Art is the conscious and intelligible process by which new expression is given to the human response to experience embedded within primal events and to ultimate themes which seek new expression in every age.

Lewis's focus then as an artist is on the story to be told, the matter to be conveyed to the receptive reader, the insight or messages to be conveyed in narrative form. The primary aim is to express meaning; the form of expression is secondary in importance. Lewis does not spend time elaborating basic rules or formulae for various art forms. This does not mean that he ignores matters of technique and style; far from it. His essays and letters to literary friends are full of critical judgments on matters such as dialogue, narrative technique, and symbolism. His recognized aversion to the new formalistic critical method of literary study should, however, be sufficient justification for placing emphasis on his theory rather than on his interest in the technical aspects of literature.

As we turn from his theory of literature to that of criticism, it is well to note, again, the subsidiary role criticism has for Lewis. He repeatedly makes clear that, in the relationship between author, work of fiction, and reader, the keynote is openness and receptivity. Anything which impedes the line of communication is pushed aside. Lewis, despite Robson's suggestions to the contrary, might agree with Robson that the function of literary criticism is finding the truth about books.[51] One of Lewis's clearest statements about the role of the critic is found in his essay "On Criticism." The critic should give us more than mere evaluation; he should inform us as well as direct our judgments.[52] A critic should possess certain simple qualifications: he should be honest, know by careful reading what he criticizes, and not say more than he can verify by reference to the text.[53] The critic is in business to tell us more about the book and judge it.[54] What a critic emphatically must not do is to invent possible explanations or make guesses about why a book becomes good or bad in the reading.[55] The critic interprets as well as he can the author's intensions and the meaning of the book. In arriving at the intention of the author, Lewis warns that the critic should beware of the easy method of psychoanalyzing about the intention. Too often these critics mistake their psychological motive for the real one which Lewis calls the "plastic impulse," the desire to shape and make which is the real impulse to creativity.[56]

In a related essay on "The Anthropological Approach," Lewis would point to a similar confusion among the anthropological literary critics who mistake the repetition of anthropological material, the trivial similarity between things modern and ancient, for its true significance as a "new invention."[57] Anthropology like psychoanalysis, can only be successful in literary criticism when used as a tool. When it blocks the direct and real experience passing between object and reader, it has invalidated any critical aid its method might offer. Both methods substitute a secondary fiction of their own making for the real experience communicated by the author through the story to the reader. It is the direct response to what the author has made which weighs most for Lewis and should, for his critics, not some substitute fashioned according to a scientific theory of the operation of the psyche or of historical sources.

With attention thus focused on the experience of receiving what the author has to give us, we are faced with the problem, the critic's problem, of interpreting meaning. Readers need to know what a book or story means. If we are to take a book directly rather than filtered through the "fictions" of different schools of criticism, we need to know what it is that we receive, and how a critic is to help us interpret what a book means.

Lewis defines meaning essentially as a system of attitudes or responses or feelings produced by reading.[58] This definition seems as highly subjective as the "fiction" of some psychological critics. Yet within the context of Lewis's critical theory, it is clear that he intends meaning to be relative to the receiver, shifting through time and historical conditions, capable of growth and susceptible to many dimensions of response and interpretation.

The ideally true or right 'meaning' would be shared (in some measure) by the largest number of the best readers after repeated and careful reading over several generations, different periods, nationalities, moods, degrees of alertness, private pre-occupations, states of health, spirits, and the like cancelling one another out when (this is an important reservation) they cannot be fused so as to enrich one another.[59]

Ideally, criticism is the record of response to a work of literature from which, by judicious canceling of opposites, we can arrive at the essential consensus of meaning at any given point, and this would be the true meaning. The critic's role is as compiler of responses to a given work and judge of the consensus of responses. He creates nothing new, and his evaluation is based on the broadest possible sample of reactions to a work.

The essay "On Criticism" is unfinished, closing with a list of fragments, presumably indicative of what Lewis might have discussed, and it should not be considered his final statement since the very essence of his criticism is flexibility, responsiveness, and the possibility of growth and evolution for the response to works of literature.

There are many parallels between Lewis's statements on the nature of literary experiences and on critical attitudes toward works of literature and his writing on the religious experience. Those who are familiar with the whole range of his work will be and have been tempted to see one as the extension of the other, the literary as a manifestation of the spiritual belief. Much that has been written about Lewis's fiction begins with that assumption. Lewis became a Christian and then a writer of fiction, and seen in this perspective the works naturally appear as the creative response to an inner feeling of extraordinary force. Thus Lewis is variously praised or blamed as a writer of religious fiction, and much to his displeasure during his lifetime, his works were interpreted only as allegories of Christian belief and ritual.

It should be clear from the study of Lewis's response to literature that has preceded this section that he was committed to a philosophy of literary response long before he became an active convert to Christianity and that his reactions, though tempered by his changed views of spirit, still reflect much of their original quality undiminished in intensity and only redirected toward a new source, not taking a new route. Lewis never confused art and real life. Some of the "unliterary mistake art for an account of real life...They wish to be deceived; they want to feel that though these beautiful things have not really happened to them, yet they might."[60] Even though he may have expressed a wish to be able to pass the watchful dragons of conventional religious response by his use of fairy tales, he never lost sight of the artificiality of literature, and in his religious life, as nearly as we can see it reflected in his writing, literary experiences, both those of writing and reading, never replaced the vastly more important direct experience of spirit at the center of Lewis's faith. Thus when we talk of Lewis's Joy as it manifests itself in his fiction, we must beware the easy assumption that that explains all there is to the fascination of readers with what he wrote. Far from it. The response to his writing is as multifarious as he could ideally have wished, and it continues to be so. The reason that most readers give for enjoying his books is not basically their appreciation of the spiritual meaning.

Following his outline for criticism, we should, as readers of his work, analyze our responses. We shall assume in the next section that we are his good readers, open and responsive to what comes to us through his fiction, asking how we react and why, and whether the fiction is compelling enough to draw us up and away from our petty egocentric world, offering us an opportunity for self-transcendence, drawing us on to deeper imaginative pleasures, giving us new insights and a broader understanding than we had before. We should ask if the fiction challenges us to come further in and higher up, revealing some primal or mythic experience in a way that we cannot fail to grasp and in such form that we feel compelled to keep on reading. We must judge whether these books permit, invite, and compel Lewis's "good reading." We also must judge whether or not what Lewis has to say is best said in the way he has elected to say it; whether the *Logos* and *Poiema* are organically linked and what effect these formal structures and devices have upon our response. And finally, as critics we must deliberate on the intentions behind the author's choice of such forms as his mode of expression and the meaning of the works themselves. Our task here is both the easiest and the hardest. It is easy in that by Lewis's direction we are free to operate without external restriction of formal critical framework or doctrine and because we have a variety of critical opinions to sample before arriving at the consensus. It is hard because the very freedom which Lewis allows gives such a great flexibility of response that we find it difficult to settle on one final response. As we would be critics in the Lewis mode, we must determine what good moments there may be which deserve the safeguarding and reinforcement which a critic can give to the good reader.

We have reached a major division in this study. Behind us lies an extended review of Lewis's ideas about what it is to be attracted to a piece of literature, respond to it, and then accept and receive its meaning so that we become something more than when we began the process. The process is simple, requires little more than an openness to new imaginative creations, and profits the reader beyond almost any gauge we might apply because the experience goes in and up to affect the very spirit of the receiver.

For Lewis, the act of reading, like any other creative activity such as planting a garden, is a religious experience. The reader is thus like the gardener or the pilgrim, as he embarks on an adventure each time he opens a book. Each book offers a new avenue to the truth. So, though the process of reading is simple, the end result is serious because of the consequences that a truly imaginative work may have on the receptive reader.

If we want to understand why Lewis's own work strikes us so forcefully, giving us a feeling of satisfaction, nostalgia, or longing, then we need to move ahead and study Lewis by these guidelines. The value of using Lewis as his own critic is that it places us on the firmest ground for understanding what Lewis intended us to receive when we read his books. Many critics have told us what they think. Lewis has allowed us the freedom to choose for ourselves as critics of his or any other work. So we proceed to a systematic and informative study of his literary attitudes as he put them into imaginative and creative practice. We are in no way obliged to see Lewis solely from this single perspective, but at least we can be certain of being well-grounded before we accept the theories of other critics. We will have looked directly at what matters most, those first things Lewis always directed his attention to, the actual works themselves, starting with *The Pilgrim's Regress* and ending with *Till We Have Faces*.

III

The Fiction

A study of Lewis's fiction seen in the perspective of his critical theory is admittedly one-dimensional. There are, however, several reasons for using this type of approach. By applying Lewis's own standards and methods of criticism, we may come to a better understanding of his purpose in writing these particular stories using the forms he did, and in the process we may gain greater understanding of the usefulness of his critical method. Critics approaching Lewis from a variety of other directions have passed by questions that deserve answers. We want to know if Lewis dogmatically forces his prejudices upon others as immutable law and fails as a critic because he gives out moral advice rather than critical evaluation.[1] We want to know if Lewis, as moralizer, takes all the life from a work and gives us instead fireworks and sophistry.[2] On the other hand, we must look to see if Lewis is a great modern allegorist, defender of the faith, a new Chesterton, the spokesman in fiction for the Christian revival. Lewis would probably brush all this speculation aside and tell us to get on with it, on to the central issue, the primary literary experience. So his method may serve to help us to analyze how readers read his books, and what sort of response they have, and what opportunities the books offer for self-transcendence.

These are important questions for any critic to answer. Applying Lewis's critical approach to his work in no way insures that we will even approach Lewis's own critical estimate of his work. We know that he disliked the immense popularity of *The Screwtape Letters*, felt that *The Pilgrim's Regress* was misunderstood and unappreciated, enjoyed the writing of the *Chronicles of Narnia*, and thought that *Till We Have Faces* and *Perelandra* should rank highest among his works. Lewis was not his own best critic. We have the opinion of many other critics who have given valuable testimony to the variety of responses elicited by Lewis's fiction.[3] These critical responses, many centered on the theological or at least spiritual and Christian implications of Lewis's fiction and thus admittedly biased, balance the evaluation of Lewis's fiction which forms the next section of this study. What has been missing in the study of Lewis's fiction up to this point is a recognition that the works are fiction, not just homiletic commentary in disguise, and as fiction they should be studied along conventional literary critical lines and evaluated on their own terms. They should not be either praised or blamed for their message, which being spiritual somehow, for particular critics, excuses stylistic deficiencies or if one objects to messages, overshadows obvious narrative or descriptive art. If Lewis is as Robson says a bad novelist, whose fairy tale country was insufficient to embody his sincerely felt themes, then by this method we ought to be able to test the validity of such remarks by judging the fiction for what it is and not for what it says or cannot say.[4]

No critical study can tell us all that we wish to know, but I hope that this attempt will strike a new balance by giving the works an opportunity to stand for scrutiny as works of fiction, and by using Lewis's own critical views on fiction to place the fiction in this new perspective. Using references in the letters, many unpublished, and Lewis's published comments on each work, and the outline for criticism developed in the preceding chapter, I will cover the basic questions of (a) Lewis's intent, (b) the book's meaning, (c) the reader's response, (d) how successfully the form conveys the meaning, and (e) some suggestions on what a "good reading" might include.

1. *THE PILGRIM'S REGRESS:*
An Allegorical Apology for Christianity, Reason and Romanticism 1933

There are no references in *The Letters* to indicate that in December 1932 Lewis was engaged in writing this book.[1] Surveying his correspondence with Arthur Greeves, to whom the book is dedicated, we see the effect of his conversion in relationship to his reading, which he always reported to Greeves, and to his writing. Although the full chronicle of his conversion, which forms the basis of this novel, is not found in these letters (*see Surprised by Joy*), the effects of that changing outlook are reflected in many comments, especially on literature. In early 1930 Lewis's interest in the homely aspect of life and nature, the "mysteries of living stuff," began to gather in strength. He was reading Jacob Boehme, Tolkien's *Hobbit* in manuscript, and William Morris, seeing now in Morris that a holy light shines through his romanticism.[2] He worried to Greeves over the sensuality of his own romanticism, questioning the role which tenderness and luxuriousness should play in the Christian life and in response to romantic literature. It was not until *The Four Loves* [1960] that he would answer questions on this subject, which he had somewhat summarily dealt with in *The Pilgrim's Regress*.

We know that his chief delight at the time was in reading the *Paradiso*, Tolstoy's *War and Peace*, and Morris; that he was deeply interested in the image of the road as a symbol of life's journey; "the road is always turning round and going back to places we seemed to have left—but they are *different* (yet in a way the same) when you come to them the second time."[3]

Throughout 1930 and 1931, he came to recognize that he had not succeeded as a writer, that as a reader he valued the moments in drama or novels when great myths found expression by any artifice, and that he enjoyed novels most when they escaped the traditional novelistic love business by way of religion, fantasy, or force. His growing interest in the Christian myth centers around his recorded turning to belief in Christ after a long talk with Hugo Dyson and J.R.R. Tolkien. It is not surprising that he should announce in December 1932 that,

I aim chiefly at being idiomatic and racy, basing myself on Malory and Bunyan, and Morris, tho' without archaisms: and would usually prefer to use ten words, provided they are honest native words and idiomatically ordered, than one "literary word."[4]

This letter contains one of the first references to *The Pilgrim's Regress*, which he later in a 1935 letter to Greeves would call his religious book.[5] The sources then are clearly, at least in style, epic and allegorical, and the meaning religious and mythic. Unquestionably the book is autobiographical. The preface to the 1943 edition makes clear Lewis's desire to share the route of his conversion with his readers when he realized, long after the book was published, that they found it difficult to follow his passage from belief in popular realism to Christianity.

Lewis has given us ample indication of his intention in writing this book. He wanted to trace the path toward Desire, showing the false seductions of the rationalistic and sensuous extremes characterized by the terms North and South. His Everyman, John, is tempted through a series of choices to mistake the lesser fulfillment of Desire for the ultimate object which is fulfillment of Desire beyond death. Lewis hoped that the allegory used in the book would approach the level of myth, revealing its meaning directly to the imagination. He added the headlines in the 1943 edition to make the book easier to follow, although he felt that it should have been self-evident to a reader who knew what allegory was. His intention then, as we trace it from his own comments, was as much didactic as literary. He would discount the significance of the book twenty years after he wrote it, telling a correspondent, "It was my first religious book and I didn't then know how to make things easy. I was not even trying to very much, because in those days I never dreamed I would become a 'popular' author and hoped for no readers outside a small 'highbrow' circle. Don't waste time over it any more."[6] This brief comment holds the key to Lewis's attitude toward the book. It was conceived as a religious book. Religion, the catalyst in the transformation of Lewis's romantic and sensuous response to nature and art into Christian belief, filled his mind at this period as the letters reveal. He was beginning to see that through literature, writers like his admired MacDonald and Morris were conveying that sense of holiness which was the true source of Desire and Joy.

He did not attempt, in his first literary effort in this new mode, to "make things easy." What he had written earlier as a poet had sprung from the same source, a desire to express in high literary form, the feeling of longing and desire which stands at the basis of Lewis's response to life. It was a love affair with romantic nature. When the opportunity arose in the early 1930s for a new expression of this love, Lewis chose what at the time must have seemed the most natural mode of expression, the one he had admired in Bunyan, Dante, Malory, the allegorical writers of the medieval romances, and Morris and MacDonald. The form was in itself elegant and traditional, structured to give a framework for the symbolic journey Lewis wished John to take. Bypassing popularity, he sought a highly sophisticated audience to whom the form would be automatically familiar and who would be able to appreciate the subtlety of his literary structure as well as perceive the message that lay at the center of his modern myth. I suspect that his intention was to focus more attention on the structure than on the content and that this desire unquestionably dulled the response of many readers.

The book's meaning is also clear, again with the helpful 1943 Preface in hand. Everyman (John) makes a journey toward death. He longs to reach the unattainable (the Island) and seeks many paths toward this desire, paths which lead him through the byways of sensuous and rationalistic sins, but it is through the efforts of Christianity (Mother Kirk) and Reason that he perceives that by its nature, Desire is the very unattainable or ineffable quality which has drawn him, and one that he can only attain finally in death, not by any earthly means.

It appeared to me therefore that if a man diligently followed this desire, pursuing the false objects until their falsity appeared and then resolutely abandoning them, he must come out at last into the clear knowledge that the human soul was made to enjoy some object that is never fully given—nay, cannot be imagined as given—in our present mode of subjective and spatio-temporal experience.[7]

John encounters the temptations of the flesh in the brown girls and of the intellect in Mr. Enlightenment, the Clevers, and Sigismund Enlightenment, and he repudiates successively neoAnglicanism, Classicism, Humanism, Marxism, and Fascism.[8] The meaning, however, extends beyond the boundary of a discussion of the Christian's route to spiritual enlightenment since Lewis intends the reader to see the dangers of rationalism in the contemporary church in the three pale men who are equated with the positions held by Eliot, Irving Babbitt, and George Santayana. The political heresies shown in the red and black dwarfs and Savage are Marxism and Fascism. Mr. Broad represents Lewis's disgust with the then currently popular broad church Christianity.

Whatever may be said of this book, in general it has never been, as Lewis put it, "popular." It was not written for that audience, and the response of more than one reader, even a "highbrow" reader, has been that the book is boring. Though the theme is closely parallel to that of *Till We Have Faces* and covers many philosophical and religious questions which are central to all of Lewis's fiction, the treatment given them in this book fails to catch the reader's imagination. Perhaps the method, which is antiquated and traditional, has something to do with putting the reader off. Certainly the title, carrying as it does the suggestion of close connections with Bunyan and *Pilgrim's Progress*, does little to entice the casual reader into a receptive frame of mind. We expect stock figures who personify virtues and vices, a journey with loosely integrated episodes forming the narrative path through struggle to salvation, more discourse than dialogue or narrative, and over all the pall which allegory often casts upon the more interesting elements of fiction: characterization, ambiguity, suspense, excitement, vividness of description, and narrative power. In fact, the ordinary reader might well expect, by association with historical examples of the same sort, an edifying document, even a literary landmark of the genre, but withal a dull book.

Indeed, Lewis was to discover that what had been clear to him in writing a book which in part is an elevated record and, at points, a justification of his conversion, was not clear to his readers, especially the long attack on the three pale men and on the claims of Wisdom and his brood. I have not read the book without the help of the headlines, though I found myself consulting them only when I was confused or wanting confirmation of a suspicion of meaning, so that I do not know what my response would have been to the 1933 edition, but clearly the headlines do little to improve the quality of the reading experience. The allegory without the headlines is often obscure, and frequently with them, too obvious. This observation draws attention to one major failing of the book: its attention to topical and personal matters. Lewis's objection to automobiles, though vividly attested to by Gus Halfways' machine or his later and more general attack on the machine age, even his very special and elaborate attention to Luxuria, excellent as description, tends to focus our attention unevenly on subjects which would normally not merit such close scrutiny. The book as a whole suffers from unevenness in movement, characterization, and narration.

The action in an allegory is by definition mental action given fleshly form to make it more interesting and acceptable in the process of our edification. As such, we expect structured development of logical ideas, but the movement here is erratic. Lewis attempts to help us with map and headlines, and excuses any difficulty by attributing it to his own peculiar road to redemption, but the fact remains that as a piece of literature, the book is confused in structure and uneven in the amount of attention given to certain episodes, e.g., those of Wisdom, the three Pale Men, the Clevers and Sigismund Enlightenment. Portions of the narrative move rapidly like Vertue's encounter with Savage, the meetings with Sensible and Broad, but others drag through the weighty disquisitions of Wisdom, or Freud, or History, slowing the action to a snail's pace and turning it inward to cerebral and wholly abstract matters. The reader, like John, listens without much interest, hoping to get back on to the trail of the Island soon.

Characterization is expectedly flat since we are dealing in allegory, but there are again moments of unevenness when a figure threatens to break out of the mold. Gus Halfways reminds contemporary readers of John Barth's Satan figure, Stoker, in *Giles Goat-Boy*. Mr. Sensible and Mr. Broad are more lively and convincing than Angular or Vertue, and even Luxuria is more appealing as a character than Reason. Wisdom and Enlightenment have no character at all. When a character comes most alive for Lewis in this book, it is through dialogue, and conversely when his characters begin to discourse, they lose our interest and become mere mouthpieces for a message which Lewis gives us more briefly and satisfactorily at the top of the page. An early example of convincing dialogue (I, 3) reveals John as a child questioning his Mother about the lease and Uncle George's end.[9] In contrast, the dialogue between John and Reason (III, 9ff.) is more like a catechism than an exchange of information or ideas. On the positive side, Sensible's speech to Vertue (IV, 4) has all the wit and balance, point and force, of one of Lewis's own essays or lectures. Lewis has caught him to a nicety.

"Sense is easy, Reason is hard. Sense knows where to stop with gracious inconsistency, while Reason slavishly follows an abstract logic whither she knows not. The one seeks comfort and finds it, the other seeks truth and is still seeking. *Le bon sens* is the father of a flourishing family: Reason is barren and a virgin. If I had my way I should clap this Reason of yours in the bridewell to pursue her meditations in the straw. The baggage has a pretty face, I allow: but she leads us from our true aim—joy, pleasure, ease, content, whate'er the name! She is a fanatic who has never learned from my master to pursue the golden mean, and, being a mortal, to think mortal thoughts. *Auream quisquis—*."[10]

Here we have Lewis at his best, standing off and giving us a portrait of the selfcomplacent, cultured hypocrite. The humor and irony apparent here, as well as in his more acidly etched portrait of Freud, Eliot, and Mr. Broad, are all highlights for any reader and are almost universally disregarded by even the most ardent admirers of his other works. The same humor and irony set into sharp relief many of the descriptive passages. A notable example is the early description of Claptrap by Mr. Enlightenment (II,1, pp.37-8).

The narration falls awkwardly upon the shoulders of this dreamer, John, who often stands in the way of narrative progress. An inordinate amount of time is spent in encounters between John and adversaries where the whole action is verbal discourse and no movement is made other than clarifying an intellectual position. Certainly this is an innate disadvantage of the form, but David Lindsay, so much admired by Lewis, was able to present a spiritual journey in allegorical form with such intensity that Lewis would always refer to the effect which reading the book was to have on him— not until after the publication of *Pilgrim's Regress*, however. There is evidence that his response to Lindsay's method can be seen in the works which Lewis wrote after reading it, notably *Perelandra*. The movement may be disjointed because it follows the peculiar path Lewis took, rather than one which would have made easier reading. But even supposing that to be a factor, there are moments when the movement of the action halts for a lengthy speech by the Clevers, Sigismund, Reason, Mother Kirk, Wisdom, or History and then resumes after an awkward pause. Excitement and suspense are minimal since we never seriously doubt that John will see the light. The sort of realistic psychological tension which Lewis created in Orual's story is missing here. Interest in the narration centers upon what Lewis will present as the obstacles to John's conversion beyond the normally expected vices and temptations, and what form he will embody them in and how skillfully he will do up the whole set piece in description.

It is the descriptive passages which hint at Lewis's early claim on the reader's approval. They are, without exception, adequate to the occasion, and there are many instances of really fine description. Allegory does not necessarily lay great demands on the author's descriptive ability. He must use some imagination in drawing his dragons and monsters of vice, his desolate and luxurious landscapes, but there is a wealth of historical material on which to draw, such as used by Dante, Spenser, or Milton. Lewis does not eschew the aid of such sources (his false Florimels, brown girls, and dragons have familiar faces), but there is a freshness in his descriptive passages which is unique to him. It is a characteristic on which I place considerable emphasis throughout the study of his later work since I feel it is a key to his success and an integral feature of his embodiment of the creative experience.

One of the striking features of his descriptive technique is its simplicity and directness.

There was no glass in the window and no bars; it was just a square hole in the wall. Through it he saw a green wood full of primroses: and he remembered suddenly how he had gone into another wood to pull primroses, as a child, very long ago—so long that even in the moment of remembering the memory seemed still out of reach. While he strained to grasp it, there came to him from beyond the wood a sweetness and a pang so piercing that instantly he forgot his father's house, and his mother, and the fear of the Landlord, and the burden of the rules.[11]

This example, paralleling as it so explicitly does a similar experience recorded in *Surprised by Joy* from Lewis's own life, sets the tone for the quality which is expressed by all his best descriptive writing. In it we sense exactly what Lewis is describing and beneath or within that experience the significance it had for him and the symbolic meaning which he wishes it to convey to us. In fact, it seems an almost perfect paradigm of the sense of desire or longing which Lewis designates as the basis of creativity in human art and action. The description forms a basis for sharing a moment of deeper imagination or self-transcendence with the reader. If we accept the premises of the organic theory of literature, then we are moved in proportion to the intensity with which the artistry of the author has permitted him to invest his object with his original perceptions. Thus Lewis is most convincing as a writer of fiction where he is most successful in conveying to us that sense of shared experience which brings enlightenment to us, e.g., the creation of Narnia, Eustace's humiliation and dragonish thoughts, and Orual's epiphany. Lewis can be most convincing in a rational argument, for example in *Miracles*, *A Preface to "Paradise Lost*, " "Psycho-Analysis and Literary Criticism," but there he does not move us by the art of fiction, only by the art of logic and clear and clever language.

His descriptive technique is deceptively simple. It is based on the same keen observation of nature apparent in his earliest Boxen stories and in the many descriptive passages of his earliest letters.

All round him the frost was gleaming like silver; the sky was like blue glass; a robin sat in the hedge beside him: a cock was crowing in the distance... he saw the mountains heaped up to the sky like clouds, green and violet and dark red; shadows were passing over the big rounded slopes, and water shone in the mountain pools, and up at the highest of all the sun was smiling steadily on the ultimate crags.[12]

The trees grew more thickly hereabouts and were of larger kinds—and as the valley deepened, tiers of forest rose one above the other on each side. They walked in shadow. But far above their heads the sun was still shining on the mountain tops, beyond the forest slopes and beyond the last steep fields, where there were domed summits of pale grass and winding water-glens, and cliffs the colour of doves, and cliffs the colour of wine. The moths were already flying when they reached an open place. The valley widened and a loop of the river made room for a wide and level lawn between its banks and the wooded mountains. Amidst the lawn stood a low, pillared house approachable by a bridge, and the door stood open.[13]

Primary colors and shapes predominate in a simple landscape. There is a warmth and homeliness, a flavor of deepest satisfaction springing directly out of the scene described. But it is a picture, a selected view colored by memory and intent, used here to give us an impression of self-satisfaction as John, having abandoned religion, stands on the Hill just before meeting Vertue for the first time. It is an idealized picture, excluding from view all that is extraneous to the vision, just as in Narnia we will find no weeds, humidity, or vermin.

The descriptions are not all of pleasant scenes. The view of Luxuria's pond and its decomposing inhabitants, Superbia "scrabbling and puddering" and the return journey's changed vision of North and South "only the long straight road, very narrow, and on the left crags rising within a few paces of the right, swamps and jungle sinking almost at once into black cloud," show the other face of reality.[14]

The structure of a Lewis descriptive paragraph is simplicity itself. The sentences are short and pointed, frequently paralleled and balanced; there is a tidiness about the construction. The verbs are active, the nouns directly descriptive. There is seldom any subtlety in the use of symbolism and image. What we have is basically a child's or innocent's perception, forever free, not dimmed by time, and it is this timeless quality which comes to act as Lewis's descriptive signature.

Descriptive passages in *The Pilgrim's Regress* are subordinate to the clothed abstractions on whom the action centers, and it is to their significance that we must turn in estimating the success of the book. If we take Lewis at his word, he intended the book as a discussion of Christianity as against unbelief.[15] He meant to convey by means of allegory, which he reiterates in his Preface is at its best an approach to myth and which should be grasped rather by the imagination than the intellect, the soul's progress along the path from longing and confusion through rejection of belief to final acceptance. "It is the sort of thing you cannot learn from definition: you must rather get to know it as you get to know a smell or a taste, the atmosphere of a family or a country town, or the personality of an individual."[16]

This form is surely the best for saying what he has to say at this point in time. He apparently wishes to convey the intellectual struggle of a religious conversion which had been going on in his life for several years. Allegory is the traditional literary form for such expression, and Lewis uses the traditional structures and devices, deviating only to make allusions to modern vices. The form suits the content by allowing Lewis to present dispassionately and objectively a set of choices from which his Everyman must choose the right one. *Logos* and *Poiema* work together, if somewhat unevenly, with message predominating over formal expression in the more discursive sections.

But we are bored. Lewis lacks originality in presenting his particular John's individual journey to redemption, which must somehow be different from Christian's in *Pilgrim's Progress* or the incentive to read Lewis is lost. Rather than being the stumbling block to our understanding which Lewis proposes, his personal involvement in the journey should have given it that individuality and originality which it so sorely lacks. As a study of his commitment to the Christian faith in 1933, it is a revealing document, telling us much about how he came to accept Christianity. In some ways it is a more arresting document on this subject than *Surprised by Joy* since it has the immediacy of a firsthand and front-line report. But the literary form militates against the personal record, and we come away dissatisfied with Lewis's first fiction because it is dry and old-fashioned, lacking in the freshness and vigor of expression and reaction to nature and life which his later works give in such full measure.

From this point on, Lewis's work takes a decidedly different direction, away from blatant allegory and moralizing toward an experimentation with forms like science fiction and children's fantasy. Lewis probably understood the limitations of *The Pilgrim's Regress* well enough. The restriction of character development and the episodic movement caused by the required meetings with stock characters and situations placed a damper on the spirit of free imaginative inquiry and creativity which brought Lewis to write in the first place. Once he had dealt with the theme of Christian conversion, he may have felt released to go ahead and try his creative talents in forms that were more challenging because they offered so many more possibilities for creative expression in both themes and form.

2. *OUT OF THE SILENT PLANET* 1938

Among the earliest indications of Lewis's interest in other worlds is his youthful creation of the animal land of Boxen and his preference for writers whose works center upon the unworldly or other worldly: Morris, MacDonald, and Wells. The Boxen stories are not technically "other worldly" in Lewis's sense since they deal with dressed animals in a medieval Animal Land very like medieval England.[1] As Lewis notes, Animal Land is unlike Narnia or any fairy land because of its total exclusion of wonder.[2] The often chronicled story of his *Sehnsucht* need not be repeated here, but we might note that Lewis always linked his interest in fiction about other worlds, either read or written by him, with these earliest emotional and aesthetic experiences.[3] That they gave him both pleasure and an escape from an otherwise constricting reality is clear in his repeated references in letters to Arthur Greeves about the escape to other worlds shared by the two young men in their reading and their response to the music of Wagner or the illustrations of Rackham and Dürer.[4] In retrospect, Lewis records his response to the literary influences of this sort: E. Nesbit's *The Amulet* was important in its early influence, along with *Squirrel Nutkin* by Beatrix Potter, and Longfellow's *Saga of King Olaf.*[5] In a 1929 letter to Greeves, he recalls the past in memories of *Phantastes, Bleheris, Dymer,* Papillon, T. Edens Osborne—all, as he said, jumbled together.[6]

By mid-May, 1919, he was working on a "Venus" poem which never materialized, but in the letter he gives us a bit of the story. Helen of Troy is being transported to Zeus by Simon Magus, and on the way they encounter evil powers, the Dynasties, who hold the heaven and prevent friendly powers from reaching the earth.[7] It is nearly twenty years, however, before this theme reappears, now transformed by Christian belief, in the struggle of the Oyarsa to free the silent planet from the grip of the Bent One.

Throughout the Twenties and early Thirties, there are references to his interest in the fusion of the homely and the magical which attracted him to Morris and MacDonald, and briefly to Jacob Boehme.[8] But the focus has shifted with his conversion, as he suggests in discussing his early interest in astronomy.[9] He directly attributes his interest in what lies beyond the limits of the science of astronomy to his philosophical and religious bent, which searches beneath the surface for the suggestion of what lies beyond.[10]

It is, by his admission, the reading of *A Voyage to Arcturus*, sometime between 1934 when Greeves mentioned it to him and 1938 when he finished *Out of the Silent Planet*, that sparked his enthusiasm for writing space fiction. His letter to Ruth Pitter, quoted earlier, indicates he learned from Lindsay that planetary fiction is a good medium for spiritual adventures. "Only they can satisfy the craving which sends our imagination off the earth or hurtling it another way."[11] He had attempted to assuage this craving in *The Pilgrim's Regress*, to what result we may judge from the preceding discussion. He wrote Charles Brady that *A Voyage to Arcturus* was the source of the trilogy because it showed him how science fiction and the supernatural could be combined.[12] He was somewhat more explicit in a letter to W.L. Kinter when he linked *A Voyage to Arcturus* and his planetary novels to earlier and classic models.

My real model was David Lindsay's *Voyage to Arcturus* wh. first suggested to me that the form of "science fiction" cd. be filled by spiritual experiences. And as the *Furioso* was in some ways the science-fiction of its age, your analogy works. But mind you, there is already a science-fiction element in the *Commedia*: e.g. *Inferno* XXXIV, 85-114.[13]

We know that Lewis was strongly attracted by Lindsay's style, by the unworldly quality of the descriptive passages, the sheer imaginative intensity of reading such a work. The style he felt was "crude," the proper names "superb," but the subject matter was Manichaean, nearly diabolic, and too strong for consumption by the young.[14] A study of David Lindsay by Pick, Wilson, and Visiak, *The Strange Genius of David Lindsay*, describes *A Voyage to Arcturus* as a nonallegorical *Pilgrim's Progress*, as mystic evolutionism, as Manichaean, and as Christian.[15] Out of all this richness some important aspects of Lindsay's influence on Lewis can be traced. The only one of the three authors who knew Lindsay, records that Lindsay was heavily influenced by George MacDonald.[16] The parallels are too numerous between *A Voyage to Arcturus*, and *Lilith* and *Phantastes* to pursue here, but Lewis must have seen them at once. Visiak suggests that Lindsay's eroticism in conflict with his idealism provokes the tension which accounts for the compelling mystery of the book.[17] Though I would not attempt to prove that the eroticism of *Perelandra*, for instance, sprang from either Lindsay or MacDonald, it is clear that the treatment of this aspect of the spiritual experience is closely allied with the influence of *A Voyage to Arcturus* and *Lilith*.

That Lindsay had an intense and coherent vision of the spiritual journey toward ultimate truth is unquestioned by his three critics. They differ however in their evaluation of what Lindsay means. The *Voyage* may be basically Christian, with Krag acting as redeemer, Muspel as God and Crystalman as Satan; or it may be Manichaean, with the final revelation that all Christianity is a delusion. Clearly it remains, as it was for Lewis, an absorbing and disturbing book, and its influence should be weighed in judging Lewis's reasons for choosing a planetary setting for his next piece of fiction.

Lewis may have been disillusioned by the reception of *The Pilgrim's Regress*, but he found new possibilities in *A Voyage to Arcturus*. We see in *Out of the Silent Planet* the same Christian on a journey, struggling with vices, internal and external, searching for truth, and meeting the ultimate reality at the conclusion of his spiritual and physical journey. *Out of the Silent Planet* is *The Pilgrim's Regress* in a new key. However, the elements of Lewis's personal dissatisfactions which inhabit the periphery of *The Pilgrim's Regress* here come into central prominence: his disapproval of the machine-age emphasis on "scientific progress," the inhumane aspects of scientific research, the greed of modern materialism, the sacrifice of the individual to the good of general progress.

What set Lewis to writing the book may have been his realization that people (one student triggered the reaction) were actually believing the fantasies of interplanetary colonization being purveyed by men like Olaf Stapledon (*Last and First Men*, 1930) and J.B.S. Haldane (*Possible Worlds*, 1927), and later expressed by C.H. Waddington (*Science and Ethics*, 1942). In a letter to A.C. Clarke, the science fiction writer, Lewis forcefully stated that the "moral assumptions in popular fiction are a v. important symptom" of the moral climate of an age.[18]

Look at Stapledon (*Star Gazer* ends in sheer devil worship), Haldane's *Possible Worlds* and Waddington's *Science & Ethics*. I agree technology is per se neutral: but a race devoted to the increase of its own power by technology with complete indifference to ethics does seem to me a cancer in the universe.[19]

W. Olaf Stapledon's *Last and First Men*, 1930, offers much against which Lewis might have reacted. It is the encyclopedic history of man to his ultimate extinction millenia off. Reading it after encountering Lewis, we see possible sources for some of Weston's and later Frost's scientific experiments. The earthly challenge to intelligent life on Mars and Venus in Lewis's novels is closely parallel to events in Stapledon's book. Forced from earth by devastating wars and shrinking energy sources, men invade Venus, and as a "higher type," destroy all native intelligence, justifying such action on the basis that the prime directive is to maintain the human species in any environment.[20] The group mind produces a super individual; sacred science culminates in producing a mentality like Weston's which places man at the center of the universe and makes him the germ of a world soul.[21] Early in the book there is a confrontation between a naked native woman of another planet, an American emissary, and a Chinese emissary. Lewis may have had this scene in mind when he wrote the central section of *Perelandra*.[22] There is a great brain kept alive with tubes and other scientific apparatus which seems close to Alcasan's role in *That Hideous Strength*.[23] Clearly, Lewis is reacting against the sort of heartless and godless scientific materialism he saw gaining popular approval. He claimed that Weston was a composite picture, though others have suggested that he is a portrait of Professor Waddington or of Stapledon. Ransom, Lewis suggests, was based on a humorous portrait of a man he knew (Tolkien?) but was not a self-portrait.[24] He explains later that he made Ransom a philologist

chiefly to render his rapid mastery of Old Solar more plausible. His friends in *That Hideous Strength* are a literary critic (Dimble), a Doctor (Miss Ironwood), an unspecified scientist (MacPhee), a scholar's wife, a charwoman, and a bear! It is v. important that there are 2 untainted scientists in the book (MacPhee & Hingest), and many of the Belbury Group are not scientists at all.[25]

Lewis's intention then is to deal with matters of present concern: the dangers of "Westonism," and of the scientific dream of defeating death.[26] He sends Ransom on a spiritual journey, forces him to go by abducting him, and reveals to him the glory of Deep Heaven and the peace and community of nonhuman life among the sorns, hrossa, and pfifltriggi. Using Weston and Devine as foils, he indicates, against the backdrop of the old mysteries drawn from the story of the Old One, Maleldil and the Bent One, the place a committed Christian can hold in otherworldly action. In his letter to the Milton Society of America, he places these books at one extreme of the symbolic and mythopoeic embodiment of his religious belief and *The Screwtape Letters* at the other. His comment to Father Peter Milward, "In my own view *Perelandra* is worth 20 *Screwtapes*," indicates the importance one of the three books had for him.[27]

Of the three, *Out of the Silent Planet* is closest to the traditional science fiction frame, giving considerable attention to the journey to Malacandra (though using little technical paraphernalia) and extensive descriptions of the planetary life. But Lewis is not interested in science except as a tool, and our attention shifts quite quickly away from the external paraphernalia of spaceship and weird landscape and comes to rest on Ransom and his reactions to his new environment and his development as the first interplanetary Christian.

Lewis probably intended the book initially as an exploration into a new form using themes, e.g., the necessity of moral choice, the virtues of simple love, loyalty, and devotion, obedience to legitimate higher spiritual authority, all of which had appeared in *The Pilgrim's Regress*. There is no indication that when he began the book he intended any sequel, though by the end, the postscripted "letter" suggests other installments, and Lewis wrote Sister Penelope in 1939 that the letter was a device to provide for a sequel.[28] The immediate sequel, *The Dark Tower*, is an only recently published romantic fragment involving Ransom in nontheological matters.

In retrospect we see that Lewis looked on *Out of the Silent Planet* as a prelude to *Perelandra*, indicating to W.L. Kinter that "No one else sees that the first book is Ransom's *enfances* [sic] : if they notice a change at all, they complain that in the later ones he 'loses the warm humanity of the first etc.'"[29] In an earlier letter responding to Kinter's question about whether the trilogy was an epic, Lewis replied that he considered it Romance because "it lacks sufficient roots in legend and tradition to be what I'd call an epic. Isn't it more the method of Apuleius, Lucan, or Rabelais, but diverted from a comic to a serious purpose?"[30] To Eddison he indicated that this first in the trilogy was the "less" in significance, ending as it does on a "satiric note."[31] In defending his "attack on science" in his reply to Professor Haldane, Lewis indicated that in the figure of Weston he tried for "farce as well as fantasy."[32] Again we see him in a defensive position and must judge his retrospective explanation of his intentions accordingly, but he indicates that his aim was an imaginative response to what he saw as the dangers not of science but of a "scientism" which seemed intent on remaking the world and the universe without pity, happiness or freedom.[33] In his recorded discussion with Kingsley Amis and Brian Aldis on the subject of science fiction, he commented on two aspects of the general subject of science fiction which apply to *Out of the Silent Planet*: a science fiction story forces its moral on the reader, and in science fiction, only the first journey to a new planet interests imaginative readers.[34]

The book is a romantic fantasy, a piece of science fiction introducing three characters who will reappear in later novels. It is focused on a space journey to a new world for the purpose of material and scientific exploitation: Devine wants gold and Weston's scientific experimentation will lead to human colonization and the consequent destruction of the inhabitants. On another level, it is the story of a lone Christian's growing understanding of the truth of Deep Heaven, of other worlds, of planetary influences under the guidance of superior celestial powers and his growth into fuller manhood, an expansion of his knowledge and his soul. It is an attack on "scientism" and a statement of the power of love, hope, and charity.

As good Lewis readers we look at what it means, then ask how we are to respond. Lewis tried to make the meaning clear. He alternately fumed because on one hand readers did not see the point and on the other hand because his publisher gave the point away in the jacket blurb when the reader should have been let alone to figure it out unaided.[35] He carefully explained to a correspondent the equation of eldila=angels, Maleldil=Christ, Old One=Father, Bent One=Satan.[36] But beyond what Lewis may have intended, and much which I have discussed is retrospective on Lewis's part or speculation on mine, we still question what we receive as the meaning of the book.

One of the first features which strikes a reader fresh from *The Pilgrim's Regress* is a marked improvement in characterization. Weston and Devine may remain rather rigid stock villains, cf., Mr. Sensible and Gus Halfways, but Ransom and Hyoi develop as their relationship deepens. The Oyarsa of Malacandra, though distant, is more personable than Reason or Wisdom. The dialogue becomes a true exchange rather than a prelude to discourse, and the action of Ransom, at least, is given a psychological depth not attempted in the characterization of John. There is excitement and tension generated by Ransom's fears, his growing perception of the world he inhabits, his journey to Meldilorn which is both a physical test and a symbolic approach to truth and power.

Another important feature is Lewis's use of setting. In contrasting an acknowledged allegory with an acknowledged piece of science fiction, we would expect the usual differences. In the former, the scene is stereotyped by traditional example: bogs, unscalable mountains, houses and castles of various vices, the homely cottage of virtue. In science fiction we face a similar stereotype, perhaps better known to the modern reader: complex mechanical paraphernalia, weird vegetation and planetary inhabitants, "special effects" abounding. Lewis, however, both disappoints and pleases us in that order. The specialized descriptions are held to a minimum because apparently they do not interest Lewis. But the description of scenery with its imaginative creation of flora and fauna, shows Lewis's real strength. What in *The Pilgrim's Regress* is confined to John's vision of the

Island is here unleashed in the intensely imaginative production of the *harandra, harandramit*, and Meldilorn. The full elaboration of this technique comes in *Perelandra* where Lewis's imaginative ingenuity could perhaps have profited from the curb placed on it later in the writing of the Narnia stories.

The book's meaning centers on a perceptive, intelligent, moral human being thrust unwillingly into an alien world where he expects to be a sacrificial victim. He is clearly not an everyman because he was "elected" to make contact with the forces of Deep Heaven, and we admire his ability to rise to the occasion, feeling as we do the novel reader's identification with and empathy for the outcast in an alien world. Guided by good feeling and good sense, by Christian faith and obedience, he makes his journey toward truth and self-understanding and experiences his moment of epiphany, although it is not a dramatic one since our attention is shifted to Weston's feeble attempt at the communication of his sick science. The book means the triumph of compassion, loyalty, obedience, and faith over the forces of greed, intolerance, egotism, and misguided "idealism." Its message is entirely congruent with Lewis's romantic idealism and Christianity, and the Christian significance is readily apparent and has had so many commentators that it needs no further discussion.

The reader's response to this book, to the whole trilogy, in fact, is a curious one. Those who think they will find "science fiction" leave disappointed by Lewis's conception of the type. Those who expect religious allegory find the landscape and livestock a trifle tedious, and one even finds the whole thing unpleasant or unsatisfactory.[37] For the more receptive, however, the experience of reading this book is imaginatively satisfying.

First, there is the studied balance of contrasts between the understated opening of a pedestrian holiday, a walking tour—we must forgive Lewis the pun, it was a family weakness—and the space flight. Nature versus machine, calm and storm, dark and light, simple choices and complex results; the contrasts abound. The story unfolds from the orthodox and uninviting environs of Sterk through the bath of heat and light into a pink and purple landscape with its unnatural elongation. We are drawn along with Ransom in his "love of knowledge—a kind of madness" to meet the hrossa and sorns and Oyarsa.[38] Once we are fairly caught, Lewis begins to slacken the pace for periodic discourse on the customs and habits of each species: Hyoi's dialogue on love (Chapter 12), Augray's explanation of the power structure of Malacandra (Chapter 15), and the meeting with Oyarsa in Meldilorn and the trial of Weston and Devine (Chapters 18-20).

There are climactic episodes, such as the *hnakra* battle, the journey over the mountains to Meldilorn, and the return to Earth, but by mid-book we have met most of the planet's curiosities and move toward the basic information Lewis wants to pass on. We see man as a tainted being, lusting after material goods, warped ideals, or sensuous pleasures, a small, benighted speck in a universe ruled by a hierarchy of benevolent and protective powers. By the example of the hrossa, Ransom sees his own bestiality; from the sorns he learns of his limited understanding of the invisible beyond; from Oyarsa is revealed his responsibility for the rejection of hope and salvation.

Many readers have been so drawn by these weighty matters that they lose some of the delight in Lewis's ample creative powers seen in the furred humans (hrossa), the embodied and wraith-like intellects (sorns), and the mechanics and artisans (pfifltriggi). Too serious a response overlooks the humor of the old hross sleeping through the trial, of Ransom's mistaken identification of Hyoi's accoutrements, of Weston's defense. To focus exclusively on the message, which Lewis clearly gives, is to exclude an appreciation of his delight in creating and filling another world. In a letter to Jane Gaskell, age 15, he indicates that when you take readers to another world, you have to fill it with something, and it has to be the right kind of filling.[39] If it is a fantasy world which you create, then the challenge is to create for it appropriate otherworldly material, not the sort of "stuff" that happens every day. The language and actions must be the heroic and romantic sort, high and reckless and above all the spell they cast must not be broken by an earthbound jolt.[40]

Judged by his own rules, Lewis fares fairly well, though not so well as in the Narnia stories. The unevenness which is so characteristic of *The Pilgrim's Regress* is felt here too as passages of description involving Ransom's reactions alternate with information passed down to the reader through Ransom. Some readers miss Lewis's own personal delight in crafting here the subcreation he admired in Tolkien's work. He found sheer pleasure in creating an otherworld, landscaping it, peopling it, providing it with a history and purpose. Here for the first time in prose fiction Lewis puts his literary credo into action by stirring the deeper imagination, presenting what the narrow and practical real world excludes.[41] He is giving us, too, that glimpse of possibilities, the vision of the ultimate source of desire, which governed his imaginative life and with which he hoped to infect the lives of others. There are moments that approach awe in the book: when Ransom perceives that earth is a gap and space an intense and radiant reality, or when Ransom approaches Oyarsa; but they fade and are hard to recapture on a third or fourth reading. We may feel what Lewis wants to do but sense that he has not quite succeeded. The problem rests in the conflicting claims of excitement against those of the deeper imagination.[42] The structure does not quite suit the purpose Lewis intends. We have a book of information vying with one of the deeper imagination. A comparison of the novel with its prototype, *A Voyage to Arcturus*, shows that the imagery and passion which Lewis found in that book do not wholly emerge in this one.[43] There is no adequate fusion of the imaginative and didactic elements; we can still separate our reaction to Malacandra and the journey there, within, and back, from the meaning of it, and to separate them is fatal because it emphasizes one over the other. Since critics see Lewis as theologically oriented, the book becomes for them a battleground for the exegesis of symbols, consequently the creative imagination is seen as a subsidiary device used in the performance of these prodigies of meaning.

Our impression as readers is one of disappointment. We are not entirely convinced that Ransom's trip was necessary. If he had been a bit more penetrating, he might have figured it out on earth. Weston, who changes from grouch to buffoon in his last performance, loses too much of the sinister quality needed for Ransom to react against, a defect later remedied in *Perelandra*. The idealized world of Malacandra loses some of its mystery by being so thoroughly explained that there is too much suggestion and too little suggestiveness. And there is a feeling of anticlimax, as though the whole story may be a prelude to something more, or at least more than the conclusion gives us. So if the book is Ransom's *enfance*, it stands as a portion of some larger piece and is weak on its own. It lacks, too, that indefinable sense of having caught, however briefly, the ineffable and longed-for experience of otherness which was so close to Lewis's own imaginative experience. Only in a few of the Narnia books do we feel that longing as though it were our own. If we are touched here, it is more by an appeal to our imaginations or intellects separately, not the fused experience which is the height of Lewis's achievement.

We are left, then, feeling that the *Logos* and *Poiema* do not work organically except on occasion. The plot becomes, after the cleverly understated opening, spasmodic and episodic, built upon a predictably regulated series of parallel encounters between Ransom and the hrossa, sorns, pfifltriggi, and Oyarsa. The narrative and descriptive sections alternate in the somewhat awkward way which characterizes both allegory and science fiction. The characters, although more fully realized as individuals than in *The Pilgrim's Regress*, suffer from oversimplification and lack of psychological motivation. The "trial" scene serves as an example. Robson calls attention to the undergraduate humor of Weston and Devine's trial.[44] Lewis intends to parallel Ransom's anticipated trial, which has presumably been the impelling force from the beginning, with the real trial of Weston. This culminating scene, the summation of Lewis's condemnation of scientific materialism and planetary exploitation, fails to convince us for two reasons. First, Weston has never successfully come alive as a villain, and his antics are hence comic but unrelated to the central theme. Lewis is hardly allowing him sufficient force of personality to permit a realistic trial. He is a pasteboard figure, more easily disposed of than Sensible, Broad, or the brown girls of *The Pilgrim's Regress*. Second, there is a quality of staginess about all the major scenes and their very inevitability reduces suspense and tension in the conflicts. The inevitability is not that of a fated encounter but is a natural progression projected from the moment we realize, when Hyoi offers Ransom the ritual drink and Ransom perceives the meaning of *hnau*, the ground rules of the planet and universe we have been transported to. Weston cannot win, and hence, comic though he may be, we cannot take him seriously as either villain or buffoon.

We come back necessarily to the meaning that here, as in *The Pilgrim's Regress*, controls, perhaps too firmly, the use of certain literary structures and techniques. Lewis has, again, displayed remarkable skill in descriptive writing.

The Earth's disk was nowhere to be seen: the stars, thick as daisies on the uncut lawn, reigned perpetually with no cloud, no moon, no sunrise to dispute their sway. There were planets of unbelievable majesty, and constellations undreamed of: there were celestial sapphires, rubies, emeralds and pin-pricks of burning gold; far out on the left of the picture hung a comet, tiny and remote; and between all and behind all, far more emphatic and palpable than it showed on Earth, the undimensioned, enigmatic blackness.[45]

His descriptions of the world of Malacandra and its inhabitants, of Deep Heaven, are evocative, imaginative, and believable. They do in fact stir the imagination. The general structure of the book, planned around a series of journeys and encounters, mounting in direction and intensity, and his use of humor to balance the "serious" aspects of his theme, all reveal Lewis's technical skill. Though these techniques often are overlooked, they mark his particular style, revealing both the balance of his own outlook and of his perspective on theological issues.

The form used here for the first time does not suit his purposes. Though he does not adhere to the science fiction form of Wells, or the fantasy form of Lindsay, he is using many of the conventional planetary travel techniques which he would modify in *Perelandra* and discard altogether in *That Hideous Strength*. He appears to be uneasy with the form, spending little time on the scientific aspects of travel and planetary exploitation and depending more on his impressionistic response to the new world which gives a freshness and reality to his descriptions. The theme he pursues militates against the form he is using in a way which weakens the structure and thus the attack on "scientism." For example, once Ransom has been abducted and the flight made, there is almost no description of the mechanics of life on Malacandra for the three visitors, and on the return journey, which almost demands more explanation of the scientific principles of unbodying the ship, we are given Ransom's unconsciousness through the whole thing. Lewis is caught in his theme, unable to express his anti-"scientism" in an essentially mechanical and scientifically oriented form. Furthermore, his interest is more in the message than the form, although at the outset his loyalties seem equally divided between the excitement generated by the creation of another world and the transcendence of earthly greed and egotism through spiritual progress. More time is spent on Ransom's education, his *enfance*, than on an active encounter between Ransom and Weston. The tone of the book is passive, Ransom receiving the Law, rather than active and militant as in *Perelandra*. Taken within the context of the trilogy, it is a natural prelude to later matters, but taken alone it seems incomplete and somewhat an apprentice work.

Lewis's strict commitment to either the form or the message was not lasting, as his later works show. For his purposes, science fiction *per se* was too constricting; it did not allow, as fantasy would, for the fine creative play of narrative and description which he admired in *A Voyage to Arcturus*. His central concern here expressed as a reaction against what he considered an appalling contemporary point of view, was too narrow to support the whole structure, and hence when judgment is pronounced on it by Oyarsa, other interests have already usurped first place, and we feel the anticlimax. The book suffers from a lack of focus and organic unity which *Perelandra* restores, where many modifications appear in theme and structure.

3.   *THE DARK TOWER* (1938) 1976

Readers of the space trilogy were unfamiliar with this fragment of a novel until a few years ago when Walter Hooper revealed its existence. Lewis probably began work on this unfinished novel when he was concluding *Out of the Silent Planet*. The only dates mentioned in the novel suggest that the time setting itself is 1938-9, which coincides with the publication of the first book of the space trilogy.

The narrative picks up exactly at the point where the last sentence of *Out of the Silent Planet* ends, with the suggestion of the next travel for Ransom being time travel.[1]

Assembled in the Cambridge College rooms of Dr. Orfieu are his attractive, young assistant Scudamour; Ransom, described as the pale man whose distressed, grey eyes are shielded by a green shade; Lewis, the narrator; and MacPhee, a skeptic and don at Manchester University. The discussion centers on time travel and the impossibilities of one body occupying two places in different times at once. These men form a society which recognizes that the division between real life and the fantastic is like a thin protective crust. Orfieu introduces them to his "chronoscope," a time viewer, a window on Othertime. The activating principle seems to be a material Z, isolated from the brain, which allows the reproduction of the time perception organ's function within the machine. There is some slow-moving discussion of the possibility of prevision and memory, mention of Dunne's [John William] book [*An Experiment with Time*, 1927] and experiments on the subject, and the first chapter closes on the suspenseful anticipation of looking into Othertime.

Chapter 2 reveals the scene which comprises all that we see of the other world, a massive building with a square tower. We come to realize that the dark tower, as it is called, is the Library at Cambridge University. Much later, after the discussion of the Smokehorse (steam engine railroad), we see that Lewis is projecting Othertime as a later view of England and particularly of Cambridge. Vision focuses on a heavily sculptured room, an obscene idol composed of nude bodies in states of morbid and senile decay. As though to complement the idol, we are introduced to a real life, superannuated erotomaniac named Knellie, a graduate of Oxford and don at Cambridge, who humorously confuses the chronoscope for a movie projector and Othertime with blue film "art." Focal point in the pictured room is the "stinging man," a horned creature who poisons a continuous line of young men and women as they make obeisance before the idol and effectively transforms them into automata, workers whom we then see constructing the tower and overseen by "Jerkies." The chapter has some fine descriptive passages giving a sense of the sinister quality of the room and the procedure of stinging and its effect. "The Man had stung him apparently in the spine, pressing in the needle point of the sting, neither quickly nor slowly, with a surgeon's accuracy. The struggles of his victim did not last long...."[2] The chapter concludes with the stinging man fixing his ghastly eye on those looking into the chronoscope.

Chapter 3 deals with the reaction to this initial experience. MacPhee, not yet convinced that it is not a hoax or hallucination, questions whether what is seen is past or future. Ransom suggests it is neither, for him it is simply Hell. The effect is to bring all the men into a violent disagreement which fades into new views of the Dark Tower. The social structure—workers, police Jerkies, and Stinging Man—is described. Now Scudamour's double appears, and we watch as Scudamour and Lewis watch the Double in the throes of receiving his sting and consequently the robes of his "office." Scudamour, afflicted by a headache, is moved by what he sees. He is expecting his fiancée, an unpleasant young modern woman, called in the manuscript of this fragment, Miss Ammeret (possibly playing Amoret to the Spenserian Scudamour) and later Camilla Bembridge. He is given leave to take a vacation since his long work with Orfieu on the project is getting on his nerves.

MacPhee again poses the question of whether the whole thing is not an elaborate hoax; whereupon, the perception that the Dark Tower is the Cambridge University Library is made, laying to rest any further unbelief.

Scudamour, in an uncharacteristically impassioned speech, attacks science: "This is science. And who ever heard of a new scientific discovery which didn't show that the real universe was even fouler and meaner and more dangerous than you had supposed?... I think we have tapped whatever reality is behind all the old stories about hell and devils and witches. I don't know. Some filthy sort of something going on alongside the ordinary world and all mixed up with it."[3] MacPhee has on the same page rejected the theories of Butler and Bergson and Shaw about evolution as nonscientific. Ransom, siding with Scudamour, indicates that he no longer thinks the Dark Tower is Hell. "But a world in which beastly things can happen to people through no fault of their own—or, at least, not mainly through their own fault—isn't Hell: it's only our own world over again. It only has to be faced, like our own world."[4] Through Ransom's words, Lewis points toward a future which might be prophetic of what lies ahead if Westonism is left unchecked. The parallel structure is fixed here by Ransom, and we see the possible meaning which idols, stings, and automata held for Lewis, the author. Ransom suggests that other times than past, present, and future may exist, and Scudamour's later explanations will bear this theory out. The chapter ends by setting up the "exchange" which will take the center of the stage in Chapter 4.

Lewis, the narrator, viewing the Double as Stinging Man, suggests that pity rather than horror and disgust might be the appropriate reaction. The later suggestion by Scudamour when he possesses the sting, that the desire to sting is not sexual, leads us to assume Lewis planned to develop this symbolic organ as a manifestation of human suffering. The result is a bit silly since even Lewis's and Scudamour's plans and protestations cannot deny the reader's inclination to see this stinger as phallic.

Scudamour, seeing Camilla appear on the screen about to get stung, plunges into the screen, knocking over the candle which reproduces the same situation in Cambridge as in the Dark Tower. This presumably facilitates the "exchange" as Scudamour passes into the picture and his double appears in Cambridge. There is a rather amusing scene as Knellie questions Orfieu on the "art" of the "film."

Ransom, realizing that an exchange has occurred, attempts to stop the Double, but after a hair-raising walk on the college roof tiles, the Double escapes, leaving Lewis, Ransom, and MacPhee to speculate on how the exchange occurs and agreeing on the necessity of getting the Double back bodily so that a re-exchange can be made. Whereupon the fiancée, the infernal woman, as Lewis the author calls her, rings through saying she will come round for Scudamour tomorrow.

Though we never see this Camilla, we feel that Lewis obviously dislikes her. "The rest of us, who had opportunities during his absence of getting to know the real Camilla pretty well, would put it more bluntly. She was not the sort of young woman who was likely to risk her life, or even her comfort, for the sake of truth in love or in anything else."[5] "For the real Camilla Bembridge was what is called 'modern.' She was so free to talk about the things her grandmother could not mention that Ransom once said he wondered if she were free to talk about anything else. There would have been no difficulty about suggesting to her that she might become your mistress; I do not think you would have suceeded unless you offered very good security, but there would have been no tears or blushes or indignation."[6] We wonder if there isn't a lot of the later Jane Studdock in Camilla's projected portrait, and if Lewis isn't relishing the possible encounter of the real Camilla and Scudamour's demonic double.[7]

The fifth chapter, contrary to expectation, veers away from the present to focus on Scudamour's narrative of his adventures in Othertime now that he has safely returned, and the last three chapters deal exclusively with Othertime. Scudamour's growing consciousness of his new situation is skillfully handled, though the treatment of his facility in language and the preservation of his innocence in the face of his demonic body and role are hardly interesting or convincing. He finds himself in the act of stinging the double Camilla and resists. The double Camilla is much nicer than the real, sensible one. It is her explanation which makes clear that the stung people are deluded into thinking that they are offered to the Great Brain by the lord of the Dark Tower, the Unicorn of the Eastern Plain, so that they can, as she says, drink of the fuller life, the euphemism for being made automata. This section (Chapter 5) is extremely slow and awkward as the lovers try to communicate, and it reveals the essential awkwardness Lewis found in writing domestic or love dialogue, which he carefully avoids in all the fiction.

There are White Riders, the barbarian enemy, who live in the forest. Looking for a way of escape, Scudamour sees a broken chronoscope, and turns at the chapter's end to greet a servant who relates the arrival of the White Riders.

Chapter 6 details, somewhat mysteriously, the inner order of the tower. There are apparently doors since the Riders bring a battering ram. There is evidently no escape; the windows are all too high to see from. The servants are Drones, who attempt to produce horns (stings) in a vain effort to unseat the Stinging Man.

They spend nearly all their spare time in the laboratory, concocting every kind of nostrum which they think may produce the coveted deformity. Sometimes it is drugs to drink, sometimes powders and plasters for the forehead, sometimes incisions and cauterizations. One depends on diet, another on some kind of exercises. Scudamour says they reminded him of nothing so much as of inveterate gamblers whom one finds living in the neighbourhood of any big continental casino—every one with an infallible private recipe for making his fortune.[8]

I quote this description because it reminds us of Lewis's growing concern for the manipulation of power for personal ends. He described, as a young Magdalen College tutor, his view of his colleagues in terms parallel to these and nearly as unflatteringly. (*See* the section on *That Hideous Strength*, note 16.) He was aware through his knowledge of Tolkien's work of the use made of that same theme in *The Lord of the Rings*. Though Lewis dropped this theme in *The Dark Tower*, he returned to it and expanded it in nearly every succeeding work.

The White Riders seem to sympathize with the workers, who are undoubtedly, in their pre-stung condition, closer in makeup to these Savages of the forest. The White Riders, who have placed a bounty on his horn, retire after a brief and pointless skirmish, and Scudamour learns through his servant that Camilla has been particularly chosen for stinging. There is a cryptic suggestion that she is "very like" another figure, suggesting perhaps that she may become an exchange for the real Camilla or at least a replica for the purposes of attraction. Probably Lewis intended this girl as a replica and may or may not have intended to exchange her later. To justify everyone's bad opinion of her, Lewis may have planned to yank the pleasant double into Cambridge to live happily with Scudamour and send the "real" Camilla where she can be appropriately modern.

This possibility seems even more likely when we find Scudamour in the library, throughout the fragment of Chapter 7, reading the history of Othertime. This section is the most boring and technical and may explain why Lewis stopped where he did. A second reading shows that the operation of Othertime seems to have been to effect a possible exchange by the creation or development of similar objects (Smokehorses or people), replicas which will attract the Othertime (earthly) counterpart. There are moments of real interest, as in Lewis's explanation of the time square.[9] We also learn that Othertime's time science has vastly outstripped ours and that our space science is ludicrously naive, that experiments in "exchange" have been made but the human child exchanged, proving unadaptable to the system, is finally used for scientific purposes. But little real action occurs. We get much information and are left with the experiment which apparently will produce the Othertime chronoscope.

Thus the book breaks off, tantalizing us with why it was left uncompleted and what it would have gone on to include. In the light of the trilogy, it appears a blind alley. Ransom relinquishes his position to Lewis and then Scudamour who are relatively neutral narrators. The interest seems more scientific and mechanical than imaginative, which may explain why in *Perelandra* Lewis turns so decisively away from the mechanics of space voyage and the technology of science fiction to the imaginative descriptions of the planet.

It is clear that he is toying with ideas and techniques suggested by his reading of *A Voyage to Arcturus*. The presentation of Othertime, the "seance"-like setting, the shocking suggestion of its reality, the proof of its reality all firmly placed in this world, are in sharp contrast to *Out of the Silent Planet* where Ransom is whisked away and the new world confronted as a *fait accompli*. The name Scudamour and more pointedly—permit me the pun—the anatomical protuberance—the horn-sting—are strikingly similar to those which come to Maskull on Tormance: the breve and magn in the Joiwind episode (p. 45), the sorb of the Oceaxe episode (p. 83).[10] It is difficult to do more than guess at what Lewis intended the Dark Tower and sting to represent.

There seem clear references to the ivory tower, a closed and inbred academic society in the Dark Tower hierarchy. The chosen leader infects his workers, automata, who think they are sacrificing themselves for a noble purpose: to enter the new religion's more intense life. In reality they are being manipulated for scientific purposes. There seem close parallels between the society of the Otherworld and Lewis's picture of science and the university in *That Hideous Strength*. In the inner circle, the drones attempt a power they can never achieve and lead lives of futile experimentation. Lewis may perhaps have intended the sting to represent the poisonous infection of a debased philosophy of any sort. We can hardly be sure of all the possible meanings. The sting is a potent symbol of evil, and certainly the evil of scientific experimentation seen in the trilogy is here also. Orfieu, a possibly sinister character, has called chaos into Cambridge with his machine, and like Weston and Frost and Wither, acts as a bridge between worlds. Othertime is not apparently Hell, but it is hellish in the Orwellian sense that it denies love, compassion, and humanity and is based on ignorance, superstitions, human sacrifice for experimental data, perversion and obscenity.

Having bested the human corruption of science by putting Weston down in *Out of the Silent Planet*, Lewis appears here to be turning to try his hand at a new approach to other worlds. It is significant that the other world is evil and is projected as a parallel to our own world, and that it is a corruption of our own world brought about by science. The references to the Big Brain or Great Brain and the catalogue of scientific discoveries revealed in Chapter 7 suggest his continuing interest in Stapledon's and Waddington's scientific speculations. But the focus in the fragment as it exists is unclear. We do not get far enough to know whether Ransom or Scudamour will be central, whether the technology of time travel will predominate over the prevision of evil which Scudamour recounts, whether the love story will assume more or less importance.

There is little question in my mind that *The Dark Tower* was an experiment for Lewis in literary creativity which failed to produce that stirring of the deeper imagination that the trilogy provides in uneven measure, the greatest force hitting us in *Perelandra*. On the whole, this fragment is stiff and slow in narration, thin in descriptive matter, and heavy with "information." The movement and suspense are there; but without the descriptive and thematic richness which even *Out of the Silent Planet* has in greater abundance, the chapters we have fall flat. And that may have been why Lewis stopped when he did.

4. *PERELANDRA* 1943

Between the publication of *Out of the Silent Planet* in 1938 and of *Perelandra* in 1943, falls the publication of *The Screwtape Letters*, 1942. In order to preserve the acknowledged consistency of the trilogy, I have elected to treat the three works together, delaying the treatment of *The Screwtape Letters* until the conclusion of my study of *That Hideous Strength*. Though Lewis learned a good deal about characterization by writing *The Screwtape Letters*, it hardly ranks with the trilogy even in his own judgment.

Although we cannot effectively date the beginning of Lewis's work on *Perelandra*, we know from his letters that by November 9, 1941, he had gotten Ransom to Venus and into his first conversation with the Lady.[1] He had finished the book by May 11, 1942, when he refers in a letter to the dedication of the book "To some Ladies at Wantage," Sister Penelope's sisterhood.[2] Later he indicated that the enlargement of the edition would delay the publication.[3] Between the publication of *Out of the Silent Planet* and *Perelandra*, Lewis had written the nontheological Ransom sequel, *The Dark Tower*, which he never completed or published, as well as *The Screwtape Letters*, whose popularity long overshadowed that of all his other writing. He also completed *The Problem of Pain* (1940) and began his talks to the RAF and his BBC talks.

We know from a July 9, 1939, letter to Sister Penelope that he was disappointed by the reviews of *Out of the Silent Planet* mainly because they failed to see the deeper implications of the book.[4] In the same letter, he sounds the note which captures the essence of his purpose in *Perelandra*: a writer can smuggle any amount of theology into the reader's mind if he colors it with romance.[5] Though his remark is offhand and tongue-in-cheek, it highlights his view of literature as an evangelical tool. His letters to Sister Penelope and Dom Bede Griffiths between 1939-41 tell us something of his frame of mind at this tumultuous point in European history. He explained to Sister Penelope in October 1940 that he was about to make his first confession, "The decision to do so was one of the hardest I have ever made.... "[6] As he reported later, the experience was not as devastating as he imagined in advance. Later he wrote her indicating that he now understood how "mythology can act as a *praeparatio evangelica* for the receptive," using *Phantastes* as an example in his own case.[7] In a November 9, 1941, letter to her he wrote,

I am writing really for company, for I'm a sad Ass [He sometimes referred to himself as Brother Ass, the plodding but well-intentioned Christian.] at the moment. I've been going through one of those periods when one can no longer disguise the fact that movement has been backward not forward. All the sins one thought one had escaped have been back again as strong as ever.

> And all our former pain
> And all our surgeon's care
> Are lost: and all the unbearable, in vain
> Borne over, is still to bear.

Dogs don't relapse. Cats do, and go wild. I'm a cat.[8]

It is against this background of inner spiritual turmoil and questioning, the questioning of his own obedience, his adequacy, of the nature of pain and God's purpose in using it (*The Problem of Pain*); of the psychology of temptation (*The Screwtape Letters*), and of the role of Christianity in literature, that Lewis wrote the second published Ransom novel.[9] It seems fairly clear from this distance that he was by now consciously committed to writing Christian romance, if we can apply such a loose term to his orientation. In recommending Chesterton and MacDonald to a Miss Jacob in 1941, he noted that it was the undisclosed theology beneath the work which attracted him without his knowing it.[10] He had written Griffiths in April 1940 indicating his preference for literature that was either purely recreational or clearly the tool for presenting moral or religious truth.[11] A letter to Owen Barfield in late 1940 or early 1941 focuses on the relationship of man to death and the human temptation to accept it as an escape as opposed to the divine freedom which Christ possessed by undergoing full life and death, themes which trouble Ransom in his fight with Un-man.

The correspondence records his progress:

I've got Ransom to Venus and through his first conversation with the 'Eve' of that world; a difficult chapter. I hadn't realized till I came to write it all the *Ave-Eva* business. I may have embarked on the impossible. This woman has got to combine characteristics which the Fall has put poles apart—she's got to be in some ways like a Pagan goddess and in other ways like the Blessed Virgin. But, if one can get even a fraction of it into words, it is worth doing.[12]

He had been drawn to the Venus myth early, writing as a young man a Venus poem which never developed, admiring the Botticelli "Venus," seeing in the pagan goddess more than physical generation, conceiving her to be the symbol of the creative imagination. Now by linking the purity of the Virgin with the spiritual creativity represented in the pagan figure, Lewis at last had a myth worth the engagement of his literary talents. He had written to Barfield much earlier during their "Great War," their extended epistolary debate on the nature of the poetic imagination:

A *myth* is a description or a story introducing supernatural personages or things, determined not, or not only, by motives arising from events within the story, but by the supposedly immutable relations of the personages or things: possessing unity: and not, save accidentally, connected with any given place or time.[13]

The myth in *Perelandra* is as Lewis indicates, multiple. Tor and Tinidril, Adam and Eve, Ask and Embla: it is the creation myth of a new world, pagan or Christian. It is also the myth of the Fall, or of the risks of commitment to a new world, of moral choice, of the pursuit of knowledge, of obedience, of evil. Disconnected in time, as *Out of the Silent Planet* could not be because it was an attack on contemporary scientific theory, self-generating in actions springing from the immutable relationships of purity and innocence versus experience and evil, *Perelandra* shares many of the qualities Lewis early assigned to myth.

He speculated at the same time on the value of the poetic imagination, which for Barfield lay in its giving new cognitive attitudes to reality. For Lewis the value lay in giving us "an enriched and corrected will, so that we returned not to know more, but to do and feel as if we knew more."[14] These early speculations were to be much transformed by Lewis's spiritual development, but his basic belief in the meaning of the creative imagination as it is received by man remained essentially the same. He described this area of his work as "symbolical and mythopoeic" in retrospect, and *Perelandra*, his favorite, will show that he brought together for the first time his aesthetic and spiritual beliefs in a unified work of the deeper imagination.[15]

Lewis designated *Out of the Silent Planet* as a "space and time story" in his dedication. *Perelandra* is "A Novel" and *That Hideous Strength*: "A Modern Fairy-Tale for Grown-Ups." These distinctions should tell us something of Lewis's intention. In *Perelandra*, he intended, he suggests in letters written after publication of the novel, to incorporate what he had learned from *A Voyage to Arcturus*: that planetary fiction is best for spiritual adventures, that it combines the philosophical fantasy of MacDonald and James Stephens with the adventure narrative of Wells and Verne, and that as Lindsay's book is, because of the power of its imaginative conception, potentially a force bordering on the diabolical through its Manichaean philosophy, so a book conceived along similar lines but from a Christian standpoint might be a potent force for good.[16] He would try to capture in this novel some of the evanescent quality of the paradisal state without the fall, and that intent shows in his response to a query about the feeling of nostalgia one reader felt the book created.

And oh how much sweeter is this *longing* than any other *having*.... What you are really wanting will never be in any finite *here* and *now* (God bless us. You know that as well as I do) and the rabbit in Magdalen grove may mediate it as well as a hross.[17]

Lewis had prepared the way for Ransom's future adventures in *Out of the Silent Planet*. Augray first uses the name Parelandra to describe Venus.[18] Lewis made clear that the letter ending *Out of the Silent Planet* was a device to link this book to sequels, and his Preface to *Perelandra* indicates that it is preceded by an earlier volume. But it is equally clear that he wishes the novel to stand alone, and after the experience of harsh critical responses to *Out of the Silent Planet*, he stresses the fact that his characters are not copied from life nor are they allegorical.

Thus we find a similar structure to that of *Out of the Silent Planet* with a space journey, the villain Weston, strange flora and inhabitants, and a test, a trial of wills. But there are many differences. The story is now narrated by an intermediary, removing Ransom and his experiences in space and time, allowing him rather more mystery than he has yet had. The journey is more supernatural and less scientific, and the focus of attention is not on Ransom at the center but on a drama of deep significance in which Ransom is to play an assigned role. There is considerably more time spent in description and dialogue than on information. The descriptive passages are more impressionistic and sensuous than those in *Out of the Silent Planet* and less blatantly symbolic in their use. The movement of the plot is much slower, more stately and studied, deliberately and inevitably moving to the catastrophe—eucatastrophe in Tolkien's terms—which brings Ransom out as victor, resurrected and reborn, spiritualized and made numinous as he will appear in *That Hideous Strength*. The intention is clear: to play the myth of paradise again but let human and divine experience save the day for a new world: to pretend or play "as if," which was a favorite game for the literary Lewis. If the Son were to appear to children, he might come like Aslan. Lewis asks what it would be like to be in on the creation and destruction of a world. Lewis is adhering to his theory that what is creative in art is not the attempt to give expression to a *new truth* which is an impossibility, but to give compelling imaginative life to one's personal perception of truth so that it may be both an expression of self-transcendence and an aid to others as they engage in the same process.

Thus Lewis seems to be embarking on a new venture. Moving away from the more explicitly science fiction focus on a journey to another world, he concentrates upon the myth of innocence and temptation, the demands of human submission and obedience to divine authority, and the enlargement of human personality and soul consequent to the successful passage through trial and testing. We might say that he universalizes his theme while retaining many of the features of his technique seen in *Out of the Silent Planet*, that he is mythologizing the science fiction form, or putting it to new uses. We cannot know with any certainty why he elected to use the creation myth at this point. One possibility is that here was a positive, in fact, ideal answer to the negative materialism of *Out of the Silent Planet*, the biological evolutionism and scientific materialism which the hrossa are so surely a reaction against. The choice of Venus, symbolic seat of creation, is obviously perfect. The optimism and celebratory atmosphere of the concluding pages of *Perelandra*, the "what it could have been like" atmosphere which surrounds the book, may be simple wish-fulfillment. They may be a religious man's daydream. And they may be a moral *exemplum*.

The meaning of the book is consistent, up to a point, with Lewis's intention. We see a seasoned Christian, selected by higher authority to perform a task, transported to a foreign realm. Our impressions all are developed through his vision, and after becoming acclimated, we see the central battle emerge. Satan in Weston tempts Eve in the Green Lady, but Christian Ransom helps her to resist and finally "kills" Satan, a symbolic if not absolute conquest. The new race experiences the knowledge of temptation without the consequent fall, and the *felix culpa* is thus allowed to become vicariously part of their experience. The book means to suggest that Christian obedience and perseverance even in the face of impossible odds can affect the outcome of events on the highest plane. No man is too humble to serve, and if he has faith, he can with divine help accomplish prodigies.

Taken in another key, we are confronted with the more human and personal struggle of a modern Christian faced with the task of defending his faith in innocence and with submissive virtue, symbolized by the island Paradise of Tor and Tinidril, against modern technological and scientific theorizing seen in Weston, the Un-man, the dehumanized tempter who would replace innocence with relativity. The battleground here is internal and psychological, although Lewis suggests this struggle by symbol, e.g., the heel wound, cave monsters, pool bath, rather than internalizing it in Ransom's mind. If Lewis had not forbidden it, we might say that this is a modern allegory of the Christian's position in a technological society.

On another level, we find meaning in the imaginative creation of a new paradise, a garden of the Hesperides, the idyllic green garden of Marvell's poems, of Yeats' Byzantium, of Keats' "Ode to a Nightingale," of Spenser's *Faerie Queene*. There are the obvious literary overtones which remind us of the compelling imaginative force of gardens and of pastoral imagery from earliest times. But for Lewis there is the additional sense of the lost world, glimpsed like John's Island through the hole in the wall, yearned for ever after and now for Ransom, experienced in fact for a lengthy period of intensely heightened experience. The physical descriptions which almost overwhelm the narrative before it gets well underway, indicate Lewis's delight in filling this paradisal world with the sensuous and romantic attraction which had drawn him since childhood. Here, more fully and completely than anywhere else, we feel his commitment to sensual beauty, to the elevation of the emotions which he saw as a symptom of Joy, the by-product he early mistook for the thing itself. Even the creation of Narnia, Cupid's Palace, and the real Narnia revealed in *The Last Battle* do not give the vibrant portrait of a world *in creation* which *Perelandra* presents.

This book circles around the central idea of potentiality: the unleashed creative force awaiting the proper guidance of the Lord and Lady, the potency of obedience which can lift a puny and lapsed human to his full powers this side of death, the potency of sly and warped reason to twist and distort innocence and naturalness, the potential in a mind of creative genius to create and people an Edenic world in which this drama will take place. Lewis is daring more here than in any previous fictional work, stepping outside the conventions of historical allegory (*The Pilgrim's Regress*), science fiction (*Out of the Silent Planet*), and spiritual dialogue (*The Screwtape Letters*) to stir the deeper imagination and spark the feeling of self-transcendence.

Readers do respond to all this complex design, although not perhaps to all these possibilities equally or indeed at once. One comment registered by undergraduates reading this novel for the first time is, "I really like this book better than any of his other things, but why did he have to go on so long about the islands and plants?" Reactions favorable to the book seem to be of two sorts and are oddly in opposition. There are those like the students who approve of the story and find it moving and enlightening, and there are others who delight in Perelandra, the place with its islands, sea, mountains, trees, but who find the story a positive block to their enjoyment of the scenery. More moderately, we might say that our response should be through one into the other; through the created world into the myth at its center, following the route which Lewis cleverly lays out for us as we accompany Ransom on his journey and feel his perceptions of colors and tastes as he experiences them. By placing his fictional Lewis as the narrator, he gives us both a link with reality and a foil for Ransom. This effect is especially clear in the opening chapters where Lewis feels the force of the malevolent eldila and is tempted, in a minor way as Ransom will later be, to "give up the job." He is our anchor in reality, the disbelieving companion who helps in subduing our disbelief, easing us over the edge into the other world as he comes to believe in the Oyarsa and to accept his role in the drama. Ransom, already liberated from human and pedestrian restraints, is free to launch into the high experiences required of him in mid-book.

We are already half won over to the fantasy we are about to enter by Ransom's reasonable and even humorous acceptance of the fantastic sights, like the Oyarsa and the coffin—spaceship—which confront us. The very human response of Lewis, cursing Ransom and his familiars, alternately jealous and fearful, also lends reality to the opening. Lewis the author follows the method outlined in our discussion of his literary theory: further in and higher up. With the airborne Ransom, we approach the new world now unknown but not particularly menacing as it was in *Out of the Silent Planet*, and with him we experience each new sight and touch. We move at his pace, absorbing the marvel of color and the movement of the floating world, tasting the fruit of the bubble tree, seeing the Green Lady for the first time.[19] Lewis makes us feel the movement and see the copper, gold, and green.

> There was no land in sight. The sky was pure, flat gold like the background of a medieval picture. It looked very distant—as far off as a cirrhus [sic] cloud looks from earth. The ocean was gold too, in the offing, flecked with innumerable shadows. The nearer waves, though golden where their summits caught the light, were green on their slopes: first emerald, and lower down a lustrous bottle green, deepening to blue where they passed beneath the shadow of other waves.[20]

He engages our senses, catches us in a net of feeling, as Ransom is caught, before we even meet the central characters. This is both wise and necessary, for to plunge us into the deep discourse found in mid-book would be to remove half the delight of this world which must be created believably before it can be threatened with corruption. We do not meet the Lady until Chapter 4, and Weston does not land until the middle of Chapter 6. Even in the midst of the debate, we are conscious of the movement of the three about the island, and later particular symbolic significance is given to the chase and underground battle to the death. Lewis might thus be said to lull us into a frame of mind receptive to his message.

The myth, if it is that, is united with the form which expresses it, and our response surely reflects the truth of that statement. Without the reinforcement of the setting, the argument would be a dry affair, like *Paradise Lost* without the poetic descriptions of Hell, Heaven, and Paradise. We cannot rightly separate one from the other. To take one example from many: the tasting of a berry becomes the paradigm of Ransom's experience on the planet: "so savoury, so memorable among a thousand tastes, that he would have begun to look for them and to feed on them only, but that he was once more forbidden by the same inner adviser which had already spoken to him twice since he came to Perelandra."[21] Critics might say, "Ah! the nagging voice of conscience." But that is the point. Unbridled response to sense experience is no more paradisal than the demonic pleasure of pure reason proposed by Weston. Much as we might wish to go on exploring the beauty of Perelandra, Lewis's theme calls us to account, and regretfully we turn to the serious matters at hand— Ransom's job.

Again Lewis cleverly foils our expectation by making the Lady Ransom's unexpected tutor, Ransom being throughout as a lapsed mortal, more pitiable than the Lady or the periodically freed Weston. We respond to and identify with Ransom, seeing in him the possible nobility of a man called into cosmic affairs. Ransom's confusion in the face of Weston's demonic reasoning, his utter hopelessness in responding to the casuistry of Weston's arguments, his despair in the face of the Lady's inevitable fall, his joy in realizing that all he can do is his best, all move us in a way the Lady's and Weston's dialogue cannot. Ransom is the hero, and it is through his development as a character, a major achievement here of Lewis's over what we have seen in John and the flatter Ransom of *Out of the Silent Planet*, that we receive the theme. The theme, rather than being centered on cosmic absolutes as some critics have suggested, takes its force from the application each reader can make of it for himself. Lewis's interest is much less in rewriting celestial history than in showing man the need to "do his best" in the face of seemingly insurmountable odds, trusting that God will take care of the rest.

What need for such an elaborate structure, then, responds one reader. The need is that of the artist not the instructor. Lewis could, if we take *Miracles* as an example, have convinced us with greater economy in some other form; but this form he chose because it could say best what he wanted to say, could tell Ransom's spiritual journey better than any other form could.

When we approach the question of whether the form suits the use to which Lewis has put it, we must respond to the reactions of readers. Readers of this book have frequently objected to its length or the "interminable" discourse. The form does not lend itself easily to what Lewis has done. The epic, the long dramatic poem, even the historical novel all allow more range for debate than romance or fantasy. Lewis attempts to intersperse action with dialogue. Weston splashes down while Ransom and the Lady discuss the prohibition of the fixed lands. Weston is possessed at the climax of his discourse on spiritual force. The violent flight which ends in Weston's death follows the longest debate of the book and is followed by the longest exposition on the nature of Celestial order. There is little question of the uneasy alliance between story and discourse and naturally enough since the story and suspense lie in the outcome of the debate and its effect upon the Lady. Perhaps there is some other form through which this matter could be more expeditiously presented. There is no form which suits the subject matter better that comes quickly to mind. The awkwardness lies in the attempt to develop a philosophical argument for freedom of choice within obedience and divine authority adequately and without losing the excitement and suspense inherent in the high stakes at risk in this trial of wits.

We must fall back on Lewis's distinction of good and bad reading. A bad reading would seek the superficial excitement of wagering for the Lady's soul and the thrills of small dragons, green goddesses, and floating islands. The good reading, involving the receipt of the knowledge gained from the discourse, would place much less emphasis on the expository digressions because they are expansions of the meaning of the book. There can be little question, however, that the book suffers from being too full. Faced with the need to make the Lady "older" slowly in preparation for Weston's highly sophisticated attack, Lewis could hardly condense her discussions with Ransom. He paces this section well with dolphin-back rides and the approach to the mystical, holy place where the coronation will be held at the conclusion of the book. There is some heavy going with Weston's appearance, and the ritual rebirth of Ransom is entirely too long and cumbersome for the effect it achieves. A third or fourth reading of the book brings to our attention the ingenuity of the debate and the imaginative power shown in creating the landscape, but the two no longer work together, which I think accounts for the dichotomy of critical response. The book does not consistently fuse our feelings and our intellectual response. Our interest in the otherworldly suggestiveness subsides after the initial reading into a study of Lewis's use of formal theological arguments in developing the debate. The imaginative matrix in which the debate is embedded shrinks to a subordinate position to become mere allegorical embellishment for the theological theme. If Lewis hoped to snare people into a Christian frame of mind through fictionalized theology, then this work must be counted a failure. It is at once too obvious and too subtle. The theme is so clearly Christian and persuasive that few would mistake the thrust of its intent. On the other hand, the proof and the argument are intricate and sophisticated in their logic.

We are left feeling that either Lewis has yet to find his true *metier* or he has yet to define more clearly what his works of fiction are to do, which is to evangelize in disguise, to heighten the reader's perception of beauty and truth, or simply to express whatever it is he has to say. Looking at some areas of specific difficulty in which theme and form are uneasily yoked, we can perhaps determine whether the difficulty lies with the rather intractable nature of the material or in the unsuitability of the form for this particular purpose. To complicate matters further, the novel has sections in which Lewis succeeds admirably in drawing a myth-like quality over the story.

One major awkwardness comes with the shift which occurs from the external perception of sensuous phenomenon, e.g., the undulating landscape, the unusual colors, the strange vegetation, and the experience of being in another world, to an internal perception of the intellectual or spiritual experience which is superimposed upon the perceptual one. Rarely do the two work together. They may reinforce each other as, for example, when Ransom, perceiving after some time that he is in a virgin world, feels all the nostalgia and longing for lost innocence which will support him in his acceptance of the role of defender of such innocence. Or when Ransom has his final battle with the Enemy, the underground scenery is particularly appropriate for the symbolizing of his descent and later rebirth. But all too frequently the spiritual journey is broken for a view of the countryside or a larger view; we take too much time seeing the scenery on our way to the climactic debate, and then once having arrived, we fail to look about us at all.

This alternation of external and internal, a failure on Lewis's part to fully externalize his theme since in a myth we apprehend the meaning through the picturing of it in external form, leads to an unevenness of movement. As we enter the novel, we follow one line: the exploration of an other world through the trustworthy perception of a tested narrator. This I call external as our interest is focused on what Perelandra is like, what Ransom sees and feels. His mission at this point is to both himself and us a subsidiary consideration. Here Lewis is superb. Although he tends to overdo the description of the planet in detail, he captures us in an other world. Particularly effective is the disorientation of space perception he puts Ransom through on first landing. We are more than once reminded of techniques used later by Stanley Kubrick in "Space Odyssey 2001." The creativity of these early sections is of a high order, and we are compelled onward to find with Ransom what lies ahead. His control of descriptive narration here seems an advance over that of *Out of the Silent Planet* where we find a concentration upon stylized categories of experience built up for symbolic purposes: the companionably shaggy hrossa with their primitive cult of the hunt and song celebrating victory; the elongated, tower-occupying intelligences (sorns), and the squat, earth-dwelling artisans (pfifltriggi). Here Lewis gives us a more unified world view which has a satisfying consistency.

When we have seen this world and its Lady and move on to the task set for Ransom, we pass into the other line of developing interest: the role Ransom will play in preserving the Lady and world intact in the face of apparently superior enemy forces. The battle lines are not clearly drawn until halfway through the book when Weston is possessed (X, 110). From this point on, we are required to shift our attention to theological points of increasing complexity which can hardly find, on the level of external representation, a symbolic equivalent adequate to sustain our interest. Certainly Lewis tries hard. The mangled frogs, the plucked birds, the restriction of the scene to one location all incorporate the external world, but the debate is essentially nonsensuous, and though our interest remains keen to see how Lewis will handle the temptation and what responses he will allow the Lady and Ransom, we tend to forget where we are. Unlike *A Voyage to Arcturus* where the landscape remains an inseparable part of the spiritual experience at each point, the temptation becomes here a set piece, beautifully done, embedded in the midst of a space journey.

One of Lewis's major accomplishments in presenting the tempter is his use of "story telling" as the central temptation: the temptation offered the Lady to write a role for herself in which she becomes the tragic and noble savior of her progeny and world. It is a particularly appropriate motif because it places the reader's attention on the creative imagination, indicating its God-given origin and inspiration and showing the essential fraudulence in its misuse by demonic will. Its use places this particular story and all fiction in the context of eternal truth, relegating it to the subordinate position Lewis believed it must occupy. The temptation also emphasizes the sub-creation of any artist and reinforces Lewis's belief that we create nothing new but merely uncover or embellish what is eternally true.

By using the narrative temptation, Lewis places emphasis on the emptiness of Satan's fictionalizing of cosmic history and on the feebleness of his claim to power and of the fantasies of Weston, who later reveals that the stories of Hell and damnation are all true (XIII, 167). Also by using the temptation on Ransom as well as on the Lady, Lewis is able to project the significant theme that it is action rather than stories which Ransom has been called to make, and that though fiction is powerful as a tool for evil, it cannot withstand right and might. Lewis was to confront in his other fiction the essential artificiality of storytelling and to make clear that it can in no way replace or match the force of original creation which is the true divine act.

The last half of the book becomes an elaborate debate, almost wholly internalized until Ransom acts. Chapters 9-14 reveal perhaps better than any section of Lewis's fiction, the effect of what he called his expository fault. The action lags and slumps as we begin the Lady's education by Weston, and even though Lewis indicates that much time has passed in debates which go unrecorded, what remains is more than most readers want. There are dramatic touches such as the splendid clothing of Weston and the Lady and the first vision in the mirror bringing fear with it. Even the internalized confrontation of Ransom with his conscience has dramatic appeal, but nearly the whole of Chapter 11 is dry and reminiscent of the worst speeches of Reason in *The Pilgrim's Regress*. Necessary as these expositions of God's purpose and truth are for the meaning of the book, they lack the immediacy which myth would at its best give them.

Ransom's acceptance of action as his task, of doing "his best," brings back some of the external sensuous experience which characterizes the first half of the book. The ascent in the cave, nightmarish and bizarre as it is, with the slimy crawl through the chimney, the exotic jointed insect, and the burning abyss, all pique our interest but could, like the whole of the book from Chapter 15 onward, profit from foreshortening. Lewis, once having conquered Weston, gives us forty pages of anticlimax. The battle is won and the Lady saved. These long and sometimes tedious pages, especially the unnecessarily prolix section in which Malacandra and Perelandra decide how to appear to the King and Lady, add nothing to Lewis's stature as a writer. If they do anything, they tend to make too explicit what we would prefer left to the imagination. He treats the same situation involving the creation of a world, a paradise, the naming of the beasts, the assumption of authority by Adam more gracefully in *The Magician's Nephew*. What spoils the end of *Perelandra* and comes close to spoiling the whole book is Lewis's intensity, his lack of humor, his conscious heavy-handed explanation of the protocol of the new reign in Perelandra. The most objectionable section of the book, from this point of view, is the elaborate explanation of the Great Dance by the eldila (pp. 214-218) where we are faced with pure information which once digested hardly awakens interest in repeated readings of the book. We feel most keenly that Lewis in his commitment to the theme has allowed the story to fall away, and we are left with an attempt on the part of characters, eldila, whom we hardly know, to exhort us to accept the higher mysteries. This seems neither the place nor the technique to use for such a purpose. The conclusion lacks subtlety and interest unless we are reading only for the theological information Lewis may be trying to pass on. And it is a pity since we sense that Lewis gave much time and thought to this concluding section which would embody his conception of cosmic harmony and unity. It is the very seriousness which kills it. Myth cannot exhort; it can move us only by the subtlety of its suggestion; it cannot be too explicit. The very suggestiveness on which Lewis placed such emphasis is dissipated by the overelaboration of the last half of the novel and more especially by the concluding chapter.

We are left with an unresolved problem in analyzing our response to this novel. Lewis's ability in the use of the creative imagination, of which we have such impressive proof in the descriptions of the sea world, the Lady, the bubble trees, and the dragon, affords us much pleasure. The thematic structure, based as it is on a central truth of experience, that each man is an instrument of destiny called on to do what he can and presented in the context of a myth central to our experience, that is, a test of obedience which may win or lose us a world, has a compelling attraction which the narrow theme of *Out of the Silent Planet* lacks. The myth is capable of sustaining the elaborate world picture which Lewis has created to embed it in, and the setting is sufficient to draw us into the meaning of the myth. We ask why they do not work organically to bring one another alive. Critics who are drawn to the message of the work seem to feel that they do. Almost everyone else feels that the two forces work separately to the disadvantage of both and to the ultimate detriment of a unified whole.

What Lewis is attempting in *Perelandra* is more challenging than in *Out of the Silent Planet*. He had with considerable humor and precision dissected the diabolical mind and its favorite snares and temptations in *The Screwtape Letters*. The economy of this shorter work, the incisiveness of its perception of evil as it fantasizes and feeds upon itself, its lack of an elaborate superstructure of description have made it from the first a popular favorite with readers of all sorts. There can be little question that *Perelandra* was conceived and executed as a more serious venture in the same direction, now mustering the full force of the novel to create a moving spectacle to catch the unwary but imaginative reader and draw him to belief. It embodies not only Lewis's professed evangelical desires for fiction, but coming as it does during a time of national and personal spiritual crisis and unrest, it presents a reaffirmation of faith in the necessity to stand firm and do what we can.

The book is rarely now read as coming out of the early war years, and few people would be aware that Lewis was having perhaps no more than the normal doubts and lapses of a Christian, some ten years beyond his conversion, but that context may help explain what Lewis hoped to achieve through writing the book. Among his motives, the predominant one appears to be the creative one: to write a novel creating a new world (always with the restriction that we can never really create anything *de novo*) in which an ancient truth could take on new life. The full force of his creative talent was focused on the opening section of the book with its careful structuring of narrative and the framing of journey and arrival. By mid-book the force of his theme begins to assume greater importance, and as the internal and cerebral action become predominant, the description slips into the background. Lewis could not keep both activities balanced, and by the end we have an attempted reunification through the elevated and inflated machinery of the coronation of the Lady and King.

A sequel is clearly in the offing as Tor announces the imminent siege of Earth, but *That Hideous Strength* does not prove the culmination of Lewis's attempt to embody in creative fiction the basic truth which he found in the fantasies of MacDonald and others. It is when he tries less strenuously and perhaps less ambitiously in the *Chronicles of Narnia* that he achieves the cohesion which is lacking in *Perelandra* and which he brings to his last and most serious and balanced work, *Till We Have Faces*. *Perelandra* is Lewis's adventure into Deeper Heaven, an imaginative leap of greater scope than any other he attempted, and his accomplishment should be judged in terms of the magnitude and daring of that leap.

5.   *THAT HIDEOUS STRENGTH:*
A Modern Fairy-Tale for Grown-Ups
1945

We have fairly clear documentation of the progress of composition for this last work in the trilogy. We know that by December 30, 1942, Lewis was far enough into writing the book to ask Eddison's advice on the nuptial practices of bears "for I have brought in a beare in the book I now write and it shall to bedde at the end with the other."[1] He had finished *Perelandra* in May of the same year and would write to Eddison on April 29, 1943, that he had finished some "300 sheets and come to the uncomfortable conclusion that it is all rubbish."[2] He finished the book by late 1943 or early 1944.

A letter to Arthur Greeves on December 20, 1943, indicates his intention to dedicate the book to their childhood friend Jane McNeill, whom Lewis referred to as "Tchainie."[3] The Preface to the book carries the date Christmas Eve, 1943, although the book did not appear in published form until 1945. Between the publication of *Perelandra* and *That Hideous Strength*, Lewis published *Christian Behavior*, and *The Abolition of Man*, 1943, and *Beyond Personality*, 1944. In September 1943, he wrote Sister Penelope that he had finished "about 6 chapters of the book on *Miracles*."[4] He wrote her in September 1944 that he had finished the third of the Ransom trilogy and mentioned in January 1945 that he expected publication of *That Hideous Strength* in June.[5] May 28, 1945, brought another reference to the anticipated publication in July and of *Miracles* during the next year.[6]

The correspondence with Sister Penelope, which was particularly active at this period, indicates much about Lewis's preoccupations when he was writing this book. These letters indicate a keen interest in the problem of defining creativity, literary creativity especially. Lewis suggested, in a discussion of the genesis of myth quoted earlier, that people do not sit down to compose myth at all; rather he suggests that out of a combination of diabolical and heavenly elements, myth evolves.[7] Writing is comparable to planting a garden or begetting a child.[8] "We are re-combining elements made by him [God] and already containing His message. Because of those divine meanings in our materials it is impossible we shd. ever know the whole meaning of our own works, and the meaning we never intended may be the best and truest one."[9] In reference to her work on the story of Isaac, he suggested that "On the imaginative level, I think the deepest truths enter the mind much better as arbitrary marvels than as universal theorems."[10] Though this advice is given in reference to her work, we can speculate that Lewis was arguing from his own experience and perhaps directly from the reaction to *Perelandra* in the critical reviews.

There is much in the letters of these few years which points to themes and preoccupations which appear in the book. Life at the Kilns was unsettled. Mrs. Moore, suffering from ulcerated varicose veins, was finding life a trial. The two women who helped run the house were not making life easy either.[11] One came close to a breakdown while facing an impending operation, and Lewis found himself dealing with psychiatrists as well as hysterical females.[12] These experiences certainly colored his attitude toward women and helped to shape his portrait of Jane Studdock, the first human woman of any significance in his fiction. At about the same time

Lewis had an unpleasant encounter with a young female graduate student. In a letter to Eddison he referred to her as one who "shad a better bestowed her tyme [makynge sporte for some good man in his bed and bearing children for the stablishment of this reaulme] or else to be at her beads in a religyous house."[13] We hardly need guess that Jane and her doctoral thesis on John Donne owe something to the unnamed B. Lit. or D. Phil. candidate who so annoyed Lewis.

Lewis has been accused of anti-feminism in his portrait of Jane Studdock, and there is more than a little evidence to support the belief that he held old-fashioned and conservative views about the role of women, particularly in a Christian society. In a 1940 letter to a lady, he discusses the marriage service and the *"Headship* of man."* He asks if she really likes women in authority and seeks authority in women when she looks for it in the world, an obviously rhetorical question.[14] Lewis felt that men were head of the house partly because they would be more merciful in what he termed foreign policy as opposed to domestic policy and because man's control allowed woman to assume her rightful role in protecting the family against the outer world. It is significant that this book should open with a section of the marriage service and equally significant that love and marriage should be central to the theme here in a way they had not been in any of the earlier works.

This book, a return from Deep Heaven to the harsh realities of college politics, vivisection, brainwashing and psychological terrorism, marriages of convenience, sexual perversion, and demonic experimentation, provided Lewis with an outlet for topics on which he had long vented his exasperation in the letters but not in the fiction. Although he disclaims in the Preface any similarity between Magdalen and Bracton, the fairy tale is one set in a college situation, and there are acknowledged similarities between Bragdon Wood and Magdalen Grove.[15]

An early letter (1928) to Owen Barfield gives what we must presume to be the candid and personal reaction of a young Lewis whose opinions might have mellowed by 1943.

...this college is a cesspool, a stinking puddle, *faex Romuli* inhabited by Fals-Semblant, Favel, Mal-Bouche and Losengeres: things in mens' shapes climbing over one another and biting one another in the back: ignorant of all things except their own subjects and often even of those: caring for nothing less than for learning: cunning, desperately ambitious, false friends, nodders in corners, tappers of the wink: setters of traps and solicitors of confidence: vain as women: self-important: fie upon them—excepting always the aged who have lived down to us from a purer epoch.[16]

By 1955 he could write a more charitable reaction toward Cambridge indicating the atmosphere to be somewhat more Christian and kindly than the hard-boiled feeling at Oxford.[17] Lewis's opinion of college life may have changed over the years, but it is clear from his picture of the politics of Bracton College that he was well aware of the professional liabilities of the academic life. He indicated to W. L. Kinter that the name St. Anne's was merely chosen as a "plausible and euphonious name."[18]

His feelings toward the social sciences can best be studied in his published reactions to the psychoanalytical and anthropological approaches to literature.[19] He would make Mark a sociologist and heap scorn on the possible and easy perversions of the profession. Of his attitude toward psychoanalysis and the mind-bending which becomes a perversion of it in Mark's brainwashing, we have ample evidence in some of Lewis's counseling letters and of what little stock he puts in the efficacy of such "science."

Keep clear of psychiatrists unless you know that they are also Christians. Otherwise they start with the assumption that your religion is an illusion and try to "cure" it: and this assumption they make not as professional psychologists but as amateur philosophers. Often they have never given the question any serious thought.[20]

One of his fullest statements occurs in a letter of March 26, 1940.

(2) Psychoanalysis. In talking to me you must beware, because I am conscious of a partly pathological hostility to what is fashionable. I may therefore have been betrayed into statements on this subject which I am not prepared to defend. No doubt, like every young science, it is full of errors, but so long as it remains a science and doesn't set up to be a philosophy, I have no quarrel with it, i.e. as long as people judge what it reveals by the best human logic and scheme of values they've got and do not try to derive logic and values from it.[21]

It is apparent that Miss Ironwood and the Pendragon's approach to Jane presents a form of psychological treatment, but the treatment is Christian rather than scientific and is meant to parallel and act as a foil to Mark's psychological indoctrination and behavior modification. Lewis's scorn for sociology may be felt in Hingest's statement to Mark,

There *are* no sciences like Sociology....I happen to believe that you can't study men; you can only get to know them, which is quite a different thing.

Because you study them, you want to make the lower orders govern the country and listen to classical music, which is balderdash. You also want to take away from them everything which makes life worth living and not only from them but from everyone except a parcel of prigs and professors.[22]

Lewis made clear in a previously quoted letter to Father Peter Milward that he had included in this novel "untainted" scientists (MacPhee and Hingest) and that Belbury included many nonscientists, so that he would not be accused of a blatant condemnation of science.[23] The book belies his statements to the contrary and presents more vigorously than either of the preceding parts of the trilogy, a condemnation of modern experimental science in nearly all its aspects: sociological, psychological, medical, and clinical.

W. W. Robson finds the book a mixture: fairy tale and thriller, science fiction and religious fable. He calls the book unpleasant and unsatisfactory, a work containing things that an admiring and judicious reader would rather forget. He compares the work to those of Charles Williams, which he does not admire and suggests that Lewis's work invites psychoanalytical analysis which real art fully transformed from psychic hang-ups never seems to do.[24] Lewis would perhaps have been pleased, if not flattered, by the comparison with Williams. Robson has pointed here to a useful direction to follow in approaching the book. The fantasy elements are not those we have seen Lewis using before, and there is hardly any argument with the assumption that such a dose of reality as we encounter diminishes the effectiveness of fantasy considerably.

The book is a come-down, in a sense, a return from outer space to earth, from the utopian and ethereal realm of paradisal Deep Heaven to the tawdry realities of a floundering marriage, political and scientific intrigue, and psychological warfare. We can only presume what Lewis's intentions were in shifting the ground for his final book in this trilogy to such a radically different setting.

It is not clear at what point Lewis realized that he had embarked on the writing of a trilogy. There was clearly a false start with *The Dark Tower* and a consequent return in *Perelandra* to the journey-to-other-worlds method and the development of Ransom as the evolving tool of spiritual forces about whom Lewis wishes to speculate. If *Out of the Silent Planet* is Ransom's *enfance*, as Lewis said, then *Perelandra* must be his adolescence and coming of age. The successful completion of his trial there seems to indicate that Lewis planned *Perelandra* as much as a vehicle for the further elaboration of his central character as for the projection of themes which, by their appearance in theological writings of the same period as well as in the fiction, must have held a strong interest for him at this time.

Although Lewis never devoted his full creative power to characterization, *Perelandra* shows that he was concentrating on the development of Ransom as a personality and that he spent considerable effort in portraying Ransom's reactions and his evolving understanding of his role in the drama in which he takes a major, if at first an unwilling part. We should analyze why *That Hideous Strength* moves us back and away from the other worlds and Ransom's presumed full manhood in some exploit in Deep Heaven and drops us into the niggling and backbiting world of Edgestow, Bracton, and Belbury. Lewis prepares us for this shift by giving a hint of the liberation of Thulcandra at the conclusion of *Perelandra*. The focus he suggests will be on bringing, through Ransom, the powers of Deep Heaven to bear on the silent planet. There is a certain balance in the reversal of Weston's role in *Perelandra* now played by Ransom in *That Hideous Strength* as he becomes the bridge by which the powers flow into Edgestow. Ransom becomes like Weston, an unman. He is so elevated as Director, the Pendragon with his throne in the Blue Room and his Christ-like halo of light, his Arthurian warmth and power, and his ability to compel beasts and humans to love him, that he is effectively elevated right out of the action in a way which Weston is not. Whether Lewis intended this to happen or not we do not know. It is certainly a weakness in the book as a part of the whole trilogy because Ransom here bears little common resemblance to the crusty philologist of *Out of the Silent Planet*. Ransom has passed beyond the realm of ordinary action, and like Merlin, his counterpart and foil, he is now more magician, sage, or king, operating above the level of most of the book's action and guiding it rather than participating in it.

There are practical reasons why Lewis may have turned away from outer space and space journeys to the real world of late World War II England. He said at the end of his career, as you remember from an earlier quotation, that readers never want more than one journey to a planet because the first one is the only one of any interest to imaginative people.[25] Lewis had carefully gone to separate planets in the first two books and used quite different modes of transportation. Now he came to the point where a third volume would involve the possibility of repetition, the mechanical repetition of the journey. There was also the chance of thematic repetition. Since *Perelandra* used the myths of paradise and human obedience, the remaining great Christian themes centering on sacrificial regeneration would be difficult to play out against an interplanetary background.

Given the time and place in which Lewis worked on this book, war-torn England of 1942-43, we speculate with some degree of accuracy that his reaction to the horror of war and destruction, bringing with it the end of all the cherished traditions which had somehow miraculously survived World War I, may be felt in the battleground atmosphere, the violence, the disregard for human rights and human compassion which characterize the activities of N.I.C.E.[26] I do not think Lewis is consciously picturing Nazi techniques in the SS style activities of Fairy Hardcastle or the experimentation of Frost and Filostrato or the liquidation of Hingest. But the tone of the book is more realistic than any previous work and the fantasy only an elevation of the real rather than as in the earlier two books, a separate world with hints of reality connecting it with human experience. Whatever Lewis's motives, conscious or unconscious, may have been, the book, "A Modern Fairy-Tale for Grown-Ups," is a notable departure in technique and theme from what went before.

The book presents us with such a multiplicity of meanings that there is a problem at the outset in marshaling the various lines of investigation into some order. This is the longest single work of fiction written by Lewis. On the surface, implicit in the title, is the theme of the demonic strength of fiendish confusion suggested by the shadow of the Tower of Babel in Lyndsay's quotation opening the story. If Lewis was interested in the operation of a central myth in *Perelandra*, then in *That Hideous Strength* we seem to be confronted by a veritable Babel of literary and historical allusions operating throughout the novel: The Tower of Babel itself operating particularly in the architectural imagery and in the confusion of tongues at the concluding banquet; the Arthurian legend with Merlin and Arthur's symbolic return from Avalon to succor England in its hour of need; prophetic dreams and seers, the epic banquet and destructive retribution, reminiscent of the *Odyssey*. There are also humorous hints of Toad's triumphant revenge on the stoats and weasels in *The Wind in the Willows*. The science fiction, great-brain-life-immortal-first-man superrace material, reminds us of Olaf Stapledon's book (*Last and First Men*, 1930) and Nazi fantasies; the apocalyptic conclusion with the appearance of the Powers and the consequent destruction of a modern Sodom or Gomorrah has prophetic overtones. Lewis has assembled in one work a rich variety of materials in support of his theme.

The theme is hardly unitary either. On the surface we are concerned with the relationship of a husband and wife, both unfulfilled through their egoistic pursuit of careers, sexually unfulfilled, unloving because they lack in the woman, a sense of obedience to her husband, and in the man, a sense of the beauty of the object which he possesses and is duty bound to love and protect. But this simple heroine and hero become the tools of those hideous strengths, both good and evil, which ultimately guide the action of the book. A step up from Mark and Jane are the forces juxtaposed in Belbury and St. Anne's. Mark, drawn toward power, what Lewis called the attraction of the "inner circle," the desire to be an "insider," comes perilously close to selling his soul. The powers at work in Belbury, represented in Fairy Hardcastle as brute violence and physical torture, sadism, sexual perversion; Frost as pure intellect divested of human compassion and diabolically pursuing an inhuman aim in the guise of scientific experimentation; Wither as possession by evil which saps all human feeling, a husk of a man still able to mouth platitudes and lead a "movement"; Filostrato and Straik as pawns, not wholly demonic, but deluded by pride and self-love into thinking their cause a purely scientific or righteous one—fanatics; and Feverstone as motivation by greed and pride in his skill at maneuvering between the possible options, the most human and perhaps disgusting of the Devil's party.

The powers at St. Anne's are less diverse and complex. Ransom, as Director and Pendragon, fills the symbolic role of Christ and Arthur, presiding over the Company, which includes Grace Ironwood, the hard but compassionate foil to Filostrato; Dimble, the literary critic who portrays the right way for an academic to behave toward his students, colleagues, and profession and opposed to the picture of the profession shown by most of Bracton excepting Jewel. Mother Dimble and Ivy Maggs represent femininity and serve as the positive image of womanhood and wifeship against which Fairy Hardcastle and, at first, Jane, represent the negative reflection. MacPhee, who appears as a total skeptic in *The Dark Tower*, serves his function by questioning the basic assumptions upon which the Company is founded, a function no one plays for the operations at Belbury, unless it is Mark in the late part of the book. And Mr. Bultitude and the jackdaw and mice play counterparts to all the tortured animals in the experimental laboratories at Belbury.

On the highest spiritual level, the forces in opposition are those of Satan, the Bent Eldil of Thulcandra, operating through the medium of Frost, Wither, and the Head versus the Powers, representing God and Maleldil, who assist the human forces devoted to good in their battle to overthrow Satan. The battle in the conclusion is an unequal one, and the terrifying apocalypse which destroys Belbury and Edgestow places that hideous strength in the hands of the power which can legitimately and truly wield it.

The novel thus operates on several levels of meaning: cosmic, mythic, and realistic, and like any good fairy tale it has an object lesson which may be interpreted or not, depending on the reader's inclination. For the casual reader, the story predominates with its science fiction mysteries and intrigues. The level of suspense here rests upon the meaning of Jane's dreams, the true activities of the N.I.C.E. (quite obviously sinister) and the counterplot mounted by the Company. Will Merlin be found in time and whose side will he join? The lesson, for those who see, is consistent with Lewis's earlier themes. The forces of good and evil operate through men. Evil can only operate by working through human forms—Weston serves as an example in the two previous books—having no other foothold in human life. Good may operate through humanity, having once chosen to do so in Christ; the choice must be freely made by man however, and good may choose some other channel since all power ultimately rests with it. Thus the strength which terrifies is not that assumed by the police state or the Head, or the psychological compulsions used to bend Mark's will; the hideous strength shown in Belbury is a perversion of the terrifying powers which descend for the destruction of Belbury at the conclusion of the novel. Perversion is, in fact, the keynote of the parallelism which acts as the structure of the book. As *Perelandra* shows the attempted perversion of innocence and beauty in an untainted world, so *That Hideous Strength* opens with a perversion of the idyllic marital relationship seen in the Lady and the King. Mark and Jane become a modern Adam and Eve, and their garden is the jungle of modern civilized academic life.

The lesson is clear: if we fail to love one another and serve God, we allow the grossest abuses of our common humanity to control our lives, perverting the clear dictates of good. Sexual inadequacy, sterility, and perversion result from the selfishness of Jane and Mark, and selfishness accounts for the sadism of Fairy and the eunuch quality of Frost and Wither. Only with self-realization and submission does the bliss brought by Venus descend to the bedchamber in the concluding pages of the book. The perversion of Law seen in the land grab at Edgestow, and of tradition in the despoiling of the college wood, and of faith seen in Straik's heresy are all consequences of giving over to others through greed or the desire for more power or sheer weakness of will, the basic human power to choose freely between alternatives. It is a revelation to Mark as it had earlier been to Ransom, when he felt he had gone beyond the point of helping himself, that he could simply choose to withstand what had seemed insurmountable pressures and choose to oppose by human will what appears to be an overwhelming force. Thus the book works through the two human characters to show the power of cosmic confrontations manifested on the human level. In fact, I think Lewis returned to an earthly setting here in order to ground the cosmic debate in a concrete present. Certainly by shifting the center of focus from the near perfect Ransom of the conclusion of *Perelandra* to the imperfect fallen Adam and Eve of Mark and Jane, he humanizes his message. For all the proliferation of allusion and symbol, this book speaks more directly and concretely to its readers of human problems and their solution than anything of a fictional nature Lewis had yet written. That does not mean that we are able to take the book as a manual for creating a happy marriage or for coping with the academic, social, professional, or political problems of modern life. The book is a fantasy, a fairy tale, and we are acutely aware that Lewis is not primarily giving us an object lesson as we watch him pile allusion upon allusion, beggaring our imagination to keep up with and sort out the intersecting lines of developing plot.

Fortunately he has provided a convenient if unvaried structure by paralleling the lives of his two major characters. It is always Jane we see first, muddled by her role as wife and student and then Mark, muddled by his position as tutor and drawn toward membership in N.I.C.E. Both are self-centered, unloving, and caught in problems of their own making. Jane meets Ransom and feels a flood of warmth and joy; Mark meets the Head and vomits, awaking to a sense of his captivity. The balance and antithesis operate down to the smallest detail of climate and setting. Ransom holds court in the airy, sunlit chamber, the Blue Room; the Head is encountered in the surgical atmosphere of an underground laboratory. This step by step parallelism has the effect of simplifying the movement of the plot and setting up a regulated pattern of comparisons and contrasts, and it provides a convenient structuring and movement for the suspense, which mounts to the predestined climax by a series of neatly predictable steps. There are the consequent disadvantages of regularity, but they are outweighed, in my opinion, by the unity and coherence they lend to an otherwise cumbersome plot.

One of the first responses we make to this book is to the unity and effectiveness of technique. In his previous fictional works, I have noted that there are unevennesses in the meshing of theme with form: the allegorical framework of *The Pilgrim's Regress* does not conveniently hold all that Lewis would like to make it present; the space fiction framework used in *Perelandra* does not wholly convey the materials, in the former case of direct social criticism and in the latter of mythopoeic elevation, which Lewis requires them to convey. In this novel, however, the unity of theme and form can best be judged by the smooth and unbroken development of plot, the steady and believable evolution of the central couple, the mounting suspense, sustained until the concluding pages, the skillful incorporation of "information" so that it flows naturally out of the story rather than protruding as an obstacle to the flow of narration.

We might be tempted to say that Lewis, by placing primary interest on the narrative and giving the "message" a secondary place, has come to a fuller understanding of the art of fiction. I think it would be wrong to suggest that Lewis ever placed greater emphasis on the artistry of fiction than on any other consideration such as the story itself, its meaning, or its possible effect upon the reader. He clearly and absolutely rejected art for art's sake from his early years as a writer. It is clear, however, that he leaned in that direction as a young man both in responding to literature and music and in his early poetry. But his early fiction does give evidence that if he erred in balancing the claims of what he called *Logos* and *Poiema*, he weighed what was said more carefully than how it was to be said. There are moments of great beauty in the expression of individual ideas or feelings in all his work: John's longing for the Island, Ransom's awareness of the approach of Oyarsa in Meldilorn, the sea description in *Perelandra*. But not until we read *That Hideous Strength* is there the consistent unity of meaning and form and the satisfying organic unity of unbroken narrative development which characterize the bulk of the remaining fiction.

There are no external indications of why this shift in method occurred. At one point Lewis felt that the first three hundred sheets were rubbish. The explanation, insofar as there is one, rests perhaps on Lewis's growing experience in writing fiction, his judicious choice of form here to suit what he had to say, and his greater attention to convincing characterization and the development of a structured and tightly knit plot line. None of the earlier works show such close organization of plot, setting, characterization, and tone. In fact, the one major criticism which we might make is that the very elaborateness of and precision of balance and antithesis in the structure tend to deflect our attention from the theme so that the structure becomes sometimes overelaborate and draws attention to itself.

What strikes us at once is the elaborate system of parallels mentioned earlier. Their effect is to place the opposing camps of St. Anne's and Belbury in positions of matched opposition. The struggle we hope will bring a happy conclusion, but the entertainment rests upon the suspense of a balanced opposition. It is not until quite late that we realize that Frost and Wither, unlike the possessed Weston of late *Perelandra* are no real match for Ransom, being only tools of the dark eldils; whereas, Ransom is nearly a Power himself. But so skillfully has Lewis developed their sinister potential, placing them at the core of the inner circle, that we feel their evil to be a potent opposition to St. Anne's good. And Lewis has skillfully focused on the power of Belbury to corrupt intelligence and reason before he allows St. Anne's to act.

The book follows the method outlined in earlier chapters as the one which appealed to Lewis most forcefully, that of penetration higher up and further in. We begin on the surface with a couple, symbolically representing opposite poles: sexually, intellectually, and emotionally. There is the central motif in this book of the circle, and Lewis plays many changes of meaning around this central image. Jane and Mark, primary-school book names, share certain characteristics of their modern environment which Lewis dislikes; they are cold, prideful, petulant, each still anxious to be admired.[27] Within the bond of marriage, the circle of shared life, they represent in microcosm the disunity of Britain-Logres, Belbury-St. Anne's, Thulcandra-Deep Heaven. So Lewis happily begins on the simplest, most realistic, least complicated level, quickly drawing us in to what appears on the surface as a quite modern examination of marital difficulties against the backdrop of Common Room politics. Though Lewis is not speaking from direct experience of marriage, he draws a convincing picture of these young people by showing them apart, and in fact we do not see the circle completed within the book though Jane is clearly moving to fulfill John Donne's lines, quoted ironically on the second page of the novel: "triumphant vindication of the body," when she joins Mark beyond the book's last paragraph.

By grounding the action of the book firmly in reality, a technique used successfully but not as extensively in the opening and epilogue of *Out of the Silent Planet* and in *Perelandra*, Lewis immediately gains our suspended disbelief. The "fairy tale" gains credibility by the careful shift from the concretely real to the possible and then into the fantastic, bridged by the use of Jane's prophetic dreams. Although Robson does not admire this novel, he agrees that Lewis's descriptions of the Common Room surpass those of C. P. Snow.[28]

Any academic would agree that Lewis has captured the real flavor of a college meeting in "Sale of College Property" (I, iv). It is from the security of this description that he can give us its ironic counterpart in the description of "Dinner with the Sub Warden" as Mark begins his progress into the inner circle, and its opposite seen much later as Jane enters the circle at St. Anne's. Lewis uses a technique which describes a facet of life with which he was intimately familiar and can thus reveal from the "inside," giving us the assurance of absolute realism at the outset. He also sets up the natural progress of the narrative inward to what for Jane will be an increasing awareness of real spiritual values and for Mark, the illusion of having joined some meaningful circle.

By moving between his two central characters and keeping their penetration into the circles of Belbury and St. Anne's approximately parallel, Lewis keeps the pace steady and gives ample opportunity for the ironic comparisons afforded by the structural and thematic parallels. One obvious use of the technique is the paralleled journeys to Belbury, Mark driven recklessly at high speed by Feverstone to encounter his fate, watching reality flash by in a blur, and Jane by train, rattling and jerking through an autumnal landscape to arrive reluctantly at the real terminus of the line and the end of everything.[29] This example is not even a good one because it is too obvious. Only after repeated readings do we gather how thoroughly and subtly Lewis has organized the parallels in the novel which create a sense of inevitability in the plot movement.

Within the whole structure, there are scenes which balance one another in ironic contrast. The Belbury dinner, drawing Mark further in, puts Jane's first meeting with Grace Ironwood in perspective and sets up our anticipation both for the final banquet to which the guests are bidden to be eaten by the maddened animals and the "last supper" at St. Anne's prior to Ransom's assumption to Perelandra. The violence unleashed by Belbury on Edgestow is reflected and magnified by the devastation inflicted on it by the Powers at the end of the novel. The paralleled confrontations of Jane and Mark with their "masters" echo many similar scenes throughout the book: the tramp's confrontation with Merlin, Merlin's confrontation with Ransom, Ransom's and Merlin's confrontation with the Powers, and Wither, Filostrato, and Straik's last meeting with the Head.

The parallelings of characters are too numerous to mention, but some are subtle enough to call our attention to Lewis's concern for showing the pervasive infiltration of power on the opposing sides of this battle. As the Head, "resurrected" from death, rehabilitated and enlivened by forces outside itself becomes the tool of Belbury and the dark eldils, so Merlin by much the same course comes to operate as a tool. Both are "soiled" magicians of an older order, fit for the use to which they will be put. Their deaths present the vivid contrast which concludes each antithesis: Alcasan, tortured and abused, the ultimate product of vivisection, ends as a heap of bones and flesh. Merlin, last seen on a horse galloping away from Feverstone, wins salvation as we see his translation through Jane's vision.[30]

There are clear parallels in the settings. The fog in Chapter 6 through which Jane muddles her way from Fairy Hardcastle's hands to those of Ransom symbolizes her mental confusion as it is played out against the background of revolution and turmoil turned loose on Edgestow. The unnatural warmth of Perelandra's visitation at the end acts as a parallel bringing summer in dead winter and the renewal of hope for the preservation of Logres. The settings of the two country houses are paralleled with the contrasts to be found in individual rooms. The warm kitchen and high-ceilinged Blue Room stand against the clinical coldness of the Head's room and the Objective Room where Mark spends some unpleasant hours.

Through these interlocking structures Lewis creates a growing sense of hierarchy and purpose underlying the apparently mundane plot which opens the book. The circles toward which the two characters are drawn are highly complex structures whose superficial operation hardly betrays the hidden power and purpose potently lurking beneath or beyond. Lewis draws us along with Jane and Mark into the center where the real action takes place. We are allowed to know sooner than they that the forces are cosmic and the stakes eternal. Lewis only barely disguises by symbol the confrontation which plays itself out here. By placing the emphasis on the real and mundane, drawing us gradually into the inner circle and up into the "meaning," he avoids the problems of the earlier books where information replaces realization on our part. The technique here is more subtle and satisfying, and even though we realize that we are receiving a message, we are so caught by the fiction of it that we do not object. We do not stop and say, "There is the message" since it steals over us gradually, and we respond to the unity and integration of the *Logos* within the *Poiema*.

Just as irony is an important component in this novel, used to keep the parallels from becoming stiff and merely repetitious, so the traditional Lewis humor comes into play to relieve the tension and seriousness that necessarily accompany this theme of cosmic conflicts. Neither humor nor irony had been used as extensively before by Lewis, with the possible exception of *The Screwtape Letters*, which is a less ambitious piece of fiction with close thematic and technical connections to this novel. Though Ivy, Mother Dimble, MacPhee, and the tramp are minor comics and stop just short of silliness, it is Merlin who emerges as Lewis's triumphant balance of the serious and comic. The whole conception of Merlin as the tool of Deep Heaven stretches credulity to the extreme. The Pendragon-Merlin-Logres subplot, connected no doubt with Lewis's interest in the subject and his interest at the time he was writing the book in Charles Williams' works, presents difficulties for the critical reader. Though Lewis makes every effort to justify the inclusion of this material—Ransom cannot be the tool since he is virginal, having no knowledge of the old magic—it remains structurally rather an excrescence.[31] But by his masterful conception of Merlin's character, speech, and reactions and by the construction of a denouement which might otherwise have been ludicrous rather than profound, Lewis has justified his use of this material. Merlin fulfills all our expectations; larger than life, commanding, potent in "magic," earthy, he is one of Lewis's finest historical creations.[32] It is with humor and relish that Lewis approaches Merlin's appearance and his task, and they heighten the plot before the apocalyptic dinner. We too relish the debasement of Wither and Straik as much as the earlier interplay of wits and power between Ransom and Merlin. From the point of Merlin's long-awaited introduction up to the destruction of Edgestow, the action picks up noticeably, as with the increasing number of strands to be kept in control, Lewis uses Merlin as a center of interest.

Humor can be found relieving the tension of the final dinner at Belbury as Lewis, using the convenient device of Babel, engages in some amusing linguistic creativity and allows various major characters to reflect on the meaning of these unearthly events. The humor is like the woman guest's laughter which turns into hysterics. There is humor of a gentler sort to be found in the jovial banter of the company at St. Anne's when they chide MacPhee for his skepticism at the last supper. Here, however, it is tinged with the sadness of Ransom's parting and is relieved only by the anticipated reunion of Jane with Mark as the book closes.

Our response to the book is a positive one. It should be clear now that Lewis has mastered the technical aspect of writing fiction so well that he feels comfortable with the demands for intricate plotting and realistic characterization developing in this novel. The scope of the novel, the intricacy of the plot, the number and variety of characters, the demands for suspense and the gradual development of the psychological motivation of the main characters, he handles with skill and apparent ease. The choice of a realistic setting which involves an internalized journey for hero and heroine, dividing the central interest between male and female viewpoints rather than placing the narrative center in Ransom, shows an advancement in Lewis's narrative skill. The increased emphasis on depth of characterization, at least in Jane and Mark, also indicates an advance over the sometimes flat characterization of his earlier fiction. The gradual movement away from reality into the fantasy or fairy tale of cosmic confrontation avoids the earlier jerkiness of structures apparently slightly at variance with the material Lewis wished them to convey. It is as much his skill as the suitability of the structure to the theme which wins our approval.

There are roughnesses, echoes of past irritations. Lewis has not grown out of the "expository" delight which gave us Reason's speeches in *The Pilgrim's Regress*. There are occasions when the action dies and the tension slumps as we get some extraneous information. The appearance of the wraith Perelandra to Jane (pp. 303-306) and Ransom's dry explanation of its significance or the explanation of Objectivity by Frost and Mark's subsequent Objectivity training (pp. 295-300) are examples of information which Lewis fails to incorporate into the flow of action. However, there are many more examples in which far more intractable material is more skillfully handled. One example is the descent of the gods, a more difficult bit of narration where Lewis's acknowledged descriptive skill, seen before especially in *Perelandra*, comes into full play. By shifting viewpoints from the actual presence of the gods in Ransom's room where their naked power is felt to the muted effect below stairs on the lesser company, Lewis expands their potency and gives added scope to his descriptions. The language itself reflects the shifting atmosphere charging the room: "Viritrilbia," Mercury, "a kind of boiling and bubbling in mind and heart which shook their bodies also" (p. 321); "for all the fragments—needle-pointed desires, brisk merriments, lynx-eyed thoughts went rolling to and fro like glittering drops and reunited themselves" (p. 322); Venus, "Laden like heavy barges that glide nearly gunwale under, laden so heavily you would have thought it could not move, laden with ponderous fragrance of night-scented flowers, sticky gums, groves that drop odours, and with cool savour of midnight fruit it stirred the curtains, it lifted a letter that lay on the table, it lifted the hair which had a moment before been plastered on Merlin's forehead. The room was rocking. They were afloat" (p. 323); Mars, "He heard the snap of the bows, the click-click of steel points in wooden shields, the cheers, the howling, and the ring of struck mail.... Under the immense weight of their obedience their wills stood up straight and untiring like caryatids. Eased of all fickleness and all protestings they stood: gay, light, nimble, and alert" (pp. 324-325); "Lurga," Saturn, "its age was no mere morass of time where imagination can sink in reverie, but a living, self-remembering duration which repelled lighter intelligences from its structure as granite flings back waves, itself unwithered and undecayed but able to wither any who approached it unadvised" (p. 326); Jove, "Glund-Oyarsa," "Kingship and the power and festal pomp and courtesy shot from him as sparks fly from an anvil. The pealing of bells, the blowing of trumpets, the spreading out of banners, are means used on earth to make a faint symbol of his quality. It was like a long sunlit wave, creamy-crested and arched with emerald, that comes on nine feet tall, with roaring and with terror and unquenchable laughter" (pp. 326-327).

The descriptive power is yoked firmly to thematic development, reinforcing and deepening our imaginative response exactly in the way Lewis suggests that sensuous experience in art should operate and not, as in some of his earlier descriptions, acting either as embellishments or distractions. There are many other examples of such linkage such as the luxury and opulence of the attire the women select for each other on the last night which strikes just the proper note. Lewis can turn his descriptive power to effect the reverse. More effective as pure description of evil than the bloodbath of the dinner or the consequent destruction of Wither, Filostrato, and Straik, is the much earlier and nearly obscene vision of Frost and Wither, clutching, giggling, grappling to the floor in a paroxysm of mutual devourings (p. 243). Lewis has in fact, made us feel what joy and evil are like rather than telling us what they might be like.

The other great strength of this work over all that has come before is the grasp of human characterization found in the development of Jane and especially Mark. In earlier works, Lewis's characters have either been men on the verge of spiritual elevation or beings of superior moral or immoral order like Ransom, the Sorns, and Weston respectively. With Jane and Mark we have fallible and malleable human material ready to the novelist's hand, and Lewis molds them psychologically to his purposes. Through them he is able to give the story direct impact on the reader. John and Ransom had been too much removed from everyday life to provide direct access to the human experience. As we follow Jane and Mark, we feel some pity for their ignorance and pride, some fear for their stupidity, blindness, and selfishness. Through his careful delineation of both characters, but especially through Mark who as the worse but more tempted and freer agent shows the more dramatic human choice, we see the power of his characterization.

Mark is presented initially as an intelligent but unlikable toady. However, against the backdrop of Curry and Feverstone, Cosser and Steele, we see that he is not entirely without character. Lewis is careful not to let him come too vividly alive for us until he is thoroughly enmeshed, partly through his own choice and partly by the circumstance of being Jane's husband, a humiliation he is to become fully conscious of later. The remedial treatment which is to bring about his rehabilitation is played off against his growing rebellion, casting ironic light on both Frost's temptation to ultimate power and the methods used. Mark's physical escape from Belbury only confirms his mental enslavement and works neatly as an indicator that the evil of Belbury has already overwhelmed Edgestow. His interview with Dimble, exactly contrasting Jane's with Fairy Hardcastle, reveals his unreadiness to choose sides and is capped by his arrest—symbolizing the slight beginnings of self-realization, and the offer of membership in the innermost circle, his temptation, and his joining the battle and the straight fight (p. 267). It is as much by Frost's deflection to the problem of Merlin as by Mark's own will that he is saved, but Lewis clearly intends us to see Mark accepting the responsibility for his free will, after withstanding the demonic attack in his cell. Called later to desecrate the crucifix as a final seal of his joining the inner circle, he elects the straight and normal, has his first moral experience (p. 299) and chooses sides. His moment of epiphany (p. 310) is not perhaps as clearly defined as Jane's. "In this height and depth and breadth the little idea of herself which she had hitherto called *me* dropped down and vanished, unfluttering, into bottomless distance, like a bird in a space without air" (pp. 318-319). We leave him, not a shining convert, but a humble lover, waiting to grow in his love for Jane, and assume his place in the human circle, "between the angels who are our elder brothers and the beasts who are our jesters, servants and playfellows" (p. 378).

Thus the trilogy closes with hope in love obedient to duty and in the preservation of Logres in Britain. Science of the Westonian sort is vanquished temporarily, and the Progressive Element in college and society put down in favor of traditional virtues found in hearth and home. Ransom is translated to Perelandra, and the evil of Belbury self-destructs and is swept away by the upheaval of nature. Of the three books, the last is the most satisfying technically because it gives us the least cause for complaint and is the product of an increasing facility on Lewis's part in the writing of this type of fiction. There are those like Robson who find the conclusion opera bouffe.[33] Others will persist in preferring the descriptive brilliance of *Perelandra*.

That Hideous Strength brings the end of more than the trilogy. Apart from three stories, "The Shoddy Lands," "Ministering Angels," and "Forms of Things Unknown," Lewis was not to use science fiction or the space voyage *per se* again.[34] Though many of the techniques elaborated on here find their way into the *Chronicles of Narnia* and *Till We Have Faces*, the science fiction story or novel ceased to interest Lewis as a form to embody what he had to say. It may be just as well since one built-in problem which Lewis recognized in the genre was the tendency to mechanical repetition. Lewis had finished what he could effectively say here. The conclusiveness of the last novel and the abortive redirection of the Ransom fragment point out the end of a creative cycle along these lines. He would turn to new forms as the vehicle to express what it became important for him to say.

6.   *THE SCREWTAPE LETTERS* 1942

The conception of *The Screwtape Letters* can be accurately dated by a letter to W.H. Lewis *Letters* (p. 188) of July 20, 1940. Lewis recounts that the idea for a book which he thought might be both useful and entertaining struck him at the end of a church service. He planned first to call it "As One Devil to Another" and intended it to consist of letters from an elderly retired devil to a young devil just starting work on his first assignment. The idea would be to give, as Lewis wrote, all the psychology of temptation from the other viewpoint. The now titled "Screwtape" letters appeared in *The Guardian* on May 2, 1941, and November 28, 1941; on October 9, 1941, Lewis committed the manuscript to Sister Penelope for safe-keeping.[1] He indicated in a letter to Ruth Pitter that the names in *The Screwtape Letters* owe something to the proper names in *A Voyage to Arcturus*.[2] His letter to Harry Blamires of March 14, 1954, suggests "I had thought of having letters to the guardian angel from an archangel side by side with those from Screwtape to Wormwood in my *Letters* but funked it."[3] He indicated to Dom Bede Griffiths that:

it still seems to me that *far* the strongest card in our enemies' hand is the actual course of the world: and that, quite apart from particular events like wars and revolutions. The inherent "vanity" of the "creature," the fact that life preys on life, that all beauty and happiness is produced only to be destroyed—this was what stuck in my gullet.[4]

The Preface indicates that Lewis's conception of Hell is one where everyone is eternally concerned about his own dignity and advancement, where everyone has a grievance, and where everyone feels the deadly serious passions of envy, self-importance, and resentment.[5] This description sounds rather like one of Belbury and Bracton.

The letter to the Milton Society, as I indicated earlier, places *The Screwtape Letters* at the extreme end of the symbolical and mythopoeic forms of which theologized science fiction is the other. Since Lewis makes allusion to what is a clear distinction between these types of writing, we should examine how *The Screwtape Letters* differs from the trilogy.

First, its purpose is simpler: to be useful and entertaining. Without much emphasis on style, Lewis draws particular attention to the purpose; he wants to show what Hell is like in modern terms, removing the romantic haze cast over evil by Milton and Goethe, replacing the illusion that evil is a liberating force by showing the facts of hellish motivation like fear of punishment and hunger for other souls. This is no game and was no fun for Lewis in the composition. The references to war and the time of its initial publication both indicate Lewis's utilitarian purpose. The method, he announces is humor because humor involves a sense of proportion, a way of seeing ourselves from the outside.[6] Humor gives the objectivity which allows Lewis to approach war and death, imminent for his readers in 1942 England, to see the humor of their lot, to lighten their burden, to give them hope. He was wise not to produce the archangelic counterpart where humor would have been difficult if not impossible. The book for believers is symbolic and because they believe in Hell it carries a sense of immediacy and truth. For others it is an allegory. Its general and widespread popularity rests on neither of these factors but on the humor which undercuts the humorless Screwtape. Lewis must have admired Browning, for much of the quality of "Soliloquy of the Spanish Cloister" can be felt in Screwtape's self-revelation.

What is not part of Lewis's purpose is any attempt to stir the deeper imagination. He would perhaps hardly consider this work literature, by his definition. Its initial newspaper publication, his initial response to its popularity, and his unfavorable comparison of it with *Perelandra* all reinforce this speculation. Written wholly in implied dialogue, the book lacks any significant opportunity for the display of descriptive power which is an integral part of his other fiction. As he noted: once conceived, the form exploits itself spontaneously.[7] So I will not belabor his technique but will confine my discussion to noting themes and stylistic mannerisms that reflect on other works. I do not mean to belittle the achievement of either *The Screwtape Letters* or *The Great Divorce*, but they are by Lewis's own standards, slighter works of the imagination than the others and require a less elaborate examination.

The method which Lewis follows in his epistolary presentation is that of mockery on several levels. Screwtape mocks the inefficiency of Wormwood and the inexplicable aims and methods of the Enemy. The inversion of meaning by reversal gives the whole work the witty bite which produces the effect Lewis suggests by quoting Luther and Sir Thomas More as openers. There are certain inherent disadvantages of the epistolary style: limited narrative viewpoint, restriction of verisimilitude of other characters or scene, limitation of immediacy of the action and of the scope of such action. But here Lewis has overcome these difficulties largely by a happy unity of theme and form and by his clear-sighted conception of Screwtape as a character.

It is the technical mastery of Screwtape's characterization which is the significant achievement of this book when we look at it within the context of the other fiction. No character in *The Pilgrim's Regress* or *Out of the Silent Planet* is so fully and realistically realized as this devil. He moves through cool assessment of his protege's prospect to cogent analysis of the appropriate temptations and on to a paroxysm of rage over the inscrutable meaning of the Enemy's "Love" for his creatures which culminates in the comic climax of the work, the letter dictated while Screwtape is transformed into a centipede. The mounting ingenuity of his proposed attack on the escalating defenses of the subject and the reflection of Wormwood's failure in the opening of each letter reach their culmination in the luscious prose of the last letter, fairly dripping with the anticipation of the feast to come.

A reader starting with this work first might well wonder where Lewis learned to draw such a convincing portrait. We might start our explanation with his presumed personal observation of the devilish in his religious life. Also Screwtape does share in the qualities of some of Lewis's earlier characterizations: the peevishness of Sensible, the slickness of Devine, the measured prose of Broad. A single figure placed in the dramatic center of a "lesson" offers certain advantages to the author. He does not have to engage in direct dialogue; he controls the world he presents; and he sets the limits of our expectations by what he elects to tell us. This is not to say that Lewis had an easy job; only to suggest that Screwtape may have been less challenging for Lewis, who was after all a lecturer, logician and seasoned dialectician, than say Mark and Jane Studdock portrayed in a domestic quarrel.

Certainly *Screwtape* is a masterpiece. In dealing with a subject matter which would have been deadly without humor, Lewis brings that balance of hard truth with a light touch which makes us marvel, even after several readings, on the justness of his analysis, the rightness of his presentation. The book is popular because it simplifies, humanizes, and universalizes the truth of evil in a way instructive illustrations, religious art, and tales of the bogeyman never have.

The attack is a frontal one, not drawing the reader "past watchful dragons" as in the later fiction. We know that we are in for a discussion of human frailty and temptation and that part of the fun which helps the dose down is the inversion of meaning which sets up the basic irony. Some of our respect for Lewis's achievement rests on his skill with a phrase. "Humans are amphibians—half spirit and half animal" obeying the "law of Undulations."[8] Joy, Screwtape defines as "a meaningless acceleration in the rhythm of celestial experience...."[9] There are numerous examples of the felicitous phrase which reveal Screwtape's delusion and the full force of the power which has caused Screwtape such concern.

The themes are in no way exceptional. Lewis has allowed their particular application to life in the twentieth century without limiting them to a specific time or location for an "attack." The temptations of the World, the Flesh, and the devilish mind are all suggested by Screwtape and then fumbled by Wormwood. The order in which they appear reinforces the progress made by the "patient" in rejecting them. Thus each step builds on the last, giving an orderly progression from venal to heinous sins. Though we do not directly identify ourselves with the young man, we do feel the accuracy with which Lewis has analyzed those temptations which will be most attractive to him at a given point in his development as a Christian, from an appeal to fantasy and emotions to that of self-love and spiritual pride.

Some of the basic themes which appear here and in the later fiction are: the impotence of evil as Screwtape indicates that real virtues and real pleasures are utterly unavailable to devils as temptations, the effective use which can be made of the normal course of events in the world, such as wars, fashions, moral and social trends—and in a human life, such as relationships with mother and fiancée, and tendencies to pride, sloth, greed, and self-indulgence and self-pity all inherent in the creature. The dramatic application of these specific circumstances comes later in the fiction which follows *The Screwtape Letters* rather than in *The Pilgrim's Regress* or *Out of the Silent Planet*. We see in Ransom's decision to act, Jane and Mark's treatment and regeneration, and the education of all the Narnia children in free choice, and finally Orual's dramatic conversion in *Till We Have Faces*, the most dramatic statements which Lewis constructed from the basic themes employed in *The Screwtape Letters*. The method used in Orual's narrative, though illuminated with descriptive elaboration in a way Screwtape's monologues are not, shows close parallels to the central focus on characterization used here.

A great part of the effectiveness of *The Screwtape Letters* rests on the fact that it does not draw us higher up and further in except in a purely rational way. We do not become involved in the characters as real personalities, and we laugh at Screwtape's peevishness, temper, and cringing fear of blackmail much as we laugh at Rumpelstiltskin stamping his way out of the story given his name. We are treated to a feast of diabolic power without fearing for our own direct temptation or damnation. We are not really invited to indulge our imagination in the creation of a view of Hell or of England in 1941. Lewis has engaged our wit and reason but not much of our imagination here, and the fictional world does not depend for its effect on the stirring of the deeper imagination or our emotional responses. It is in fact only through Lewis's objectivity and tight control over the humorous presentation of these themes that he avoids the pitfalls that caught him later in *Screwtape Proposes a Toast*. Written for the *Saturday Evening Post*, as Lewis tells us, and against his earlier and better judgment, it is a falling-off from the tension of the original *Screwtape Letters*. Now Lewis gives us less universal themes, and some of Screwtape's speech reveals certain of Lewis's pet peeves: conformity, democracy, leveling in education and the arts, in fact leveling in all aspects of life, "modern" women (the normal twentieth-century girl is "a minx, a moron, and a parasite."[10])—Screwtape's observations, not Lewis's—and the regulated State. The effect is raillery rather than wit, and whether we are to see this as a sad decline in Screwtape, an inversion of his observation of the sad decline in the quality of devilish fare or not, remains to be seen. The effect is certainly flat compared to that sparkle of wit behind all Screwtape says in his *Letters*.

The Screwtape Letters are in some ways an ingenious exercise in a well-established genre, the debate, turned here to the purpose outlined at the beginning of this brief discussion. Lewis is not attempting a new imaginative creation as he was to a degree in each of the space trilogy novels individually. What he does is to take a traditional form and treat it imaginatively and wittily to produce a classic of its type.

7.   *THE GREAT DIVORCE* 1945

Warren Lewis's diary records on April 17, 1932, that his brother had an idea for another religious work centering on the idea that eternal punishment may be intermittent. Lewis was proposing a book about a day trip to Heaven.[1] In January 1945, Lewis wrote to Sister Penelope that the anticipated publication of *That Hideous Strength* would take place in June 1945, and he referred to *Who Goes Home?* or *The Grand Divorce* the early titles of *The Great Divorce*, indicating that it had no connection whatever with *That Hideous Strength*.[2] The next letter to her indicates that *The Great Divorce* is set to appear in August 1945.[3] There are singularly few references in his correspondence to this particular piece of fiction, but that does not, I think, allow us to infer a lesser regard for it on Lewis's part. He wrote Jocelyn Gibb in 1954 that he was always glad to hear of anyone's taking up that "Cinderella," *The Great Divorce*.[4] Earlier in the same year he had written W.L. Kinter, indicating, evidently in answer to a query, that he was indebted to Dante in *The Great Divorce*, noting that he consciously modeled the bus driver on the angel at the gate of Dis [*Inferno*, IX (79-102)].[5]

The preface to the first edition characterizes it as a "small" book, a "fantasy" with a "moral" and acknowledges that its purpose is to stress the separation of Hell from Heaven. Lewis is keen on putting that division between two spiritual realms into perspective, putting first things first. Hell will not evolve into Heaven, and the process of becoming a spirit is an arduous one involving the rejection of much we hold dear, even in a purgatorial state. The unwillingness to choose between the alternatives is the first step in final damnation. The dwarf cannot bring himself to choose Heaven over the Tragedian he has created, while the ghost must ask that the red lizard of Lust be killed before he and it can be transformed and their roles reversed.

This book is the shortest and most clearly didactic of Lewis's fiction. His intention is apparent, and the reader's response is direct and simple, not requiring the deeper imaginative response of a work like *Perelandra*. Lewis is not setting out to reach us on that level. The fantasy is a simple one of stock allegorical figures like those of *The Pilgrim's Regress* variety engaged in an encounter where information concerning their spiritual future will be passed on to them through a series of examples. The connections with Dante are rather remote and tenuous since Lewis is making little effort at heightened literary experience for the reader. There are the traditional elements of the guided tour through celestial regions. The guide here is Lewis's literary idol, George MacDonald. The small book ends with the revelation that it has all been a dream. But there is no attempt to categorize the ghosts or place them on ordered levels.

Among the noteworthy aspects of this book are the speech mannerisms which Lewis uses effectively to catch the nature of a particular character. The Big Ghost, who only wants what is his right, is a fine example, as is the episcopal ghost. The *Biography* suggests that E. W. Barnes, a free thinker and Bishop of Birmingham, is the model for the episcopal ghost. Lewis is attacking the liberalizing and demythologizing movement within the church which found expression in Barnes' book, *Rise of Christianity*. Lewis spends little time describing external characteristics but allows each ghost to present himself. The most effective example of this device is the dwarf and actor where the will and speech are separated, and the self-created image absorbs the soul which refuses love and forgiveness. In comparison with the stock allegorical figures of *The Pilgrim's Regress*, Lewis shows that here he has developed the technique of character presentation to a high level.

There are occasional examples of Lewis's descriptive power. The grey landscape of Hell gives way to the hard and bright vision of Heaven. "I could see what might be either a great bank of cloud or a range of mountains. Sometimes I could make out in it steep forests, far-withdrawing valleys, and even mountain cities perched on inaccessible summits."[6] But these descriptions do not encourage the stirring of the deeper imagination. Lewis's interest in the theme of Heavenly solidity and the need to choose to go up and on, overshadows any strictly literary or aesthetic considerations. There is the bittersweet moment at the end, reminiscent of "The Piper at the Gates of Dawn" in *The Wind in the Willows* which stirs our feelings in the way the best of Lewis always does:

The eastern side of every tree-trunk grew bright. Shadows deepened. All the time there had been bird noises, trillings, chatterings, and the like; but now suddenly the full chorus was poured from every branch; cocks were crowing, there was music of hounds, and horns; above all this ten thousand tongues of men and woodland angels and the wood itself sang. "It comes! It comes!" they sang. "Sleepers awake!"[17]

But the tone of the book is that of instruction rather than self-transcendent enlightenment, just as the method used is that of a lecture illustrated by examples. There are some examples of Lewis's traditional humor like the irony of the fashionable lady who refuses to be seen in Heaven, but the lightness of observations on board the bus and on arrival fade into the instruction which the fictional Lewis receives and passes directly to us. The imaginative fantasy then is really not so much a creation of another world as the vision of choice which Lewis places at the center of this piece of fiction. The reader who comes to this book expecting to find what we might rightfully consider by this point as Lewis's literary trademark: the creation of believable other worlds with characters acting out symbolic dramas of spiritual significance in a setting which engages our imagination and which works organically to underline the theme, will feel some disappointment. *The Great Divorce* is not a debate because the argument is all on one side, and as a consequence it fails to hold our imaginative interest and must rely on a rational engagement which comes close to being dry at times.

Although one critic finds this book "a triumph of didactic fiction" and sees it as the "quintessential Lewis," the majority of readers have found greater interest in the more creative work.[8] It would not be inappropriate to suggest that one of Lewis's motives in writing this work was to answer the vexing question he expressed in a letter to Sister Penelope about the exclusiveness of Heaven.[9] Whether it stands up to some of the compliments paid to it like "rich and sensuous texture which ranges from the grim to the glorious," "Almost as dramatic and sensuous as *Perelandra*," remains the decision of individual readers who may prefer this type of writing to more imaginative creations.[10]

8. *THE CHRONICLES OF NARNIA* 1950–1956: *An Introduction*

The history of the composition of these seven "children's" stories has been drawn in considerable detail by Walter Hooper in "Past Watchful Dragons" and more recently in *A Biography* so that I will not rehearse these facts in detail, being satisfied merely to point to significant aspects which relate to this study.[1]

John Haigh, one of Lewis's critics, has suggested that Lewis moved into the new form of children's fantasy because he wanted to avoid repetition.[2] Lewis was, he felt, saying the same things but simply using another vehicle. Lewis himself commented that his children's stories were side chapels off the nave of his basic work, which suggests an acknowledged consistency running through all the fiction.[3] Even Robson grudgingly admits that these stories did embody "things" which Lewis was profoundly sincere about though the form was inadequate to what Lewis tries so hard to make it accomplish.[4]

There can be little question of Lewis's sincerity and seriousness in writing these books. Numerous letters attest to his interest in catching his readers, of all ages, off guard. "If I am now good for anything it is for catching the reader unawares—thro' fiction and symbol."[5] "The fairy-tale version of the Passion in *The Lion* etc. works in the way you describe because—tho' this sounds odd— it by-passes one's reverence and piety....Make it a fairy-tale and the reader is taken off his guard (Unless ye become as little children....)."[6] His credo, stated in the letter to the Milton Society, makes clear that the imaginative man was "he who brought me, in the last few years to write the series of Narnian stories for children; not asking what children want and then endeavoring to adapt myself (this was not needed) but because the fairy tale was the genre best fitted for what I wanted to say...."[7]

The Lion, the Witch and the Wardrobe began, we know, with a picture of a Faun carrying an umbrella and standing in a snowy wood. The picture had been in Lewis's mind since he was about sixteen.[8] An early draft was begun in 1939 and put aside until the mid-1940s. Stimulated by reading Roger Lancelyn Green's *The Wood That Time Forgot*, Lewis had more mental pictures of a queen on a sledge and a magnificent lion and nightmares about lions.[9] He read his developing story to Green, who liked it although Tolkien did not, and Lewis records that with the entry of the lion, all the rest of the story came together as the Lion soon pulled the other six Narnian stories in after Him.[10] He began to fill in the events before the action of *The Lion, the Witch and the Wardrobe* but produced only the Lefay fragment.[11] The Lefay fragment, unpublished, is Lewis's first attempt at what later became in completely revised form, *The Magician's Nephew*. *Prince Caspian* (other titles: *Drawn into Narnia, A Horn in Narnia*) was finished by December 1949, and by February 1950, *The Voyage of the 'Dawn Treader'* was ready in manuscript. July 1950 saw the completion of the manuscript of *The Horse and His Boy* (other titles: *Narnia and the North, The Horse and the Boy*); November brought *The Silver Chair*. By October 1951, a version of *The Magician's Nephew* was shown to Green, but Lewis finished *The Last Battle* in March 1953 before making the revisions suggested by Green to *The Magician's Nephew*.[12]

There is little else that can be drawn from firsthand sources concerning the genesis of these stories. We may speculate on why Lewis came to write them when he did: the wartime evacuee children in his home in 1939, his lifelong admiration for Kenneth Grahame, George MacDonald, and E. Nesbit, the resurgence of his interest during the late forties after the success of *The Screwtape Letters* and the space trilogy in a form he last used in 1939, and his growing conviction that fantasy could act as a spiritual preparation for young minds. Retrospectively, in a series of essays on the subject of stories and fairy tales, Lewis made his intentions in using the genre quite clear. Moving from the general "On Stories," through "On Three Ways of Writing for Children," to the specific "Sometimes Fairy Stories May Say Best What's to be Said," we arrive at the following rationale for the writing and reading of stories. One might be tempted to say "use" of stories had Lewis not forbidden that as a possibility.

Stories move us by casting actuality into another perspective, catching us off guard, challenging our deeper imagination and sending us back with a renewed pleasure to the actual world from our sojourn in what Lewis calls plausible and imaginatively moving other worlds.[13] Stories, unlike realistic novels, do not set themselves up as actuality, fact or information, but they do intend to give us an exciting glimpse of the "as if," a sense of the unexpected, an adventure into possibilities, an image of what reality might be like at a more central region.[14] Art, the art of the story specifically in this case, is an invitation to come further in and higher up. We are not, as F. R. Leavis suggests, attracted to the thing in itself, its plot, characters, symbols, irony, or structure. Through the artistry, the "net" of plot or adventure and excitement, we are drawn out of ourselves and into meaning which we had not dreamed of before. Here it is tempting to suggest that the whole process of transcendence which is central to the *Chronicles of Narnia* is a metaphor for Lewis's mature view of the art of fiction, and that these stories were written to exemplify this theory, further in and higher up symbolizing the author's method and the reader's road as well as the evolution within each book and across the *Chronicles* as a whole. But an honest look at the facts forbids such neat theorizing, and the second essay on how one writes for children indicates that Lewis was observing what had happened in his own case and that of other writers, not giving us the outline of how he went about writing fairy tales. It is this delight in organic creativity which throughout acts as a balance to Lewis's otherwise overpowering rationality. He makes no attempt to explain the mechanics of writing stories or how an author succeeds in moving his readers. We are given no practical advice.

Having firmly established children as legitimate readers, not a group to be written at or down to, Lewis defends his use of the fairy tale on the basis of its appropriateness to his subject. His defense rests on the premise that life and art are organic and evolutionary. The creative acts of writing and reading are also evolutionary, a progression from meaning to meaning. Lewis's statements on his own writing and the evidence of his work show that writing is as much a journey of discovery for Lewis as reading his work is for us. He discounted, especially in the *Chronicles*, any preconceived program which Narnia would flesh out, and the facts of composition recently revealed in the Hooper and Green *Biography* bear him out.

The form attracted Lewis, he said, because of its restrictiveness, on the one hand, and on the other, the opportunity which fantasy and the fairy tale offered him to convey meaning in a way which is generally unavailable to the novelist. He particularly appreciated the enforced condensation, the check on his expository demon, the curtailment of length and scope, the exclusion of erotic love, the equally balanced chapter lengths, the restraint on description, and the virtual exclusion as he said of analysis, digression, reflection, and "gas."[15] Fantasy offered the chance, when presented in fairy tales, for using as Lewis said "giants and dwarfs and talking beasts.... an admirable hieroglyphic which conveys psychology, types of character, more briefly than novelistic presentation and to readers whom novelistic presentation could not yet reach."[16]

It seems fair to suggest, having seen in some detail what Lewis's fiction had developed into by this point, that he had come back, in a sense, to write the sort of fiction which had intrigued and delighted him as a child. But that was not his only motive. He had much to say about the achievement of Joy and to an audience whom from his own experience he knew to be turning away both from the literature which could suggest the sources of Joy and from the Church which should teach it. His motives for writing may have been multiple. First he wanted to convey the pictures he saw. Next came the expression of longing, the *askesis*, the spiritual exercise now identified with the creative act of fiction writing; third was the challenge of whether he could keep in control, not letting either description or argument overbalance each other. Finally he wanted to steal past the ever watchful dragons, the stereotyped responses to religion. Perhaps there were other reasons hidden even from himself: a desire to rival the *Hobbit*, a wish to emulate MacDonald, the psychological insistence of his pictures, dreams, and nightmares. We cannot know with certainty what all his motives were. The result, however, was Narnia, which expresses thematically and artistically all that is central to Lewis's art and theory of literature and which many critics feel will be that part of his fiction which gains him permanent literary recognition.[17]

Since I wish to trace the evolution of Lewis's technique as he wrote the stories without losing the overall pattern which emerges from reading the seven in the order he recommended, I will begin where he began, with *The Lion, the Witch and the Wardrobe* and deal with *The Magician's Nephew* just before *The Last Battle*, putting the framing books side by side in their compositional order. In the final analysis, I think this will do less damage than might be supposed since the greatest affinity is between *The Magician's Nephew* and *The Last Battle*, with the other five books falling into an order with an inner consistency. I do not propose separate chapters on each book since I have found them exemplary of Lewis's organic creativity, and thus I think they would profit by examination in one long chapter with subsections devoted to individual works. Critics have already cited many sources and parallels to other works admired or read by Lewis, so I shall confine myself to a study of his technique and themes in the light of the earlier chapters on his work to this point. Much has been written about the Christian allegory and symbolism to be found in Narnia; again, I leave the reader to other readily available sources since my attention will be directed toward the integration of meaning in the form Lewis chose rather than an exclusive selection of meanings.

THE LION, THE WITCH AND THE WARDROBE
1950

As Lewis paused on the verge of a new creative adventure in the use of the imagination, the form he had chosen for what he had to say must have presented certain problems. In his earlier fiction, we have noted his use of traditional forms and the growing skill he displayed in adapting them to his particular purposes. Lewis was not a technical innovator, the creator of new forms. In fact, his belief in God's unique role as creator rather denied that possibility to him.[1] Authors never originate anything in the sense of creating it; they rearrange the pieces in new kaleidoscopic combinations. Bunyan stands behind *The Pilgrim's Regress*, Wells and Lindsay behind the space trilogy, and Milton lurks behind *Perelandra*. There are sources, if we want them, for everything Lewis wrote. So with fairy tales, there were daunting examples before Lewis as he began, tales he had admired as child and man; and his challenge was to offer something distinctly new, something imaginatively fresh. There were the problems of keeping the story simple without juvenilizing it; of treating his readers with respect without giving them analysis, digression, reflection, and "gas."

The form he chose was conventional: four children, an adventure in an old and mysterious house, and an unexpected journey to another world. There are echoes, as critics have noted, of E. Nesbit and others, but once the adventure begins, we start to see Lewis's distinctive quality.

One striking feature of his prose throughout the *Chronicles* is its consistent simpleness and evenness. There is a reasonableness and steadiness about the measured and balanced sentences which reassure us of the reality of whatever Lewis narrates or describes, whether it is the cold white arm of Jadis revealed to Edmund or the whiskery face of a beaver which greets Lucy upon her waking. Lewis evidently enjoyed the discipline which helped to maintain this basic tone because he repeatedly mentions it as a positive feature of writing these books. The calm, measured movement of the story, eminently readable by children and adults, moves the narrative along at a steady pace and provides that solid basis, the created reality, from which Lewis can depart on occasion without shaking our belief in his manufactured fantasy. The sentences are simple and short, the language carefully chosen to be expressive but not showy or eccentric. It never draws attention to itself, which is a great credit in a genre where some authors depend for the effect of their tale on the uniqueness of their descriptive language.

The descriptive technique used by Lewis here and throughout the *Chronicles* is worth studying at the outset since it carries the burden of convincing us of the reality of these adventures and is the heart of Lewis's technique for touching our deeper imagination. To say that the whole thing "began with a picture" may seem trite and repetitious, but it is the key to Lewis's method. We know that the whole process of creation of these stories was the accretion of pictures and their coalescence into thematic unity—a moving and evolving picture. This is much more an organic method than most critics are willing to allow Lewis, but we must, I think, accept his honest statement that he began not with a full-blown chronicle of Christian themes for children in mind but with pictures which formed a pattern and were fitted to a theme which had run through all of his earlier fiction. The technique depends on appealing to the reader's feelings through descriptions and thus moving him to thought by use of sublimity, as described by Longinus rather than by dialogue, as used by Socrates. The dialogue in all the stories is less effective generally than the descriptive sections, especially where the children are first introduced in *The Lion, the Witch and the Wardrobe*, and we sense that Lewis had never listened closely to how children say things though he caught what they would talk about. Later when they become kings and queens, their courtly language strikes a strange note, but by then we are so deep in the fantasy, the "as if," that we are hardly bothered by that incongruity. When the Witch, Aslan, and all the created world of Narnia appear, Lewis is on new ground and makes the speech of his creatures believable and appropriate.

John Haigh has pointed out the fact that images of sound and color predominate in Lewis's descriptions of Narnia; the aural and visual are used to present us, especially young readers, with the series of sensations which Haigh feels are characteristic of Lewis's method here.[2] He suggests that children respond to the narrative and descriptive interest; whereas, adults prefer the moral and spiritual vision.[3] On the contrary, it seems clear that you cannot have one without the other, and that in fact the strength of the method lies in the embodiment of meaning in imaginative description that is clear, moving, and credible.

Lewis's method parallels the already discussed organic creative process of the novels in a now more condensed and organized fashion. We are presented with pictures which create the most memorable and effective impression of Narnia; Edmund meeting Jadis, the children confronted by Aslan, Aslan being comforted by Lucy and Susan, and his death on the stone table. The pictures are drawn together by a slowly evolving theme which only at the climax reveals its central significance. The organic process works to draw us into Lewis's vision naturally, and it is the aptness of the pictures and the appropriateness of their prose description that does what Lewis wants, drawing us further in and higher up.

The plot structure follow that of Lewis's earlier fiction: a straight line, single thread development of tensions centering on a journey into the unknown, on tasks and choices which determine the outcome and establish turning points thematically, and on the lives of certain characters. A simple paralleling of two characters develops through reciprocating scenes where analogous actions serve as ironic commentary on the choices of these characters. The climax is a battle setting to rights the near catastrophe which precedes it, and the story ends in Tolkien's words, "eucatastrophically" or happily, sliding gradually off the tension of epic acts to the low normalcy of real childhood games in an old house, and thus coming full circle. This pattern is used with slight variations—the journey to Narnia is always managed in a different fashion each time—in each novel as it had been in *The Pilgrim's Regress* and the space triology and to an extent in *The Great Divorce. The Screwtape Letters* is the only work which lacks it. The plot pattern is hardly unique and shares such diverse probable sources as epic, and Arthurian legend, and medieval romance, as well as the romantic novel. The basic pattern of journey, perilous choice, battle, and victory are not new, but Lewis molds them to his purpose with great skill. Balance is one key feature of his method. Chapters are carefully balanced for length and ease in reading. Scenes are given equivalent scope so that there is little lingering over particular scenes of the sort that retard the movement of *Perelandra*. The movement is consistently forward with few episodic interruptions, the only serious one being the appearance of Father Christmas, who nearly jolts us back to London and whose intrusion may or may not improve with additional readings.

Turning to the book, Lewis shows us his considerable skill in opening the story. From the altogether understated beginning, "once there were four children whose names were...." " through their stilted initial dialogue, he quickly and expertly draws us into Narnia with Lucy, the sweetest and most susceptible, youngest of the Pevensie children with whom we identify and through whose eyes we judge what we see.[4] Her innocence and trust are the spectacles through which we see the unfolding action. Lewis could hardly have been more clever in disarming an adult's skepticism and disbelief. The wardrobe is a master stroke though it was to cause Lewis some worry resulting in the humorously overstated warning that it is very silly to shut yourself in a wardrobe, even if it is not a magic one. The genius of Lewis's choice of event and description lies in their appropriateness. Perhaps because he knew the archetypal state of childhood so well, though he knew little about children from first-hand experience such as one has as a parent, he invariably chose the appropriate image, action, or response for his children. Lucy's response to finding Narnia rather than the back of the wardrobe is the most natural thing in the book, and though she is surprised by Tumnus, she is not frightened but rather intrigued, and so she goes further in. The progress of the story and of the *Chronicles* as a whole is "further in," a phrase repeated in "She took a step further in" (p. 6), "Further in, come further in. Right in here" (p. 62), and symbolized in many ways by Edmund's descent into misery and Lucy's ascent to Aslan, and by the physical movement into Narnia and to Cair Paravel on the eastern shore from the western wilds; and finally by the spiritual penetration into the mystery of the incarnation and crucifixion.

Lucy, after a meeting with the faun reminiscent of that of Alice with the White Rabbit, returns to the "real" world, and Lewis cleverly plays off our budding allegiance to Lucy and Narnia, of which we have had just the taste to whet our appetite, against the disbelief of the other children, especially Edmund. Her adventure sets up theirs, and the questioning of her honesty firmly establishes us on her side and certifies Narnia's reality. The parallel scene done with such effect is Edmund's antithetical meeting with Jadis. Lewis uses the children's reaction to climate and food as a barometer of their spiritual condition, most obviously seen later in Eustace who is seasick and then dragonish. Lucy, without a coat, does not react to the cold and is treated to a lovely English tea and chat by the fire. Edmund, who went wrong by going to a "horrid school," finds himself in a strange, cold, quiet place, and throughout his adventures in Narnia he suffers from the cold. His alienation from his brother and sisters is reflected in his lonely rationalizing while awaiting the Witch. Their interview, ironically and almost humorously in contrast to Lucy's with Tumnus, sets up the basic antithesis between greed and pity, egotism and self-sacrifice, which governs the thematic development of the book. Food becomes the principal symbol of the difference between Edmund and Lucy.

The Turkish Delight is another master stroke. Whatever it was in Lewis's childhood, it is in fact now a highly overrated sweet, in my opinion. The name, with its Oriental and romantic overtones, suggests more than the product gives, and Lewis uses this idea simply but with great force in making the Witch appeal first to Edmund's greed and then to his desire for power. "I want a nice boy whom I could bring up as a Prince and who would be King of Narnia when I am gone.... I think I would like to make you the Prince—some day.... You are to be the Prince and—later on—the King;... " (p. 34). The meeting which parallels Lucy's first encounter with Tumnus where he admits his temptation to do her harm and is forgiven, discloses Edmund's ready acceptance of betrayal in order to gain self-satisfaction and power. And with the advent of the Witch, we have Lewis's first maleficent fairy tale creation, caught in the phrase, "You shall know us better hereafter" (p. 28).

In the chapter, "Back on This Side of the Door," Lewis gives us further preparation for the final plunge of all four into the other world and allows Edmund to clinch his horridness and the Professor to prove logically that Narnia is a possibility. The third return is to a landscape now familiar to the reader, and Lewis cleverly shifts the basis of suspense to a larger arena: the Witch versus Aslan, Winter versus Spring, Old Law versus New Law. The children are immediately caught up in a momentous action, an epic struggle beyond their small sphere. Though they have roles to play: Edmund the betrayer, a Judas; Peter the Knight, a St. George against the Dragon; Lucy and Susan as the two Marys; the action has swept them up into great events, the significance of which they can hardly realize. Lewis had used the same technique in all three of the planetary novels, perhaps with greatest success in *Perelandra*. Here he gains the advantage of deepening and heightening the meaning of the adventure by suiting the tasks more judiciously to the capacities of those on whom they fall. Unlike our reaction to Ransom, who must be canonized and Weston who is dehumanized, with these children, we can place ourselves in the Beavers' paws and see if we can "get through."

The devastation of Tumnus's cave puts the homeliness of the Beavers' den in the delicious peril of the Witch's wrath; and the dinner, a classic in Lewis's fiction and children's fiction at large, is too long to quote but stands as an example of the effective reinforcement of meaning by description. The simple, domestic, homey fare echoes the mood and emphasizes the trust Lewis places at the center of his fellowship of animals and men. Edmund significantly trusts the Witch who appears human but is clearly unnatural ("Her face was white—not merely pale, but white like snow or paper or icing sugar, except for her very red mouth" p. 27). The Beavers reveal that she is nonhuman, suggesting that there isn't a drop of real human blood in her (p. 77). Beaver advises "when you meet anything that's going to be Human and isn't yet, or used to be Human once and isn't now, or ought to be Human and isn't, you keep your eyes on it and feel for your hatchet" (p. 78). The robin which Edmund suggests is a false guide, is true to nature and leads the children to safety. Nature is to be trusted, and it is the unnatural distortion of seasons which symbolizes the Witch's desire to destroy humanity. Freezing represents death and cold represents the inhibition of natural joy.

The choice on Edmund's part to defect initiates his journey to the Witch, paralleled by the children's journey into spring, and the ironic reversal of his expectations of a reward. He gets dry, stale bread instead of Turkish Delight, and his "reward" is played off against the Beavers' true meal. Edmund's policy and guile are appropriately rewarded as is the trust the children place in the Beavers.

The mention of Aslan's name, which has such a pronounced effect on all children, initiates the suspense with which Lewis prepares for his later appearance. By using this device, the mysterious effect of a "sacred" name, Lewis produces an aura of meaning around Aslan which is reinforced by the Beavers' explanation of what he is: "'Course he isn't safe. But he's good. He's the King, I tell you" (p. 76). As the antagonist of the Witch, the savior of Narnia, son of the Emperor beyond the sea, the King of the Beasts, he becomes the focus of our anticipation, as he is for the children, and ultimately the ruling symbol of the *Chronicles of Narnia*.

It is not for me to try to explain why Aslan works. An individual reader's reaction to an animal figure endowed with human and symbolic qualities is a very personal thing. Who would try to explain why we feel so drawn to Pooh, Tigger, Piglet, Toad, Mole, or even Badger? The essence of their ultimate appeal very probably springs from that personal response lying beyond the reach of analysis or critical dissection and examination. By the time the children hear Aslan's name, we are comfortably settled in a world of talking animals and a maleficent witch. We simply take it on faith that Aslan's very name has the power to affect the children, and even though we may not feel it, Lewis invites us to associate that feeling with one he knows we have all had.

Perhaps it has sometimes happened to you in a dream that someone says something which you don't understand but in the dream it feels as if it had some enormous meaning—either a terrifying one which turns the whole dream into a nightmare or else a lovely meaning too lovely to put into words, which makes the dream so beautiful that you remember it all your life and are always wishing you could get into the dream again. It was like that now (p. 64).

Thus Aslan becomes the embodiment of longing. He is the satisfaction of all longing, the source of all longing. He is good and terrible, huge, solemn, playful, golden, king, son, sun, beast, god, and father. He is nothing other than Lewis's Joy incarnate in a concrete form. And although Lucy and Susan can clutch at and romp with him on his reappearance, he disappears at the end before the festivities at Cair Paravel.

It is Lewis's craftsmanship in molding Aslan to his purpose more than any sources he may have drawn upon, like the Lion of Judah, which produces this astonishing and compelling centerpiece for the *Chronicles*. We are two thirds of the way through the book before we come face to face, and the extended preparation is justified by the effect of that meeting. Unlike the Witch who appears unannounced and is then described, we find Lewis first describing Aslan's effect and then showing him in fact. This preparation, perhaps symbolizing the *praeparatio evangelicum* which the book witnesses, is carefully keyed to the shifting balance of power reflected in climatic change. Edmund's cold and lonely journey to the Witch's house, his disfiguring of the stone lion, and his "reward" are placed in contrast to the coming of Father Christmas with rewards for trust in the particular form of utilitarian implements such as, sewing machine and sluice gate for the Beavers and sword, dagger, horn, and potion for the children's use in the coming battle.

Frankly, Father Christmas, for all Lewis's attempts at his rehabilitation as a Christian figure, strikes the wrong note, reminding us all too forcefully of childish pleasures and frivolous fantasies. In the freshly created newness of Narnia, he brings us with a shock back to reality, breaking the spell, if only momentarily.[5] It may be our fault as modern readers who associate St. Nicholas with the commercial Santa, but the fact remains that there is a momentary bump even though Lewis makes the occasion rather solemn and the gifts useful.

Lewis's descriptive power is at its height in the noises and sights of spring. Symbolically the turning point, the thematic shift of power from the Witch to Aslan, it is the heart of the book's beauty, and significantly it is Edmund who, tied to the dwarf and driven along, first sees it.

In the wide glades there were primroses. A light breeze sprang up which scattered drops of moisture from the swaying branches and carried cool, delicious scents against the faces of the travellers. The trees began to come fully alive (p. 118).

Then the others feel it, too.

They walked on in silence drinking it all in, passing through patches of warm sunlight into cool, green thickets and out again into wide mossy glades where tall elms raised the leafy roof far overhead, and then into dense masses of flowering currant and among hawthorn bushes where the sweet smell was almost overpowering (pp. 119-120).

Edmund, having experienced the silence of the stone courtyard with its immobilized creatures, is first to hear the change.

A strange, sweet, rustling, chattering noise—and yet not so strange, for he knew he'd heard it before—if only he could remember where! Then all at once he did remember. It was the noise of running water. All round them, though out of sight, there were streams chattering, murmuring, bubbling, splashing and even (in the distance) roaring. And his heart gave a great leap (though he hardly knew why) when he realized that the frost was over (p. 114).

Edmund's rebirth, kindled on the spark of his pity for the stone figures who had recently been celebrating Christmas, moves through the rebirth ritual to his near death and rescue, twice repeated. Aslan saves his soul, Lucy heals his body.

The other children reach Aslan, portrayed as a medieval king in his cloth of gold pavilion and surrounded by his courtiers, in this instance, centaurs, dryads, unicorns, and the like. Battle is joined, Peter winning his knighthood by killing the wolf Maugrim. As we move further in, the conflict takes on deeper and more clearly spiritual significance. This point is a crucial one, for here the message is closest to the surface and most nearly at the center of focus. Often before when Lewis reached his point as in *Out of the Silent Planet* at Meldilorn or the debate of Weston with the Lady and Ransom in *Perelandra* and later the apocalyptic conclusion of *That Hideous Strength*, the message eluded his control and declaiming itself, seized the lead, and the delicate balance of the creative structure wavered. Here, by keeping the theme firmly grounded in the children, who are our link with deeper meaning and our window on inner truth, he keeps the significance of Aslan's action in perspective. It is for Edmund's sake that Aslan suffers, and Edmund, barely deserving such sacrifice, makes Lewis's point absolutely clear. It is Susan's and Lucy's grief we feel, and their joy when Aslan appears transformed. It is the understatement which Lewis achieves here in his picture of sacrifice and redemption which affects us so keenly. The Deeper Magic of mercy triumphs over the Deep Magic of the law of justice. But solemn as the outcome is, it follows explanation with a celestial romp. Lewis thus preserves the special quality of Aslan: playful but solemn.

There are only a few passages in Lewis's fiction such as the creation of Narnia in *The Magician's Nephew* and the apocalypse of *The Last Battle*, which equal the organic sanctity of meaning of the chapter titled "Deeper Magic from before the Dawn of Time." By organic sanctity of meaning, I refer to the fusion of meaning with structure which makes the implicit deeper significance an inescapable reality in the experience of reading such passages. The form and meaning are so organically fused that our inhibitions are dispelled and the clamor for rational proof by the intellect totally quieted. The meaning sanctifies the form and the form the meaning, lifting the whole experience beyond pleasing instruction to belief. It is here that Lewis achieves the enviable result of making the reader feel the Joy, the sublimely indefinable exaltation of the spirit, which he sought throughout his life.

From Aslan's transformation to the end, the tension is released, and we move back gradually to the bare room with the wardrobe. The Witch's death, now a foregone expectation, is followed by the release of the captives, containing one of Lewis's finest descriptive touches, the description of the stone lion's release. "Then a tiny streak of gold began to run along his white marble back—then it spread—then the colour seemed to lick all over him as the flame licks all over a bit of paper—then, while his hindquarters were still obviously stone the lion shook his mane and all the heavy, stony folds rippled into living hair" (p. 165). We meet the giant Rumble-buffin, one of Lewis's more original creations, a giant with character, and we see the children safely enthroned. The anticlimax lets us gently back to earth and leaves us with the expectation of further adventures.

PRINCE CASPIAN: THE RETURN TO NARNIA
1951

After the abortive attempt to give Lancelyn Green the origin of the lamp-post and the history of events preceding *The Lion, the Witch and the Wardrobe* which produced the Lefay fragment, Lewis turned back to the Pevensies and sent them back to Narnia, called by Susan's horn. It was the idea of the horn summoning the children back which started Lewis on the sequel and gave the book its early titles *Drawn into Narnia* and *A Horn in Narnia*.

Though we are dealing with the same four children and a journey to the same world of Narnia, hundreds of years after the first adventure, only a year in our time, the structure of the book and the thematic interests are quite different from those of *The Lion, the Witch and the Wardrobe*. There are no preliminaries before we are dragged bodily into Narnia along with the Pevensies, yanked into the other world off the railway platform. The first half of the book is much slower in pace than *The Lion, the Witch and the Wardrobe*. There is a certain ingenuity in Lewis's presentation of the slow realization by the children that they have returned, and that aids in acclimatizing both the children and the reader, who may be unfamiliar with the early story. The focus of attention is not, however, on the world they reenter but on what they are to do, which remains a mystery for the first seven chapters.

There is, in fact, little suspense while we listen to the recounting of the history of Prince Caspian, his wicked uncle Miraz, who acts as a representative of grown-up rationality and tyrannical policy, and Caspian's tutor Cornelius, who plays Merlin to Caspian's Arthur. This section of the book suggests a medieval romance framework with emphasis placed upon dynastic palace intrigue, usurpation, the flight of the rightful heir, the magic horn to be winded only in greatest need, and the wild ride into a kingdom where loyal followers await the true prince's call to arms. We have already been prepared for high and noble exploits by the children's discovery of the treasure room, the recovery of their "gifts," and the returning sense of obligation which kingship has laid upon them. Peter advises Susan to cheer up and grow up because in Narnia, she is a Queen (p. 21). At this point Lewis introduces us to the Old Narnians: Trufflehunter, "I'm a beast, I am, and a Badger what's more. We don't change. We hold on"; Trumpkin, "Whistles and whirligigs!"; Nikabrik, who is the Black Devil and counterpart of Miraz in Old Narnia; and the three Bulgy Bears, Pattertwig the squirrel, Glenstorm the Centaur, Giant Wimbleweather, and Reepicheep, who will show both the gravity and humor of courtly life and be a more significant character in the next novel.

Though there are amusing moments and some lively description of characters and a few arresting depictions of scene, such as the dance of the fauns at the end of Chapter 6, the movement is slow and sometimes tedious. Lewis presents us with two worlds. The first is the Narnia we know through the children's recollection and our knowledge of *The Lion, the Witch and the Wardrobe*. This idyllic world, freed from the tyranny of the Witch, was one where the principle of *hnau*, drawn from *Out of the Silent Planet*, operates. Men and beasts are unified in a rational fellowship, all subjects of Aslan, guided under the headship of King Peter, the High King. There is a hierarchy, a Great Chain of Being, reflecting the order of the celestial

Great Dance, and we see a fantasy world which is a microcosm of the great world of paradisal reality, or at least a reflection of it. Pagan and Christian elements mingle, as do men and beasts, in a world where mercy has triumphed over the claims of Mosaic justice and pagan blood-sacrifice. We see a fantasy Golden Age.

The other world, symbolized by Miraz and Nikabrik, is the modern, corrupted descendant of the Golden Narnia; it is a world of rationality, apostasy, tyranny, pessimism, and fear. The Telmarines we find are pirates who have unwittingly stumbled into and corrupted Narnia. But they are not alone in their destructive effect. The power of the Witch (you can always call a witch back, says the hag [p. 165]) abets the apparently natural pessimism and cynicism of the Black Dwarfs, whose disbelief we see again in *The Last Battle*, and brings degradation even within the remnant of Old Narnia to which Caspian flees. Lewis seems to see in Miraz all the adult, no-nonsense, unimaginative rationality which his fairy tales, at least on one level, represent a protest against. Miraz's disbelief in magic, in history, and his fear of water and woods, the two aspects of nature endowed with almost magical significance by Lewis, reveal him as the titular villain: Captain Hook, the authority figure who would spoil all daydreams and who is underneath the bluster rather comic, as Miraz is when he accepts Peter's challenge. A more serious and less comic menace is Nikabrik, cold and hard, a hater of humans and half dwarfs, a pragmatic rationalist, a racist and a traitor to the Tao; he is in fact immoral where Miraz is not; Nikabrik betrays his better instincts.

The story centers on the theme of belief. Each major character either accepts the truth, tests and accepts it, or rejects it without test. The Pevensies are not convinced they are in Cair Paravel until they find their "gifts." Trumpkin, a skeptic but not an apostate like Nikabrik, must be shown that Edmund and Susan are King and Queen by competitive feats of arms, an amusing trial which clearly reveals Lewis's theme—"we're awfully fond of children and all that, but just at the moment, in the middle of a war—but I'm sure you understand" (p. 97). Miraz and Nikabrik learn through death where reality lies. The recalcitrant lords of Telmarine are left on this side of the door, like *The Last Battle* dwarfs huddled in the stable, unwilling to test the truth.

It is the test of faith in Aslan which forms the basic and central theme of the book since it is Aslan who comes across the sea to put all things right. Once more, Lucy is the focal point of this test of belief. It is Lucy who senses the movement of the tree spirits and who calls them to life, and later it is to Lucy that Aslan appears. In scenes parallel to those on the same theme early in *The Lion, the*

Witch and the Wardrobe, Lucy attempts to bring the others to her faith. She is supported by Edmund and democratically vetoed by the others for various reasons: Trumpkin out of ignorance, Susan from sloth, Peter from pride or expedience. Here Lewis reveals his disgust with the application of political principles to personal belief. You cannot legislate either faith or obedience. All the characters fail the test and are led on a pointless and symbolically exhausting rocky descent and ascent. Lucy, chastised by Aslan, realizes that belief must be seconded by obedience and thus the corollary theme appears, as it did in *The Lion, the Witch and the Wardrobe.* The emphasis here is on individual belief and obedience. As the four follow Lucy and Aslan through the night, they see him gradually materialize as their growing belief permits his revelation.

This relatively brief section of the book (pp. 121-150) is the thematic and structural center, the only portion of the book containing that organic sanctity of meaning which we see pervades *The Lion, the Witch and the Wardrobe.* Here rather than history or chivalric battles or rites of celebration, we have the children again acting as our window on the world of eternal truths. If you believe unquestioningly—"'Oh, don't be so stupid,' said Lucy. 'Do you think I don't know Aslan when I see him?'" (p. 122), then you obey unquestioningly. The result of blind obedience to false gods for Miraz, pride; for Nikabrik, self interest is death.

Lewis's descriptions in this central section shine with some of the same luminous quality we find in *The Lion, the Witch and the Wardrobe.* Whether this should be attributed to the numinous quality of his subject matter or to the elevation of the theme remains a question of individual response, but undeniably they have the same quality and effect felt in Aslan's appearance in the earlier book. Lucy's first taste of the Old Narnia comes with associations of light, odor, and sound.

It was cool and fresh; delicious smells were floating everywhere. Somewhere close by she heard the twitter of a nightingale beginning to sing, then stopping, then beginning again. It was a little lighter ahead. She went towards the light and came to a place where there were fewer trees, and whole patches or pools of moonlight,... (p. 111).

Later she joins the dancing trees and enters the charmed circle to meet Aslan. Then, accepting their obedience, Aslan roars, commanding the reawakening of nature, and a great romp begins.

Pale birch-girls were tossing their heads, willow-women pushed back their hair from their brooding faces to gaze on Aslan, the queenly beeches stood still and adored him, shaggy oakmen, lean and melancholy elms, shock-headed hollies (dark themselves, but their wives all bright with berries) and gay rowans, all bowed and rose again, shouting, "Aslan, Aslan!" in their various husky or creaking or wave-like voices (pp. 151-152).

With the arrival of Bacchus and Silenus, the ecstatic moments drop back into a pageantry which will characterize the conclusion of the book. In quick succession comes the victory over Nikabrik and his Hag and Were Wolf, symbolizing hatred, hunger, and thirst, the "practical" powers he prefers to Aslan. The challenge and single combat bring victory to Old Narnia, and the trees take a vengeance not unlike that of Fangorn in *The Lord of the Rings* though not so vicious. The story ends with a prolonged romp highlighted by the liberation of the young school mistress and the old nurse and the proper punishment of Miss Prizzle and the dumpy and prim little girls with fat legs. Reepicheep steals the show with his deathbed revival and his demand for a tail, and the book ends happily if a bit frivolously. Susan and Peter, grown too old, pass beyond Narnia; Edmund and Lucy will return to help Caspian find the seven lost lords in *The Voyage of the 'Dawn Treader.'*

In theme and structure this work follows the pattern which appears in the first story. The children give us our viewpoint on events, and Aslan's appearance is the focus of anticipation and the high point of our imaginative response. The journey, trial of faith, and test of obedience all reappear, and faith justifies the happy outcome, won by strength founded on trust in Aslan. We are introduced to a host of interesting characters, some highly imaginative creations like Reepicheep and Trumpkin, but on the whole the book fails to measure up to the pleasure we feel in reading *The Lion, the Witch and the Wardrobe.*

In addition to the pervasive theme of faith and obedience, we are given related but less pertinent and universal ideas to contemplate. Lewis seems to have been deflected from the theme of the incarnation of Joy which controls our response in *The Lion, the Witch and the Wardrobe*, to a host of lesser themes which are neither as engrossing nor as stimulating. Though Lewis brings medieval chivalry and high romance to Narnia with court intrigues and knightly combat, the struggle of adult skepticism and pessimism, the lost faith that leads to false idols simply do not stir us in the way Aslan's epic encounter with the Witch does. Neither the risks nor the triumphs are as great, and we leave the work feeling a bit let down, rather like Lucy, having called the trees into life and then feeling "that she had just missed something: as if she had spoken to the trees a split second too soon or a split second too late, or used all the right words except one; or put in one word that was just wrong" (p. 113).

Structurally the book suffers from the apparent division of purpose which the themes reflect. Though the children are drawn to Narnia to assist Caspian in gaining his throne, the first third of the book laboriously recounts past history. The adventure theme of the book, the surface plots, suggest that our interest will rest in Caspian's attempts to overthrow the power of Miraz, returning Narnia to its true nature, dethroning pragmatic rationalism and replacing simple faith in natural reason, the *hnau* quality Ransom admired on Malacandra. But Caspian is a pawn in Aslan's paws, and the plot descends from the promise of a deeply imaged mid-section to the anticipated battles and celebrations which alternate with disturbing regularity throughout the last anticlimactic third of the book. The emphasis is unevenly divided between the children's reunion with Aslan and their trial by faith, and the adventures which they have been called in to Narnia to pursue. Our loyalties as readers are thus divided between the expectation of another numinous book like *The Lion, the Witch and the Wardrobe*, and a children's chivalric romance. Tolkien faces a similar problem in *The Two Towers*, and only by the organic incorporation of Rohan and Gondor within the larger scope of the action does he succeed in keeping the chivalry in check under the master theme. Of Lewis's achievement here, we can say that the book is an interesting episode in the *Chronicles*, just as the orientalism of *The Horse and His Boy* is a curious highlight showing another side of Narnia and a new approach by Lewis. But we are not left feeling that either book gives us the essential Narnia found in *The Lion, the Witch and the Wardrobe*, *The Magician's Nephew*, and *The Last Battle*.

Having noted how the book fails to meet my demanding expectation, it is only fair to point to the very fine features which it does offer. Lewis has many reasons for limiting the number of characters when he introduces Narnia; and as it is, there are a great many who appear in *The Lion, the Witch and the Wardrobe*, but few are drawn with the care he lavishes on Trumpkin and Reepicheep. They reappear later, but their basic qualities are developed here. Reepicheep is his masterpiece in this book. A more unlikely figure would be hard to imagine as the representative of dauntless courage. Were he anything larger than an overgrown mouse, he would be insufferably pompous, and were he portrayed less skillfully, he would be ludicrous or insipid. As it is, Lewis hits that happy balance between humor and awe which is reflected even in Aslan's capitulation over the renewal of the tail.

It is around Reepicheep and Trumpkin that the humor, which is more strongly felt in this book than in *The Lion, the Witch and the Wardrobe*, circles to puncture the solemnity of the various ceremonial occasions which we witness. Trumpkin, the unbeliever, is shaken till his teeth rattle, the final proof of Aslan's reality. Reepicheep does not quail even before his hereditary adversary and overlord; his name hints of mouse "squeeks" as well as "cheek."

Humor and good feeling take many other forms in a book where evil hardly has a foothold. Miraz and Nikabrik talk an evil line, but they are essentially empty and easily toppled. Lewis must have loved bears. His brother wrote after a trip to Whipsnade Zoo that Lewis intended to introduce a bear into the family menagerie a the Kilns and name him Bultitude. The Bulgy Bears remind us of Bultitude and the old hross at Meldilorn. They represent all the sleepy, comfortable virtue of an uncomplicated existence, hibernating and sucking honey from their paws even as marshals in the list. The romps which counteract the heat of Peter's battle, though somewhat stagey with the appearance of Bacchus and Silenus, have the effect they were evidently intended to have, signaling the new reign of the Old Narnia—a Narnia that would belong to the Talking Beasts and the Dwarfs and Dryads and Fauns and other creatures quite as much as to men. The imagination and fancy are reenthroned as the Pevensies end another adventure.

THE VOYAGE OF THE 'DAWN TREADER'
1952

Finished by February 1950, *The Voyage of the 'Dawn Treader'* came from Lewis's pen needing hardly any revision or correction.[1] The seamless, uninterrupted flow of this book reinforces the biographers' analysis of its composition and reflects the union of theme and form which signals Lewis's subjection of his material to his purpose. After the faltering of the Lefay fragment and the somewhat uneven jumble of possibilities present in *Prince Caspian*, Lewis came in *The Voyage of the 'Dawn Treader'* to the simplest and perhaps most effective plot structure he would ever employ. His intention seems from the beginning to have centered on sending Caspian and the two children on a journey of adventure, which as the story developed came to represent their penetration into the heart of Aslan's mystery by their arrival at the frontier between life and physical death. Thus the physical adventure becomes a spiritual quest which ends in revelation.

The plot line is simple and straightforward. The journey, fore-shadowed in *Prince Caspian* by the history of Miraz's disposal of the seven lords in the original quest, fulfills Aslan's promise that Lucy and Edmund would return. The method of return, a unique one "through the picture" into Narnia, brings Eustace Scrubb along as the disagreeable skeptic; the modern and progressive child, kin to the dumpy little girls with fat legs in Miss Prizzle's class; and the vicious children at Eustace's and Jill Pole's school later in *The Silver Chair*. Eustace acts also as a foil to the adult pride, egotism, and apostacy seen in Miraz and Nikabrik, for this story is child-oriented. Even Caspian is young, only three Narnian years older than in his first appearance, and the spirit of the book is that of the limitless expectation of possible adventure which subtly catches our belief and lends credibility to our increasingly exotic experiences of dragons, sea serpents, Midas pools, fallen and retired stars, and lands where nightmare and heart's desire come true. Age is repre-sented by Coriakin and Ramandu, whose great antiquity places them apart in authority and experience, but there is little threat that they will step in to spoil the fun. It is ironically Eustace, made old before he is young, who must grow young by symbolically sloughing his skin and bathing, which represent his rebirth to wonder as well as to goodness. In this sense, Ramandu acts as Eustace's foil.

Thus almost no time is wasted in beginning the journey or in the physical return from the end of the world. Our attention is focused on a series of adventures that lead us steadily in and up. The image is descriptive of both our physical and emotional reaction to the journey. We move steadily eastward, past the last habitation of man into the unknown and uncharted seas, arriving finally at the great wave which represents, among other things, death and the end of time. Symbolically the journey stands for many possibilities. It represents for all on board the journey which tests man's courage and bravery, and Caspian's speech to his men on Ramandu's island reminds us forcefully of Henry V's to his men at the battle of Agin-court. It is, on another level, a journey of mercy, bringing the lost lords home, returning order to the kingdom, saving the hopeless and befuddled, setting things to rights. For individuals on board it permits the fulfillment of their greatest desire; for Reepicheep, to pass to the uttermost East; for Caspian, to fulfill the quest he promised to Aslan; and for others like Eustace, it brings unwanted but necessary change, a blessing undesired but gratefully accepted. For Lucy it brings the story that forever is desired, symbolizing both joy and the beatific vision. For Edmund and Lucy it brings the knowledge of salvation and points out for them a road through the real world as their true path.

On the deeper levels, the journey is the quest for holiness, the penetration into the mystery of the lamb and lion, mercy and justice, meekness and power. The way is beset with fears and some tests of courage, but the movement is inexorable. Here Lewis has shown the brilliance of his choice of a sea journey. Beyond a point there is no return, and the very elements combine to compel the ship on to the ultimate East.

The movement upward in the book is one of emotional and perhaps spiritual elevation which provides us with a fine example of Lewis's theory of the compulsion toward deeper understanding developed through highly imaginative literature. We are drawn along with the ship, not resisting as forcefully as Eustace, whom we begin by despising, but resisting the pull of the inevitable immersion in glory, the drinkable light, which envelopes the end of the book.

The journey begins with understatement. Lucy and Edmund, chafing under the hostile environment of Aunt Alberta's home and rather pitying themselves on being "left behind" are ripe for an escape. Susan is already turning away from Aslan and is losing our sympathy. She is no good at school and very old for her age. Their escape is clearly that of the prisoner, not just a wish-fulfillment.[2] Of the seven books, *The Lion, the Witch and the Wardrobe*, *Prince Caspian*, and *The Last Battle* represent variations of this motif. The children's longing helps to bring the picture to life: first movement, then wind, then the briny smell, the pause on the frame, and then the plunge. It might almost be seen as an outline for the achievement of a mystical experience. They literally fall into their adventure, *in medias res*, and the paralleling of their gusto with Eustace's seasickness provides a fine irony which Lewis preserves unabated until Eustace's conversion.

The events of the first five chapters are admittedly preparatory. Aslan does not appear, and the action centers on Caspian's assumption of power, his proof of his kingly authority, with the help of Lord Bern, and the conquest of earthly evil: Pug, the pirate slaver, enslaving men's bodies; Gumpas, the slothful and self-seeking governor, a slave to greed. There are some fine ringing lines given to Caspian. "'Have you no idea of progress, of development?'" says Gumpas. "'I have seen them both in an egg,'" said Caspian "'We call it *Going bad* in Narnia'" (pp. 47-48). Lewis now seems more comfortable with the dialogue and the children's speech. He shows considerable cleverness in the colloquial speeches of Pug and his thugs and later in the Chief Voice among the Dufflepuds. Eustace's diary acts as an ironic commentary on the action, especially during the storm, though Lewis becomes a bit disingenuous in his portrayal of the water butt confrontation of Eustace and Reepicheep.

On the whole, the first five chapters are literally and figuratively the calm before the storm. With the last inhabited island passed, the *Dawn Treader* begins the quest in earnest. How Lewis hit on the transformation of Eustace, the metamorphosis into a dragon, as the first incident in this part of the journey, we can only wonder, but there is no question of its absolute appropriateness, and that of Pauline Baynes' picture of the weeping Eustace. It is a comic but pointed version of Kafka's *Metamorphosis* more akin to Apuleius than Ovid. The point is clear; however, Eustace's punishment, like that of a soul in the shadowy city of *The Great Divorce*, is to have his faults become externally manifest like the red lizard on the man's shoulder or the dwarf with his Tragedian. Set in the first of many impressionistic and symbolic landscapes, the comic account of Eustace's dawning realization that the claws and fire are his own, blunts our self-righteous "that's only what he deserves," attitude and prepares the way for his conversion. Aslan's appearance is related to us through Edmund, appropriately enough since Edmund understands better than the rest because he was, as he says a traitor, Eustace only an ass.

One of the unifying features of these episodes which furnish the journey with action is that in each instance there is a conversion of some sort taking place; some spiritual process is involved which underscores the pervasive journey or quest theme. Eustace's conversion begins when he recognizes his need for others; he feels lonely, perched high above the activity he has scorned and sought to escape. But greed and dragonish thoughts prevail, and the transformation is complete. The descriptions of the dying dragon, baffling and disarming our expectations of Eustace's probable fate, are perfect, especially when seen through an imagination fed on exports, imports, and drains. It is the very untypical action of the dragon in fact and later of Eustace as a dragon that makes both portraits so arresting. Eustace's rehabilitation strikes the right note, too, presented as it is almost as if it were a dream. There is the poignance both of Eustace's feeble attempts at change and the heartfelt hurt which brings the new soul from its hardened shell. As Lewis says, the cure had begun.

One of Lewis's great strengths here and throughout the spiritually charged remainder of the book is that he neither overstates his case nor makes anything too explicit. Too many analyses of Eustace's conversion spend time drawing parallels from other works by Lewis or other Christian writers, finding sources, and explicating symbolic meaning when the richness of the episode rests on its suggestiveness and not directly on its explicit message. The moral clearly does not require or invite elucidation, but the creative imagination has given us a feast of possibilities, touched with gentle humor.

Chapter 8 is an interlude. No sea voyage into the unknown would be complete without the Great Sea Serpent, here a rather mindless worm bent on wholesale destruction. The encounter gives Reepicheep and Eustace an opportunity for valor and praise and does not require Aslan's appearance. Deathwater Island's Midas curse affords a temptation of a serious nature. The escape is from the lust for gold which strikes at least Caspian and Edmund before Aslan can restore their perspective and then erase the memory altogether. Lewis's achievement lies in the ironic contrast of the innocent appeal of the pool and the death that lurks in its very touch.

Chapters 9 through 11 bring Lucy to the foreground. She is now firmly established as Lewis's favorite, for he gives her the gravest task, a most serious test by temptation of a mature kind—vanity and self-love. She proves herself charmingly capable and wins through to a secure place in Aslan's promised country. This description makes the encounter with the Dufflepuds seem a very serious business indeed; whereas, the reality is quite comic. But only the reader realizes that Lewis wishes to test the children's credulity; the children themselves remain blissfully ignorant. Confronted by Silence, which always looms in Lewis's imaginative use of it as a menacing vacuum into which the celestial music of the Great Dance has not penetrated, cf., the "Silent" Planet, the Grey City of *The Great Divorce*, the Dark Island, and Charn, the children waver. Silence envelops them as they move across the apparently deserted beach and persists even into the house. It is the absolute quiet of the long hall and the wizard's room that daunts Lucy as much as the task of finding and performing the spell.

We know the moment the Chief voice speaks and the other voices agree that we are in for some fun. The island is a proving ground for the Dufflepuds, moving from common dwarfs up to manhood, body is becoming soul, ignorance is moving toward wisdom. For Coriakin it is a purgatory where the patience and obedience he lacked as a star are tested and strengthened. For Lucy it is a test of courage and loyalty to her companions and to Aslan and Joy. Because Lewis has already made us love her simple, generous soul, the test is poignant but not sentimental. She is nearing the crisis of adolescence which Susan has passed into, and her temptations are appropriate to her age. With Aslan's help, she resists vanity but succumbs to self-admiration and the desire that her friends should like her. The spell for "refreshment of the spirit," the unrepeatable experience which Lewis repeatedly tries to capture in his fiction, brings her to the end of her test, and chastened by Aslan, she finds explanations in her conversation with Coriakin. The episode subsides into a romp. For all the joviality here, it is clear that Lewis intends us to understand the moral responsibility which those placed in positions of authority over others must exercise. Coriakin's relationship to the Dufflepuds is analogous with Aslan's to Narnia, of Caspian's to his subjects, of the wise to the foolish.

The humor of this interlude is sharply contrasted with the pall of darkness which confronts the *Dawn Treader* in Chapter 12. The irrational fear of the unknown, the unleashed nightmares which countermand Reepicheep's insistence on adventure at all costs, culminate in an agony of pure fear from which only the heaven-sent albatross can guide the ship. This description of stark fear is almost unique in Lewis's fiction. Usually he resorts to the feelings of characters to convey qualities of fear or despair, cf., Ransom facing the task of destroying Un-man or the encounter with him in the fiery cave, but here we have the palpable thing.

Except for the creak of the rowlocks and the splash of the oars there was nothing to show that they were moving at all. Edmund, peering from the bows, could see nothing except the reflection of the lantern in the water before him. It looked a greasy sort of reflection, and the ripple made by their advancing prow appeared to be heavy, small and lifeless. As time went on everyone except the rowers began to shiver with cold (p. 154).

The test is one of courage, and it is Reepicheep who shames the rest into accepting the challenge. He implies that a refusal to accept an offered adventure, of any kind, is an impeachment of their honor.

Chapters 13 and 14 bring us to the enchanted table at the beginning of the end of the world. Though this section is both interlude and prelude, it strikes the solemn and mysterious tone that will prevail to the very end of the book. It is to Lewis's great credit that he can sustain the mounting tension and unworldliness of these concluding four chapters. Throughout the book, the journey has moved inexorably in this direction, and by slow degrees Lewis has prepared us for the approach to the uttermost East, the holiness at the end of the quest. The magician Ramandu, a star retiring back into starhood, parallels the regenerative roles of Aslan and Coriakin. The mysteriously replenished table with its sacramental overtones and magic sleepers, deepens the mystery.

But the old man came on without speaking to the travellers and stood on the other side of the table opposite to his daughter. Then both of them held up their arms before them and turned to face east. In that position they began to sing.... it was high, almost shrill, but very beautiful.... And as they sang, the grey clouds lifted from the eastern sky and the white patches grew bigger and bigger till it was all white, and the sea began to shine like silver (pp. 176-177).

Like Aslan's song in *The Magician's Nephew* creating Narnia, Ramandu's weaves a spell which engulfs the children and the reader. From this point, we are drawn with increasing rapidity toward the end; the action is centered not in the search, but rather in the irrepressible attraction of the sought after. The dialogue becomes, along with the description, stately and solemn, and we begin to acknowledge the old spell of high seriousness and deep meaning which characterizes the climax of *The Lion, the Witch and the Wardrobe*. Lewis allows nothing to intrude to break the spell. We travel on an enchanted sea where sea kings ride to the sea hound and where the quality of light is that first felt by Ransom when he entered Deep Heaven in *Out of the Silent Planet*. I cannot really capture the essence of the last two chapters by judicious quotation. It is so seamless and superb in its movement that I can only say, read it and feel it, if you question that Lewis can move our deepest imagination by his creative originality. For the voyagers, each day brings an increase in brilliance, and the tension mounts as we near the end. Much of Lewis's success depends upon his appeal to our sense perceptions. What appears to be a white wall, mysterious, hard and impenetrable, becomes a sea of water lilies. Sailing beyond the point where Caspian halts because he is unprepared for the ultimate voyage, the children and Reepicheep reach the wall, the wave separating them from Aslan's country. They come to the final wall: "It looked as if the sky came down to meet the grass in front of them. But as they went on they got the strangest impression that here at last the sky did really come down and join the earth—a blue wall, very bright, but real and solid, more like glass than anything else" (p. 214).

One false step, one lurch into sentiment, and the whole aura would have collapsed, and Lewis nearly took that step. The Lamb-Lion was a daring exposure of this theme, and perhaps for some readers it does break the spell. For most, however, it has always been a possibility if not an expectation.

If one paragraph comes close to capturing the mood of the conclusion it is this one:

After that for many days, without the wind in her shrouds or foam at her bows, across a waveless sea, the *Dawn Treader* glided smoothly east. Every day and every hour the light became more brilliant and still they could bear it. No one ate or slept and no one wanted to, but they drew buckets of dazzling water from the sea, stronger than wine and somehow wetter, more liquid, than ordinary water, and pledged one another silently in deep draughts of it. And one or two of the sailors who had been oldish men when the voyage began now grew younger every day. Everyone on board was filled with joy and excitement, but not an excitement that made one talk. The further they sailed the less they spoke, and then almost in a whisper. The stillness of that last sea laid hold on them (pp. 203-204).

The near poetic invocation of Joy, the incarnation of nature, and the idyllic serenity of this journey to the "very end of the world" are reflected in Lewis's lucid and evocative prose. When elaborate phrasing and verbal ornaments might be used to heighten the effect, Lewis uses the simple and direct. The hush of Joy, the quality of light and air, are described as a child would experience them, uncomplicated by sophisticated distinctions and evaluations. It is a tribute to Lewis's mastery of prose that he can make the last chapter moving without making it mawkish and pathetic.

Scenes like this one display Lewis's mastery of narrative and descriptive techniques and serve to reinforce my suggestion that his style is essentially a rational rather than an emotive presentation of fantasy. Lewis's fantasy is always firmly anchored in Christian principles and in the artistic control of his material. It is the rationalist's control of his material coupled with the traditionalist's beliefs that keep the most dramatic scene from toppling either into moralizing or sentimentalized anticlimax. Lewis is perilously close. Here the climax is the last moment of the book, and the children are balked at the wall, turned back from Joy, forced to give up fantasy for more mature belief. "... you must begin to come close to your own world now.... This was the very reason why you were brought to Narnia, that by knowing me here for a little, you may know me better there" (p. 216). But the baptism of their imaginations, signified in Eustace's conversion, will lead them all to a spiritual maturity beyond this last childhood adventure. Eustace, a relative latecomer, will be given one more trip to act as Virgil to Jill Pole's Dante.

Lewis's achievement here is of a very high order. The adventure of discovery and the quest for the seven lords gradually merge with the quest for Joy, and so skillfully has Lewis developed the movement of the plot that, with the exception of the sea serpent episode and perhaps the Deathwater Island adventure, the sea voyage moves unwaveringly toward this ultimate goal. There is no discordant diversity of episode and meaning, no particularly expository or discursive section, as in *Perelandra* or *Prince Caspian*. We forget, in fact, that we are in another and foreign world, so homey has Lewis made us feel, and the watchful dragons are asleep as we glide past them into the safe haven of heart's desire come true, the striking reverse of the Dark Island.

This book, certainly the last portion of it, epitomizes Lewis's definition of a "good" book as one which ideally permits, invites, or compels what he calls good reading. We can safely say that a good reading of a fairy tale is one which enlarges our being, as Lewis says, to our "everlasting benefit." The enlargement and the self-transcendence have one ultimate goal, and there is no serious doubt by "good" readers that we attain that goal at the end of this story. There may be other of Lewis's works of fiction which convey deeper or weightier matters, but there are none which convey his meaning in a more superbly suitable form and with as much ease and gracefulness.

THE HORSE AND HIS BOY 1954

This book, written fourth but published fifth and generally read sixth in the *The Chronicles of Narnia*, reveals its history in its variant titles. Read on June 26, 1950, by Green under the title *Narnia and the North*, referred to as *To Narnia and the North*, it was later to have as suggested titles: *The Horse and the Boy, The Desert Road to Narnia, Cor of Archenland, The Horse Stole the Boy, Over the Border, The Horse Bree* (these latter seven were Lewis's suggestions to his publisher Bles) and finally with Bles's suggested revision, *The Horse and His Boy*.[1]

It is not at all clear why Lewis elected to publish this novel after *The Silver Chair*. Perhaps he wanted the continuity of Eustace's reappearance and the historical continuity of Rilian's position in Narnian dynastic descent. The various titles reveal the emphasis on horses, even Lewis's playful remark about the title *The Horse and the Boy*, indicating that the title might attract the "ponybook" reader, suggests that the direction of this book might be somewhat different from what had come before.[2] That in fact is the case. Of the seven books, this one has the least connection with the others in terms of theme, characters, and plot. Though not totally divorced from the others, it is unique because of its lack of obvious relation to the rest.

The main characters, despite the title, are children, but they are otherworldly, Narnian and Calormen children, not earth children on a journey of adventure in Narnia; and this is the only book in which Lewis gives his earth children a rest from Narnia. The journey is from south to north rather than west to east as before, and it is an escape rather than a search, though it results in discovery at the end. Aslan appears but more as a symbol than a personality. The predominant theme is courage in the face of adversity, but the quest for Joy is suppressed and interest centers upon more mundane and frivolous matters attendant upon an extended flight to safety. The prevailing tone is that of a rather flat description of the adventures of a boy and girl in the Arabianesque court of the Tisroc, "may he live forever," and Lewis relies more heavily than ever on dialogue, horse and human, to move the plot along. His interest in a sort of exotic Orientalism is most pronounced in this book, though it comes to the surface again in *The Last Battle*. Here it colors the tone and atmosphere, drawing attention away from Narnia and providing a contrast to the previous books with its descriptions of the paynim luxury of the Tisroc and his court. There is an increased reliance on humor and irony which replace the imaginative elevation of *The Voyage of the 'Dawn Treader,'* and the book gives the uneasy feeling, when read in this order, of a falling off in creative force.

We might be tempted to assume one or two possible reasons for Lewis's choice of this type of story. He was perhaps tired of the formula of bringing children into Narnia and thought a change would be salutary for him and his readers. He may have thought that it was time to internalize the fiction in Narnia, giving the history and character of Calormen and Archenland. He may have been indulging his acknowledged delight in talking animals and Oriental splendor. Or he may have wanted to show that the trials and tests of obedience, understanding, courage, and loyalty which earth children had undergone, could be developed with just as much force in Narnian characters. What he is saying is not radically different from what is expressed in the three preceding novels, but the form is different and the effect is less potent.

The plot in this book is a double-stranded one, closer in structure to *The Lion, the Witch and the Wardrobe* than any other early *Chronicle* story. The adventures of Shasta and Aravis cross and mingle with those of Susan and Edmund. The Shasta-Aravis plot predominates, and there is not much parallelism between the plots, but the introduction of the Narnians in Tashban serves as a convenient device for complicating and slowing the main action and permits the introduction of Corin, Shasta's double, and the romantic medieval theme of chivalry and battle with its attendant courtly dialogue and pageantry, allowing the action to move beyond the scope of the children's escape and up to higher matters. As we see in earlier stories, it is Lewis's method to embed the central adventure of the children in a larger context in order to sharpen our perspective on the children's actions, to add scope to the work, and by placing the children within the larger world they inhabit to diminish their role in the face of larger meanings. Lewis never lets the microcosm of his children's world dominate the macrocosm of Narnia or Aslan's country.

I call this plot a Cinderella plot. The children, Shasta and Aravis, both motherless and suffering under the yoke of tyrannous authority, escape under the aegis of talking horses rather than a fairy godmother. Mistaken for a prince, Shasta is at last confirmed in royalty and becomes the king. After the trials, both physical and spiritual, the children are rewarded and live happily ever after. By choosing children of opposite sexes, social scales, and races, Lewis sets up occasions for innumerable parallels and ironic contrasts which embellish the plot. Shasta, uneducated and untested, presents a complete contrast to the authoritarian equestrienne Tarkhenna, Aravis, at their first meeting. Her pride and self-satisfaction make a nice contrast to his steady and commonsense good nature and courage. To add texture, Lewis makes Shasta a slave escaping to freedom, and Aravis must pretend that she is a slave to Lasaraleen, who with her frivolous round of clothes and parties and gossip is all Lewis abhors in young women. We might remember Susan's "maturity." A further irony appears in the two horses whose roles reverse those of their human beings. Bree, the war horse, is boastful and commanding, but underneath a coward when it comes to lions, and it is Shasta who alone "saves" Aravis. Hwin, the demure and self-effacing mare, has the common sense and courage to urge them on when delay might mean the fall of Anvard. Her good sense puts into ironic contrast the impetuosity of Aravis.

The movement of the plot follows a straight line, from the escape, Chapters 1-3, through the mid-section centered upon the complications in Tashban, Chapters 4-8, and concluding with the desert flight and the battle, Chapters 9-13, and with the anticlimactic resolution of Chapters 14 and 15. The altered direction of the journey from south to north, rather than the traditional west to east of the earlier books, may merely be a geographical fact. We may be intended, however, to see some symbolic significance in the direction. The north is Narnia, country of true faith, land of free and of talking animals, home of blue-eyed, blond-haired, open, friendly, and generous men and proud but gentle ladies. Calormen and Tashban represent by contrast, the dark, sinister, decadent, specious, groveling, infidel-worshiping slavers, whose glozing language Lewis delights in parodying, one suspects for more than just the effect. The movement from evil to good here is placed, by the time frame of Peter's reign as High King, within the action of *The Lion, the Witch and the Wardrobe* and, with the conquest of the White Witch, evil is externalized in the threat of invasion from the South. Peter is away fighting Giants on the northern border, so Lewis gives us a kingdom besieged by enemies in contrast to the peace of *The Lion, the Witch and the Wardrobe* conclusion. I suspect however that the choice of Calormen as the adversary here has more to do with Lewis's own delight and interest in creating Calormen, the Tisroc, and Tashban than it does with his wish to give us a symbolic picture of the medieval infidel at war with the true believer or of the symbolic south of *The Pilgrim's Regress* with his old passion for northernness, though the influence of these factors can not be discounted. It is the lack of seriousness characterizing the whole book which gives us a sense of his thematic disengagement as much as any single scene such as the Tisroc's interview with Rabadash or Rabadash's transformation. We have only to compare our reactions here to those in *The Last Battle* when Rishda meets his fate and the later treatment of Emeth, in order to judge the range of Lewis's use of Calormen in the *Chronicles*.

The meaning of the book seems quite clear and offers, apart from the previously noted descriptions of Calormen itself and of Calormen characters, no notable departure from the now firmly established pattern. Children, placed in a strange environment, make a journey of discovery, undergoing certain tests or trials which strengthen their character and prepare them for the role which they will play in some larger action which concludes the book. Here the journey is an escape from slavery into freedom; the children complement rather than contrast each other like Eustace and Lucy of *The Voyage of the 'Dawn Treader.'* Their tests take the form of coping with a hostile environment rather than with the evil machinations of witches or men. Their tests are those of their courage and humility, and they move sporadically through the last half of the book often interrupting the action rather than reinforcing its movement. The temptations offered the children usually are to sins of omission rather than of commission like Edmund's and Eustace's. Shasta, because he knows no better, must be taught what to do: to ride, to be courageous in face of danger, to rule. Aravis must be brought down to an understanding of the need to accept responsibility for the results her decisions may have on others—the ten scratches equal the lashes given her slave on her account by her step-mother. There are no dramatic conversions, except the humorously inverted one of Rabadash into an ass, *a la* Apuleius's *The Golden Ass*, and of all the *Chronicles*, this one probably carries a less pointed message or allegorical meaning.

Perhaps because of a relaxation of the tension, so keenly felt in *The Voyage of the 'Dawn Treader,'* produced by the counterpointing of theme and structure in an organic union, we are tempted to feel that Lewis here takes a rest, a pause in the movement of the *Chronicles*. In this sense it is the least intense of the seven, the one closest to a common fairy tale. There are few if any moments of strongly felt description and almost no sense of the organic sanctity of meaning that illuminates the previous story. But that criticism hardly gives credit to what is certainly a fine story, albeit not up to the standard of the best of the *Chronicles*.

In terms of description, we are treated to Lewis's only serious foray into an exotic and oriental Narnian land. We are to have Charn and Underland, even Bism, but here Lewis indulges his longstanding delight in Araby in order to produce a memorable Turkish delight. Certainly the description of Tashban with its Tisroc's palace and great temple of Tash, its terraces of orange and lemon trees, its spires, battlements, minarets, pinnacles, is both economical and evocative. The contrasting descriptions of the desert crossing and the arrival at the oasis are well-handled. Arrival in the North is heralded by sweet scents, green grass, water, and the song of a nightingale. The homey dwarf house, redolent of the homes of Tumnus and the Beavers is more effective than the hermit and his pool, reminiscent of Galadriel and her mirror in *The Lord of the Rings* and Lloyd Alexander's Medwin in *The Book of Three*. Aslan's appearance to Shasta in the aura of blinding light is evocative but lacks the power in this context to move us much since it is both anticipated and repetitive. The description on the whole is good but unexceptional in view of what Lewis had achieved before.

Dialogue, used more in this book than in the previous *Chronicles*, is effectively managed. The contrast between the children's and horses' informal conversations with the court language of the Narnians, Archenlanders, and Calormen is appropriate, and Lewis manages a creditable presentation of horse talk without becoming cute. Even the pompous and elaborate ornamentation of the Tisroc's interview with Rabadash is good though it goes on far too long for the matter it conveys. What Lewis might have given but did not was more concrete and emotive descriptions of the palace, gardens, and general atmosphere of the city of Tashban.

With the crossing into the North, the narrative falls into a confusion of cross purposes. Perhaps because the desert represents the physical gulf between slavery and freedom and yet the quest does not end with the arrival in Archenland, the tension slips away in the divergent actions which confuse the end of the story. Bree, Hwin, and Aravis are shunted into the Hermit's enclosure. Shasta completes his quest by meeting his father and then Aslan; however, the straggling plot ends must be brought together with Edmund's and Lucy's arrival and with the battle, inexplicably related through the Hermit's mirror rather like the broadcast of a football match. The book then descends into anticlimax as the doubting Thomas, Bree, finds that Aslan is, by his paws and tail and whiskers, a true beast, and Rabadash is transformed.

The real climax comes far too early and with too little preparation to be fully effective. When Aslan reveals himself to Shasta, the apotheosis is too sudden to epitomize the revelation Lewis usually associates with it. This fault is symptomatic of the failure of the book as a whole to bring the spiritual and thematic moments of impact together. The tension trails away from Shasta's temptation to self-pity and Aslan's appearance to his recuperation in the Dwarf's house—parallel to Aravis's in the Hermit's and uncomfortably reminiscent of Snow White and the Seven Dwarfs—and concludes in the lengthy and predetermined battle.

Why Lewis elected to drag the story out with Chapters 14 and 15 remains a puzzle. He could easily have dispensed with Bree's disbelief and Rabadash's presence without a chapter each. Though we would not want to forego the joke on Rabadash the ridiculous, Lewis runs the risk of further diluting the tension after an already anticlimactic battle. The awkward reunion of Corin and Cor, made princely and pompous by Lewis, reminds us of the dangers of keeping on. We never see Huck Finn back in Hannibal.

The overall effect of reading this fourth book is not, for me at least, like Green's initial enthusiastic response.[3] It is the only "internal" book of the seven, depending on the material of Lewis's created world for its interest and excitement. Though the themes remain the same in general outline as those of the other books, the interest in this book rests on the surface rather than in the depths. Lewis engages our interest by the novelties of setting and of the use of Bree and Hwin, but we fail to become involved in the course of events, remaining as perhaps too critical spectators when greater compulsion could have disarmed our disbelief. There are unevennesses in the movement of the action, particularly in the last third of the book, and the general reaction is that for whatever reason, the story fails to hang together and compel a response from us. It does not work to produce that elevation of the spirit which we associate with the best of Lewis's books.

THE SILVER CHAIR 1953

After toying with such titles as Night Under Narnia (Green's suggestion), The Wild Waste Lands (Joy's and Warren's), Gnomes Under Narnia, and News Under Narnia, The Silver Chair emerged as the title of the fifth book, completed by March 1951. Here we come back to Eustace and begin our trip to Narnia with another escape, now from the precincts of a "co-educational" school in the term following Eustace's miraculous conversion from nasty to nice recorded in *The Voyage of the 'Dawn Treader.'* The linking of this story with the action and Narnian time of *The Voyage of the 'Dawn Treader'* would suggest that Lewis may have felt that after *The Horse and His Boy* he should return to the sequence of events which seemed to develop naturally out of the action of the previous story, a method he followed in both *Prince Caspian* and *The Voyage of the 'Dawn Treader.'* We know that the Pevensies will not return this side of death, and that Eustace may. The time elapsed is some seventy Narnian years. We are introduced to a new character, Jill Pole, replacing Lucy and balancing Eustace as dual main characters, and the Green Witch who seems either a relative or reincarnation of the White Witch.

The envelope framework which Lewis uses here is an interesting variation of a structure which he used before, and it tells us something about the meaning of the book. Opening abruptly behind the gym of Experiment House, a mixed, progressive school which is the epitome of Lewis's abhorrence for modern education, the action quickly draws the children through the wall into Aslan's country. It is Aslan who frames the action of the work, appearing clearly to Jill, using the children as tools for the rescue of Rilian, and testing them and their belief in order to bring them to their salvation. Though they call on Aslan, it is he who calls them for his purposes. Thus firmly established at the outset is a task and a quest. The children, through sloth and selfishness, will become lost at Harfang and deflected from their purpose. They will be deceived by the Giants, the Witch, and their own fears, but they will succeed and be healed in the end. The movement of the plot is from the "real" world of adolescent persecutions and psychologically damaging progressive education to Aslan's mountain: an escape from the warped fantasy of an educational theory to the reality of Lewis's imaginary world where truth rules. This movement is up the hill ("Jack and Jill went up the hill"), through the gate, and on to Aslan's mountaintop. The air is clear and bracing, and Jill's responses and perceptions are almost unnaturally clear.

From the point where Jill "sins" in acting so foolishly that she causes Eustace to fall over the cliff and is then baptized by drinking the living water of Aslan's grace, the action descends. First the descent is into Narnia and then overland with the children following the clues to their goal. The clues can be seen as commandments, the Tao, moral strictures, or simply as external guides on the path of the pilgrim seeking redemption and union with God in Christ. They lead the children on an arduous journey in which they have as guides first the wise owls and then the estimable Puddleglum. As they move across the wintering landscape, their path is blocked by natural and symbolic obstacles. Escaping the peril of the Giants, they fall into Underland and the real center of their adventure. Thus the movement, after the initial ascent in Chapter 1 to Aslan's mountain, is descending, an escape from the rarefied spiritual atmosphere, which the children are not yet prepared for, to the plane of the quest. The quest leads underground and reveals even further depths in Bism, and then turns upward, with the rescue of Rilian, to break out at last into Narnia. The physical restoration of Rilian prefigures the resurrection of Caspian in Aslan's country, and the children's return to harrow Experiment House.

Religious and psychologically oriented critics are certain to point to the underlying significance of these movements. The fall from the cliff is original sin, Jill and Eustace are Adam and Eve, and their search and ultimate discovery of Rilian are the discovery of their salvation in Christ. The psychological interpretation suggests that the fall from the cliff is the loss of innocence, the journey is experience, even sexual exploration in the Underworld, and finally rebirth as Jill emerges from the birth canal, half in and half out of Narnia.

Lewis urged images like these many times. Ransom descends with Hyoi, rises to meet Augray, and descends to confront the Oyarsa. He rises with Tinidril to the fixed lands, descends with Weston to the underground, and is reborn in the pool where he recuperates from his wounds. The journeys of John in *The Pilgrim's Regress* and of Orual in *Till We Have Faces* show similar uses of these images of ascent and descent. Lewis would answer critics who attempt to pin his meaning to a single point by saying that they mistake the secondary meaning for the primary. All these examples show Lewis's consistent concern for the truth: that what falls will rise.

The themes of escape, the escape of the prisoner, and the test by quest ending in spiritual rejuvenation are already familiar from previous works. To these Lewis has added new interests. The theme of mutability is important in *The Silver Chair*; for the first time in Narnia we see age, sorrow, and death. Caspian and Trumpkin, in serious and comic manner, bring home to us the inherent changeableness of even a fantasy kingdom. Though Aslan remains immutable, Narnia does not. It is not paradise but just another world where evil may enter, change dull beauty, and death bring sorrow. The autumnal winter landscapes clearly represent the mood which surrounds the action and reinforce this theme. Lewis is not, of course, focusing on death and decay exclusively. They are simply aspects of his fantasy world which had not appeared before, but they do foreshadow the creation and apocalypse which dominate the structures of the last two books in the *Chronicles*, *The Magician's Nephew* and *The Last Battle*.

The other major thematic development in the book centers on the nature of the temptations which confront the children on their quest. Lewis has shown in earlier stories the simpler temptations of gluttony for Edmund in *The Lion, the Witch and the Wardrobe* and pride and greed for Eustace in *The Voyage of the 'Dawn Treader.'* *The Silver Chair* brings more subtle temptations in the form of self-deception and the purposeful confusion of appearance and reality. The children are tempted to confuse their own desires with their task. Given a set of clues as guides, not rules, they muff three out of four, and would have failed that one but for Puddleglum's courage. Part of the thematic structure deals with self-deception. Jill does not want to admit that she caused Eustace's fall. Puddleglum's pessimism forms both a parallel and a contrast. Though he always supposes the worst, "he'll want to have the leg off at the knee, I shouldn't wonder" (p. 205), he is never confused through self-interest about what is right. "We're just babies making up a game, if you're right. But four babies playing a game can make a play-world which licks your real world hollow. That's why I'm going to stand by the playworld. I'm on Aslan's side even if there isn't any Aslan to lead it. I'm going to live as like a Narnian as I can even if there isn't any Narnia" (p. 159).

The Green Witch is the symbolic center of this deception. She represents the power of intellectual deception which can invert good and evil and dethrone reason. She has, of course, the advantage of enchantments like oppressive odors and monotonous music which cloud the perceptions, but her attack upon the children's reason depends upon linguistic inversion, the denial of meaning. "Your *sun* is a dream; and there is nothing in that dream that was not copied from the lamp. The lamp is the real thing; the *sun* is but a tale, a children's story" (p. 156). Here Lewis comes to the thematic heart of the rationalist's and skeptic's rejection of belief and of the creative imagination which gives artistic form to such belief. Faith and trust in what the characters know is real—here in Aslan, the signs, and Narnia itself—and the courage to pursue the task assigned without succumbing to the deceptive appearance of things; that is Lewis's theme.

The meaning of the book develops as we look at the theme just stated. The characters are paralleled for ironic effect. Rilian, the chief victim of deception, is seduced by the beauty of the Witch, who reminds of us Spenser's Duessa and her Red Cross Knight. So enchanted is he that he becomes subject to his mother's murderess and confuses his short periods of sanity with madness. The instrument of his enchantment, the silver chair itself, is a mockery of a throne and a fitting symbol, with its straps and restraints, of the punishment which his delusion brings upon him. In contrast, his father never falters, believing that he will find Rilian if he seeks long and far enough, and in searching for his son (sun), is symbolically looking for Aslan. He comes to find his eternal life, restored by Aslan in the final chapter.

Against Puddleglum's counsel, the children are drawn by the anticipated luxury of bath and food at Harfang only to discover, almost too late, the irony that they have been sent to be bathed and then eaten. They are deluded just as Rilian is deluded into thinking he has real power when he is only a tool in the hands of a force of unreason which seeks the dethronement of truth.

Even the Underworlders, freed of the power which had called them up against their will, ironically misinterpret what they see when Rilian comes to liberate them, so that confusion continues to reign even after the Witch's death. The apocalyptic destruction of Underland signifies both the restitution of normal order by the return to Bism of those who belong and the departure of Rilian and his party for the Overworld, and the restoration of reason and clear-sightedness which is tested as the lights fail. Even at the very end, there is the comic confusion of Jill's escape and the boys' fears that she has had a further misadventure.

The structures and techniques which Lewis uses here are also familiar to us, many having appeared in earlier books. The plot is single-stranded and the movement steady and even. There is a balancing of chapters and a sense of ordered proportion about the whole book. Chapters 1, 2, and 16 are framed by Experiment House and Aslan's mountain. Chapters 3, 4, and 15 give us Narnia, and Chapters 5 and 6 the journey to Harfang; Chapters 7, 8, and 9 the arrival at the buried city and then Harfang; and 10 and 11 the descent to Underland. Chapter 12 brings the climax with the defeat of the Witch and Chapters 13 and 14 the escape and journey to Narnia. Each episode leads naturally into the next. Lewis makes greater use here than in any other of the *Chronicles* of the story within the story. The technique is significant here because it establishes the ironic contrast between true stories in which belief can reasonably be placed and the lies of the Witch which masquerade as truth. Three separate stories are told here: one by an old Owl, the story of the lost prince; one by Rilian, his deluded version of his enchantment; and one by Golg, the story of the gnomes' enchantment. These stories help to provide information about the factual history of Rilian's disappearance seen in the Owl's account, and in Rilian's own account, we are given an example of the power of deception to warp the truth.

There are fewer major characters here than in many of the other *Chronicles*, and it is Puddleglum, modeled on Lewis's gardener at The Kilns, Fred W. Paxford, who stands out as a master stroke. Anyone who knows Tolkien's stories immediately senses the physical similarities shared by Gollum and Puddleglum. Both are aquatic, lean, frog-like, and cold-blooded. But the parallels stop with physical likenesses. Perhaps Lewis had in mind to give the other side of a froggy character. Certainly Puddleglum is the hero, preserving by faith, courage, and action the belief that slips through the children's and Rilian's grasp under the Witch's enchantments. He is, too, a character, in the best sense of the word, capturing in speech and thought all the canny wisdom and careful deliberation of a man close to the soil. His personality perfectly suits his role in the book, and rather than acting as an embellishment, as Trumpkin or Glenstorm do, he has an integral function to perform. His skepticism acts as a test of the truth of appearances which are designed to attract and delude the children. His pessimism, though, is never close to despair. When it comes down to the basic confrontation, it is action which counts, and he elicits real speech from the Witch. "Dare to touch my fire again, mud-filth, and I'll turn the blood to fire inside your veins" (p. 158).

Lewis seems less intent in this story on presenting the personalities of his characters than in projecting a situation which requires their obedience to a suggested path and temptations to deviate from that path. Jill and Eustace consequently receive less attention as personalities than Lucy in earlier books or Shasta in the previous one. We are amused by Jill's antics in Harfang, but apart from her hesitant capitulation to Aslan which rouses some empathy from us, the story moves more by external than internal motivation. Lewis is never entirely convincing nor perhaps comfortable when he internalizes the action in his children, and perhaps that is why we are not often given the opportunity to get the full range of response to a given situation which more fully drawn children might have provided. Rilian remains the least convincing of characters partly because he is a pawn rather than an actor. The Queen, the unnamed Green Witch of Underland, remains more a voice and a beautiful physical appearance than a rounded character like Jadis. Except for Puddleglum, the book has few memorable characters because the temptation being offered here is studied in its universal effect, rather than its peculiar appeal, and the characters all fall, to a greater or lesser degree. The thrust of Lewis's theme is toward the universal deception of illogic manipulated by evil power seekers like the Witch-Serpent.

As a consequence of the flatness of character development, emphasis is thrown on description and action. Lewis had, by the time he wrote this story, moved away from the Orientalism of *The Horse and His Boy*. We are back to a recognizable Narnian landscape although we explore regions we have not encountered before. For the first time, Lewis describes Aslan's mountains, seen from afar at the end of *The Voyage of the 'Dawn Treader.'* Autumn sunlight, smooth turf and blue sky reveal a riot of music and color and movement: "level turf, darting birds with yellow, or dragonfly blue, or rainbow plumage, blue shadows, and emptiness. There was not a breath of wind in that cool, bright air. It was a very lonely forest" (p. 11). His masterpiece of perspective is the view from the precipice.

Imagine yourself at the top of the very highest cliff you know. And imagine yourself looking down to the very bottom. And then imagine that the precipice goes on below that, as far again, ten times as far, twenty times as far. And when you've looked down all that distance imagine little white things that might, at first glance, be mistaken for sheep, but presently you realize that they are clouds—not little wreathes of mist but the enormous white, puffy clouds which are themselves as big as most mountains. And at last, in between these clouds, you get your first glimpse of the real bottom, so far away that you can't make out whether it's field or wood, or land or water: further below those clouds than you are above them. (pp. 11-12).

Here Lewis is not playing with words like "sun" and "lamp," "cat" and "lion," but using their reality to create a response in the reader, feelings which are natural adjuncts of his theme. The artificial odor and thrumming are rejected in favor of field, wood, land, and water.

The device of using a story within the story gives Lewis an opportunity to display his virtuosity in catching a tone, the winding of a tale in courtly and solemn owl tones, and to comment by example on the meaning and value of tradition and imaginative elaborations on abstract truth. Rilian, looking like Hamlet, owes his tale to older stories of royal murder. His tale is stately in language and movement. "It was great, shining, and as green as poison, so that he could see it well: but it glided away into thick bushes and he could not come at it" (p. 49).

The description of Underland, a contrast to Aslan's mountain, is in some ways a disappointment. It is dull and drowsy rather than sinister, lending atmosphere to the Witch's later delusions.

It was full of a dim, drowsy radiance, so that here they had no need of the Earthmen's strange lantern. The floor was soft with some kind of moss and out of this grew many strange shapes, branched and tall like trees, but flabby like mushrooms. They stood too far apart to make a forest; it was more like a park. The light (a greenish grey) seemed to come both from them and from the moss, and it was not strong enough to reach the roof of the cave, which must have been a long way overhead. Across the mild, soft, sleepy place they were now made to march. It was very sad, but with a quiet sort of sadness like soft music (p. 125).

Lewis may have wished to create here a sense of the enchantment which delusion casts over the senses, dulling the perceptions—Underland is an unreal estate, the creation of the Witch, an infernal delusion without the vibrant life and reality of either Bism or Narnia.

It is both Golg's description of living jewels and salamanders talking mysteriously from the fire and our own view of Bism which bring it into sharp contrast with pallid Underland, a poor substitute for Narnian or central reality.

A strong heat smote up into their faces, mixed with a smell which was quite unlike any they had ever smelled. It was rich, sharp, exciting, and made you sneeze. The depth of the chasm was so bright that at first it dazzled their eyes and they could see nothing. When they got used to it they thought they could make out a river of fire, and, on the banks of that river, what seemed to be fields and groves of an unbearable, hot brilliance—though they were dim compared with the river. There were blues, reds, greens, and whites all jumbled together (p. 180).

The same giddy perspective is used here to suggest limitless depth as we have felt it on Aslan's mountain, and Lewis parallels the descriptions to reinforce the message that reality in its true form is multifarious and potent.

The most dramatic section combines Lewis's descriptive skill with his formidable dialectical powers in the linguistic analysis which symbolizes the Witch's almost hypnotic control of the children's minds. Whether or not it is inappropriate in a work of this sort, as some critics suggest, it works both as a powerful statement of Lewis's belief in the validity of language as an expression of truth, and of imaginative literature as a moving and credible picture of that same truth. If there is an edge of personal criticism directed toward some of Lewis's colleagues who engage in the Witch's method of relativism and reductionism, that only serves as sauce to the meal.

In her summation, the Witch comes to the central issue for Lewis. She implies that literature, especially of the make-believe sort, is merely an elaborate copy, a toy.

You have seen lamps, and so you imagined a bigger and better lamp and called it the *sun*. You've seen cats, and now you want a bigger and better cat, and it's to be called a *lion*. Well, 'tis a pretty make-believe, though to say truth, it would suit you all better if you were younger. And look how you can put nothing into your make-believe without copying it from the real world, this world of mine, which is the only world. But even you children are too old for such play.... Come, all of you. Put away these childish tricks. I have work for you all in the real world (p. 157).

This statement from the Underworld is perhaps the clearest summary Lewis ever gave in his fiction of the negation of meaning and value in a world view which divorced facts from their imaginative significance. As *The Screwtape Letters* suggests, the gradual erosion of belief in apparently insignificant matters greases the path to disillusionment and apostasy. Tangible physical reality, what I touch and see, becomes all there is in the Witch's existential world, and fairy tale and make-believe are in her warped vision Plato's imitation of an imitation, or worse, the fancy of a child enlarging on a dull object and endowing it with a meaning it cannot have. All creative response to life becomes an elaborate game of no practical use, and those who indulge themselves by playing it are childish and deluded.

The Great Snow Dance, comic and stately, rhythmical, orderly, and yet childlike in its simplicity and its compelling movement, is Lewis's counter ritual to the Witch's distorted logic. It is silly and pointless, serves no purpose other than the expression of delight in order and harmony, but it is a meaningful expression of a joy in life which no amount of logic can express, define, or deny. Jill's perception of the dance from the halfway position of her first view, stuck between Underland and Narnia, indicates the juxtaposition of the two worlds and her dawning understanding of what she perceives.

...then she saw that they were really doing a dance—a dance with so many complicated steps and figures that it took you some time to understand it. Then it came over her like a thunderclap that the pale, blue light was really moonlight, and the white stuff on the ground was really snow (p. 192).

The concluding chapter with its moving portrayal of Caspian's death and resurrection and the harrowing of Experiment House, is an anticlimax. The tension is most intense in the confrontation with the Witch, and once she has been vanquished, the rest is, like most of Lewis's endings, a steady descent back to the children's world. Though Lewis uses the ultimate example of mutability in Caspian's death, his immediate resurrection forestalls any lasting sadness we might feel and rather undercuts the application of this "lesson" for the children and the reader. We are inclined to feel that this episode might better have been left out since it contributes so little to the main theme. Though we are forewarned that Caspian will die, and trusting Aslan, know that he will rise again, we really gain little by seeing how Aslan does it. The harrowing of the school however is more successful, ending the book on the right ironic note with the appalling reversal of the bully's expectations which serves as a final comment on the theme of appearance and reality.

Lewis has not ventured in this book beyond the techniques of his earlier stories. Returning to the single and direct one-strand plot and concentrating on fewer characters and episodes, he has regained control over the general movement of the *Chronicles* after the wavering of purpose and technique apparent in *The Horse and His Boy*. If, in terms of theme and descriptive power, this book seems less inspired than the two that were to follow or one or two of those which precede it, we should recognize that we cannot have seven books all on the same level of intensity, and it is the variety of the seven which makes them attractive. The theme of this story is not one of Lewis's most compelling though it is of particular interest because it shows that his interests are neither orthodox nor narrow. The structures used to convey the theme are adequate, if rarely so effective that our particular attention is drawn to mark them for special distinction.

The book is a good and solid one, but it does not offer those moments of special elevation and insight which I have remarked upon in *The Lion, the Witch and the Wardrobe* and *The Voyage of the 'Dawn Treader.'* We are not compelled or even invited to an experience beyond the level of an ordinary reading of fiction, and though we may admire Puddleglum as a creation, he cannot draw the book up to a self-transcending experience.

THE MAGICIAN'S NEPHEW 1955

Conceived second, written sixth, and finished last of the seven *Chronicles*, and by Lewis's direction to be read first, this story, the next to shortest of the series, might appear at first as something of an anomaly. Hooper and Green have told us that the initial attempt to provide the background of *The Lion, the Witch and the Wardrobe* produced the abortive Lefay fragment, read to Green in June, 1949.[1] Lewis returned to his characters Digory and Polly

in 1951, and under the title *Polly and Digory*, Green read portions
of the story in May and October 1951. Apparently responding to
Green's objections to the second version with its repeated visits to
Charn and the sojourn with the countryman named Piers who later
apparently became Frank, the cabby, Lewis set it aside, finished
The Last Battle, and gave the revised typescript to Green in February
1954.[2] The book is not, however, such a literary curiosity as the
history of its development might suggest.

Lewis returned to the children-into-Narnia structure he used in
The Lion, the Witch and the Wardrobe and added a late 19th-or
early 20th-century London setting. As the biographers are pleased
to note, the children are natural and believable, especially in their
dialogue and behavior, and the setting gains verisimilitude by its
association with Lewis's childhood.[3] The major additions to the
Chronicle characters are Digory (Professor Kirke of *The Lion, the
Witch and the Wardrobe*) and Polly; the earthly and otherworldly
magicians, Uncle Andrew, a comic masterpiece, and Jadis, Queen
of Charn.[4] The action is enveloped by scenes in London, and the
center of attention is divided among three worlds: London, Charn,
and Narnia, with London and Narnia sharing equally in the space
devoted to their presentation. The parallel structures used in *The
Lion, the Witch and the Wardrobe* appear again in the ironic contrasts of the themes: magic versus true creativity; the negative
power of Jadis and the destructive force of the Deplorable Word
versus the creative force and potent effect of Aslan's song; and the
contrasts of orders of being, such as queens versus subjects, magicians versus servants, Aslan's talking animals versus beasts. Children
are juxtaposed to adults, cabbies to educated gentlemen and queens,
and rational animals to imperceptive and deluded men.

In many ways the plot and movement of this story are simpler and
less complicated than any in earlier stories. Lewis retains the idea of
the quest, the test, trial, temptation, and final success of his novices.
But the emphasis here is placed on the rather natural evolution of a
simple adventure involving normal childish curiosity into a spiritual
experience. At its most basic level, the book is concerned with the
difference between magic and creativity. The magician cannot create
anything; he can, like the author, only move already created objects
about, combining them in unusual or striking patterns. In a letter to
Dom Bede Griffiths on March 25, 1946, Lewis discussed magic,
defining it as "the artificial and local recovery of what Adam enjoyed normally," but he suggested that where magic and prayer
are considered, magic is lower than prayer because the magician
expects to produce results through a ritual by reason of necessity;

whereas, the one praying trusts that the result of the prayer will be for the best, whatever it may be, and that any necessity operates beyond weak human comprehension.[5]

So with Uncle Andrew, the vain and weak magician, we have a man who does not even know the effect of the power he has invoked. It is vanity after all which, in fact, has led him to become a magician. Jadis, corrupted by power, has descended from a line of noble and good kings and queens. Her pride and greed have lead her to destroy her own world and to defy a power greater than hers by entering the garden and eating the fruit of immortality. Her power is that of destructive brute force, and throughout the book she is an Amazonian figure of strength destroying anything which blocks her path. Her tool is a word, symbolically the unleashing of the atomic holocaust. After eating the apple, a sly intellectual speciousness enters her attacks upon the children, so that she exits from the story, cast from heaven like Satan, left to tempt those like Edmund who may be swayed by self-love into joining her in her hatred of the good. In a July 20, 1954, letter to W. L. Kinter, Lewis reminded him that she was reminiscent of Circe, Alcina, and the archetypal witch of all fairy tales, a character we almost know by instinct.[6]

Aslan, echoing Jadis's words to Edmund in *The Lion, the Witch and the Wardrobe*—"You shall know us better hereafter"—says to the cabby, "You know better than you think you know, and you shall live to know me better yet" (p. 137). Aslan is the symbol of true creation, of originality, and his song, so movingly described by Lewis, is the archetype of all earthly literary or musical creations carrying only that hint of Joy and exaltation which the one act of creation, symbolized in the unfolding of Narnia, excites in the children and in each of us reading this passage or any passage of good literature. Only Aslan can make from Nothing, as Jadis describes it, the vibrant life of Narnia. So Lewis juxtaposes magic and spiritual omnipotence. We view the contrast directly, but our vision is directed, as in all the stories, through the clear and receptive vision of the children. Charn is cold, sterile, and dead. Narnia is warm, fecund, and growing. The wood between the worlds is a limbo of drowsy inactivity.

More specifically, Lewis's purpose in writing this book was to provide for an opening into the *Chronicles*, and so he needed a creation story, his Narnian Genesis, to balance what would be apocalyptic in *The Last Battle*. By waiting to complete this book last, he was able to round out the whole structure of the seven books and neatly foreshadow events which would follow: the wardrobe, Aslan's sacrifice for Edmund and Eustace, even the eventual political and moral decay which grow and culminate in the intrigues and deception of *The Last Battle*, and which are wholly man-made and owe little to direct evil manipulation by witches or wizards.

The appropriateness of the theme of magic versus creativity is revealed as we discover the various forms it takes in this book. The children, looking for adventure, fall into more than they bargain for. This is the only novel in which they are not called for some purpose having to do with Narnia itself; albeit Lucy's motivation in her initial discovery of Narnia remains somewhat problematical on this point. The adventure comes then from the same impulse that produces magicians: a desire to know, a curiosity about what is beyond, the possibility of other worlds. This is a book which stresses other-worldly possibilities and the implacable pull of the imagination more than any of the other six. Digory wakes Jadis because he cannot resist the temptation to knowledge, in this case "what will happen next," which is like the later temptation to heart's desire and immortal life which he does resist. Lewis is suggesting then, in a symbolic microcosm, that the impulse to discover deeper meaning, the inner spiritual meaning, can take the form of curiosity in children, drawing them into an adventure which may have significant results in their deepest inner life. The process of being drawn further in and higher up is shown here more simply, affectingly, and forcefully than in many of his more complex works of fiction because the process is treated as one of the most familiar of childhood experiences and gradually evolves into its full significance.

Coming to Lewis's meaning on another level, that of the test and trial of Digory, we see that the crucial questions, as in most of these books, are those of faith, courage, and love. Digory begins his adventure, not as an escape, though that possibility surfaces momentarily in his initial teary recital to Polly, only to be quickly submerged in more important issues, but as a quest—the cure of his mother. He is already being tested by his earthly circumstances before he begins his trial in Narnia. His faults are curiosity and impatience, minor ones in the scale of comparison with vanity and pride. Early in the action he is made the antithesis of both Uncle Andrew and Jadis, those who use others for their own ends. His trial is designed to insure that he and we understand that it is only by doing for others that you can be given what you need and desire. His task is to be obedient to Aslan's command, to put aside his own desire and to remove the worst of the evil he has brought by attracting pride and vanity into Narnia. The task is not a difficult one. Aided by Fledge and fortified by the faith, common sense and the good feeling needed to resist Jadis's blandishments, there is never any real doubt that he will succeed. It is a *pro forma* temptation and trial. But it underlines Lewis's insistence that only faith and belief can bring hope that all will be well. No magic charms or ritual incantations can cure Digory's mother, but faith and love do.

The "high and lonely destiny" that are elected by Jadis and Uncle Andrew, suggest another theme, the isolation of those who trust their own will to secure for them that mastery over others that is their controlling desire and joy. The ironic parallel of Jadis and Uncle Andrew reveals the truism that absolute power corrupts absolutely. Jadis is like Satan. Uncle Andrew, a comic figure, is neither a good magician nor a good man, and his gentle punishment at the paws and trunks of the talking beasts is aimed more at his dignity than his soul. He returns, if not repentant, at least a much nicer person than he went.

Lewis intended, judging from this discussion, to set the *Chronicles* in perspective by giving the group of stories a beginning. He wanted to present the theme of creativity, earthly and otherworldly, and he must have wished to reinforce the basic themes of faith, hope, and charity because these are the virtues found in Digory's character and underlined by Aslan when he calls the beasts to intelligent life. "Love, Think, Speak" (p. 116).

Structurally the book is not unique. The single line plot moves directly through a series of paralleled episodes carefully juxtaposed to place the themes in clear view and give an opportunity for ironic and humorous contrasts. Chapters 1, 2, and 15 are the real world frame. The wood between the worlds is used to add to the suspense by slowing the action, especially that in Chapter 3 where we think at first that we have arrived at our final destination, and later to offer a variety of choices. It is a clever device because its neutrality places Charn, Narnia, and London in glowing contrast, and, as a gateway to possible worlds, it adds tension.

The world of Charn is one of Lewis's finest descriptive episodes. As a dying world, it has little to offer but atmosphere, which Lewis catches in the awesome silence, the decaying palace grandeur, the dreariness and desolation.

A great stone monster with wide-spread wings stood with its mouth open and you could still see a bit of piping at the back of its mouth, out of which the water used to pour. Under it was a wide stone basin to hold the water, but it was as dry as a bone. In other places there were the dry sticks of some sort of climbing plant which had wound itself round the pillars and helped to pull some of them down. But it had died long ago (p. 45).

By the suspension of action until Digory summons Jadis back to life, Lewis adds to the mounting tension as the children penetrate the Hall of Images. Here the decay of ability is traced in the faces of Jadis's royal predecessors. The progress of history is rather pessimistically reproduced by Lewis in these images, culminating in the tyrannical Jadis and her Deplorable Word.

The contrasting portrait of the creation of a world, the birth of Narnia, is the chief episode of this story and is the single most affecting and emotion-charged piece of description Lewis created in the *Chronicles*. Its virtue is that it is an organic unity, fitting action, theme, atmosphere, setting and character into a whole which is impervious to critical dissection and analytical probing. It has, to a high degree, that organic sanctity of meaning which has become my touchstone for Lewis's highest fictional achievement.

Given the subject—the creation myth—and the already established features of Narnia-like beauty of landscape, talking beasts, and vitalized climate, one might say that Lewis had little left to do but tell how it came to be. But it is his very description of this process which forever places the gem in its setting.

Far away, and down near the horizon, the sky began to turn grey. A light wind, very fresh, began to stir. The sky, in that one place, grew slowly and steadily paler. You could see shapes of hills standing up dark against it....

The eastern sky changed from white to pink and from pink to gold. The Voice rose and rose, till all the air was shaking with it. And just as it swelled to the mightiest and most glorious sound it had yet produced, the sun arose (pp. 100-101).

You might say, "just a child's view of a sunrise," and not be wrong; yet Lewis has endowed this rising with all the excitement and nostalgia, all the longing and anticipation which symbolize his Joy and our understanding of that feeling however we may choose to title it. By using the commonest, most childlike reactions, he has managed not to overwrite for his adult readers nor to underrate the child's delight in each day and the promise of a unique adventure and the renewal of past delights.

Once we have felt the awe which Lewis manages to infuse into this description by its nearly hypnotic effect upon even Jadis, he moves on to the more practical matter of populating the new land. Here the parallels of the divine creation and the artistic creation lie close together, for Aslan is analogous to Lewis as he describes the results of Aslan's song.

When a line of dark firs sprang up on a ridge about a hundred yards away she felt that they were connected with a series of deep, prolonged notes which the Lion had sung a second before. And when he burst into a rapid series of lighter notes she was not surprised to see primroses suddenly appearing in every direction. Thus, with an unspeakable thrill, she felt quite certain that all the things were coming (as she said) "out of the Lion's head." When you listened to his song you heard the things he was making up: when you looked round you, you saw them (p. 107).

Into the solemnness of the occasion, Lewis introduces the cabby's unstifled if uncritical approval, and Uncle Andrew's contrasting distress, abated only by his perception of the commercial possibilities offered by the growing country. Humor tempers awe as we pass on to the first joke and comic misunderstanding which constitutes Uncle Andrew's punishment. In a garden of Eden and Noah's-ark abundance of animal life, Lewis sets his creation myth, giving the animals to themselves and their leadership to Frank and Helen. Again, it is the matter of perspective which determines what we see. "For what you see and hear depends a good deal on where you are standing: it also depends on what sort of person you are" (p. 125).

We move off the intense moment of awe or reverence, if you wish, which surrounds the center of the book, to the assignment of tasks. The talking animals are to serve as counselors, Frank and Helen as kindly rulers like Adam and Eve, and Digory as healer and preserver. His test is anticlimactic, as by necessity the Fall is an anticlimax to the Creation. There are, however, few biblical parallels to be found in this book. Digory's trial is not archetypal. He has in fact already fallen, is a Son of Adam, and is merely giving Lewis an opportunity to expose Jadis as confirmed in evil and giving Aslan an excuse to assist Digory by curing his mother. The effectiveness of the book then does not rest on its full-scale allegorical presentation in the simplified form of a famous story. If the book is read in that fashion, it comes up rather short of our expectation. What it does capture, I have tried to suggest, is a feeling of delight and joy in a new creation, a sense of all that creativity *de novo* brings with it.

The story trails off into the anticipated "happy-ever-after" ending which Lewis handles with a minimum of the usual sentimentality. The book is full of life and vigor and hope, but it is not free from its share of problems. One of the most glaring problems is that of the meshing of the theme and form, the *Logos* and *Poiema*. Although the plot is not as burdened and unwieldy as the plot of some of the earlier stories, it tends to remain too rigid at certain points for the material it conveys. One such point is immediately after the creation of Narnia. Lewis feels obliged to move the action ahead, following the "program," when we would be quite content to linger in the atmosphere he created with such singular effect. If we were moving ahead to matters of similarly singular importance, the consequences of the creation, we might accept the situation with resignation. But as it is, the last third of the book is a falling-off. Lewis has reached the peak too soon, and we are pulled back to a reality which jars against the aesthetic pleasure and the stirring of the deep imagination which are the real attraction of the book. If either Uncle Andrew or Jadis were more engagingly evil, we might want to see what happens to them next, but our response to the book is not established mainly through character; with Lewis it almost never is, except in the final novel, when he does succeed in making Orual come alive for us.

The other fault arises from Lewis's self-consciousness. He wanted to make this book a beginning to an already written series of novels, and he revised it more than any other work of fiction he produced. In his conscious attempt to create an opening into the series, he seems to have slipped into the uneasiness of a defensive position. There is a certain "them-us" antipathy in the book. The "children versus the adults" produces certain tensions (albeit the adults are magicians and not admirable or typical adults) which are resolved in favor of the children. The power which corrupts Jadis and Uncle Andrew is never given a fair chance to tempt and corrupt Digory and Polly, who seem blissfully immune, in a way Edmund and Eustace are not, to the full possibility of evil while they are utterly open to the beatific vision. The humble and lowly are juxtaposed to the cultured and regal, and they too are immune to the corruption which power can bring. The admiration which Lewis felt for protected innocence and uncorrupted country virtue is unconvincingly portrayed, and Frank's ennobling is one of the least credible transformations in the *Chronicles*. The book, all in all, seems to plead for too simple and uncomplex a state and is on the whole weaker than other of Lewis's pictures of virtue tested because it is too simple, easy, and nice.

It is tempting to guess at the possible reasons for what is essentially a slip in his otherwise steady and firm portrayal of innocence. He was writing and had finished *The Last Battle* before he completed this book in its final form. It is conceivable that *The Magician's Nephew* reflects a recoil from the darkness of that last book's symbolic reflection of a decadent contemporary life and a final spiritual apocalypse. It would be easy enough to see how an overemphasis on the simplicity of goodness might have resulted. Certainly the two books are poles apart in tone and location, but curiously enough they are companion pieces, like tapestries from the same loom, depicting quite different scenes, and the following study of *The Last Battle* will reveal how much the textures of these two reflect each other.

THE LAST BATTLE 1956

The last of the *Chronicles*, seventh in the series, and briefest by a few pages, this story was conceived as the concluding story which would draw the action and themes of the preceding six together, acting as a complementary volume to *The Magician's Nephew*. There is no indication that Lewis spent any considerable time in putting the book together or in revising it, and yet it shows the same seamless quality which pervades *The Voyage of the 'Dawn Treader.'* On April 15, 1954, he wrote to Joan Lancaster, "The 7th is already written but still only in pen-and-ink, and I have not quite decided yet what to call it. Sometimes I think of calling it *The Last King of Narnia*, and sometimes, *Night Falls on Narnia*."[1] In May, replying to her query about more Narnia stories, he wrote "As for doing *more* Narnia books than 7, isn't it better to stop when people are still asking for more than to go on till they are tired?"[2]

It is clear from the book itself, that he saw it as the ultimate Narnia story. Critics have pointed to the symbolic significance of seven stories and the seven friends of Narnia. I do not think Lewis said to himself, "Now we must stop at seven to keep the symbolism straight." There are many possible reasons for his ending the *Chronicles*. He had finished saying what he had to say. After completing the work on *The Voyage of the 'Dawn Treader'* and *The Horse and His Boy*, he was experimenting with material which could have drawn the *Chronicles* in another direction, but the themes remained the same, and there is a limit to the amount of repetition, no matter how cleverly handled, that mature readers will accept. There is a lagging or falling-off beginning in *The Horse and His Boy* and continuing through *The Silver Chair*. *The Magician's Nephew* clearly shows the end drawing near as he gives us the beginning of the *Chronicles*. By excluding the children from Narnia after two, or at the most three, visits, he had, without introducing new characters, either to use internal plots as in *The Horse and His Boy*, which did not use the children from our world, or draw the series to an end, since Jill and Eustace had made their first and second visits respectively in *The Silver Chair*. In terms of theme, it was inevitable that having given thought to the genesis and redemption of Narnia from evil, Lewis would inevitably give the apocalypse. And finally, his own words suggest that he felt he had written enough of this sort of fiction, and that for practical reasons, if not for artistic and thematic ones alone, it was time to stop.

The title was a happier choice than the two suggested in his letter. The tone of the book is dark, brooding, and heavy, suggesting the storm and darkness that proverbially precede the hopeful dawn. From the outset, we can hardly believe we are in Narnia; it seems so much like a possible view of contemporary England and Europe. Men are deceived; the old values are brought into question; greed, political intrigue, slavery, and destruction seem the order of the day. The old faith is either doubted by skeptics, denounced by atheists, or feebly wished for by timid believers. The first half of the book is summed up by the theme, "That sort of thing doesn't happen any more," and the first three quarters of the book show a world disintegrating under the force of irreligion and greed, the small band of believers reluctantly retreating until, losing their last earthly battle, they pass through the stable door to find their reward.

There is little question about Lewis's intention in writing this book. It serves as a fitting conclusion to the *Chronicles*, providing a highly moving finale to the preceding action. Thematically it brings the promised return of Aslan to his country and of the characters to their desired place. It fulfills the reader's desires for a conclusive and idyllically happy ending. At the same time, it provides Lewis a convenient vehicle for his reflections on the current state of life as he lived and saw it around him. Thus the last *Chronicle* is not just a fictionalized account of the world's last night, nor the necessary and anticipated but undesired end of a long story. It is the expression of Lewis's view of modern life and the situation of modern Christians on the verge of an exchange of that sordid reality for something longed for since childhood. It is the beginning of a new story.

There is significant evidence in Lewis's correspondence throughout the postwar period and into the fifties to suggest that he disliked the trends which contemporary life in all its facets was taking. His acceptance speech delivered at Cambridge strikes the same note, but more humorously. Lewis disliked "progress," both scientific and socioeconomic, when it produced what he regarded as essentially inhumane conditions in which a man could no longer claim the freedom to be himself, to work for himself, to have his privacy, to be an individual and not part of a herd. The reflection of his distrust of contemporary civilization can be seen, obliquely, in the portrait he paints of Narnia in decline.

Narnia is in decay. Shift, the comic symbol of Lewis's evolutionary inversion, is the clever manipulator of the plodding, docile, and "not very clever" ass. Lewis repeatedly referred to himself in letters to Sister Penelope as "Brother Ass," suggesting the humble role played in the passion story by the ass who bore Christ on Palm Sunday (and Balaam's ass), and the subservience which Lewis felt, the humble role which he tried to bring his pride to reflect upon.[3] Shift with his pathetic failings, his rationalizing, drinking to escape, greed and petty desires for more nuts, represents some of the worst aspects of a modern life which dehumanize man. Shift is a man becoming a beast, and it is significant that in this book alone Lewis paints animals as capable of guile and deception, perversions of their noble estate as Talking Animals, as *hnau*, rational beings created and endowed by Aslan at the creation of Narnia. The evil, for the first time in all the *Chronicles*, is *in* Narnia and is not the direct manifestation of external evil forces like Jadis or the Green Witch, though it may ultimately be traced to such sources. The fault lies within life itself. Shift is corrupt, Ginger guileful and specious, Rishda greedy and tyrannical, the Dwarfs skeptical and pessimistic materialists. What we see is nearly an existential universe where good and right are questioned and deception and disguise are the tools for the manipulation of false and enslaving beliefs based on fear. Shift first corrupts the docile Puzzle to his purpose by convincing him that the very thing which he knows he should not do is the one thing that Aslan wants him to do as a test of his faith. This argument is familiar to us from Weston's temptation of the Lady in *Perelandra* and, inverted, it becomes the offer of Paradise rejected by the Dwarfs here and by several of the passengers in *The Great Divorce*.

Throughout *The Last Battle*, the themes of deception, disbelief, and skepticism appear as the tools used by the unscrupulous for the manipulation of the gullible. There are some overtones of *1984* and *Animal Farm* in the book, but Lewis is clearly pursuing his own attack upon a society which has the capacity to be led by clever fools to its own destruction. The action moves from belief, to hope, to disillusionment on the part of Tirian and the true Narnians. This descent is counterpointed by the transparent plot laid by Shift and then Ginger and Rishda. Aslan, for the first time in the history of the *Chronicles*, makes no appearance in Narnia, only appearing on the other side of the stable door and bringing order out of chaos which the last battle has brought upon Narnia. We are shown an old civilization in which the hope for a return of good is almost dead.

Lewis seems to intend us to understand that men and their society have largely brought destruction upon themselves; it is the history of Charn and of all civilizations. Even Tirian, acting in the heat of the moment, kills the Calormen soldiers without the demanded courtesies and preparations and thus forfeits his good name. The talking beasts, confused by the false Aslan and lacking the faith needed to preserve them from the fantasy that Aslan because he is not tame can thus possibly be cruel, mistake the true source of tyranny. The key theme is that of faith since it is Tirian's firm faith which leads him to perceive the deception and to call upon Aslan and the children for help. It is the faithlessness of the skeptical Dwarfs that leads to their self-deluded and egotistical demand of Narnia for their own and their final delusion that their eternal situation is the darkness of a stable when they have been offered Paradise. It is Emeth's belief which changes his pagan devotion to good account, and it is Ginger's rational faith in the impossibility of spirits and powers which brings him to the brink of disaster and returns him alive but wholly a beast. Shift and Rishda meet a crueler, if wholly deserved fate.

Lewis uses the theme of faith throughout the *Chronicles*, but it finds its most significant expression here. The range of disbelief extends from the simple confusion of Puzzle and the animals about who or what Aslan is, to the atheism of Ginger and Rishda, and it is the cynical unbelievers who practice the cruel deceptions which characterize the life in Narnia before the end: a life of slavery, wanton destruction of life and property, fear, and tyrannous dictatorship. The hopes of Tirian, representing the last outpost of belief in Narnia, are methodically dashed until he has only his sword and his friends to stand by him in the last battle. He is overwhelmed by the power brought against him. Only the destruction of this world can reverse the inexorable order of decay.

The method which Lewis used in presenting this highly dramatic theme is simple and follows the lines of some of the other stories in the *Chronicles*. The plot is single and direct in its movement. The rapid pace of events, more action-packed and interspersed with less description than in any previous book, leads on with a rush to the slow and solemn climax with the fall of night on Narnia and ends with the happy relief of the paradisal last chapter. The children, contrary to their action in earlier stories, do not appear until the 6th chapter, and Aslan, not until the 13th. As I pointed out earlier, the focus of attention is on a world devoid of belief and remote from grace where evil has control and men manipulate others for their own greedy ends. The framework of the plot is one of movement from the decadent world, through its purging and destruction, into a celestial world, or as Lewis suggests in his reference to Plato and the cave image, from the imperfect reflection of reality, earthly joy, to its deeper or higher and ultimate source. Thus we move from fear to love, from despair to Joy. The movement of the plot and tone is caught in Aslan's call "Come further in! Come further up!" (p. 158). The movement from the stable to the garden is a transcendental one, and it stands as the most prominent and moving example of Lewis's belief and his dedication to the pursuit of Joy to its ultimate source.

Perhaps because the larger issues and themes control the action and its movement, character and incident are left rather in the background. Though the plot provides Lewis with ample opportunities for splendid characterization, none of the characters rise to the level of a Puddleglum or Trumpkin. Most of the characters whom we meet in this book are corrupt, and although Tash is a brilliant portrait of evil, none of the characterizations hold us spellbound in the way Jadis does. Even Tirian seems a less believable and significant character than Rilian or Caspian of the earlier books. The characters all seem overshadowed by the compelling movement of the events which literally sweep them up.

Lewis uses contrasts and parallels, antitheses and ironic inversions to pinpoint the issues which help to develop the action and themes. The long-planned seizure of Narnia by the Tisroc, subtle and apparently entirely successful, ends in the catastrophic destruction of all of Narnia. The subtlety of the attack on Narnia is foiled by the very simple expedient which the unbelievers overlook: that the names they manipulate have real significance and power. Thus they call down their own destruction by their pride in reason. Shift and Puzzle, Grizzle and Poggins, Rishda and Poggins, Ginger and Aslan, all represent antitheses as do the outside and inside of the stable. Throughout the central battle scenes, it is the speculation about what really lies on the other side of the door that adds to the tension and suspense.

Because the book deals with an inexorable decline, there is less in the way of suspense than in previous books. We are forewarned that the children are probably dead; we know that the battle will probably be lost; we anticipate some sort of transformation from one state to another. Our curiosity is piqued more by the questions "when" and "how" than by "whether or not." To forestall too speedy a climax in a book almost wholly climactic, Lewis uses several skillful techniques which bear closer study. One of these devices he used before, the multiplication of a single episode by varied repetitions. Shift forces Puzzle to go to market; he then forces him into the more serious task of donning the lion's skin; then Shift finds himself in a comparable position under Rishda's control, and ultimately both Shift and then Rishda find themselves under Tash's control. Similarly, Tirian, with rising and falling hopes, enters a series of increasingly more dangerous encounters, and with increasingly greater odds against him. The plot is thus extended and the suspense prolonged without undue elaboration or complicated subplots. The paralleling of the promised millennium which Shift offers the Narnian animals: "You won't be slaves. You'll be paid—very good wages too. That is to say, your pay will be paid in to Aslan's treasury and he will use it all for everybody's good.... What do you know about freedom? You think freedom means doing what you like. Well, you're wrong. That isn't true freedom. True freedom means doing what I tell you" (pp. 30-31), with the real paradisal experience of Chapter 16, helps to place the movement of the action in a structured framework which is directed spiritually upward.

The children's role here as companions of Tirian and as soldiers in the last battle is somewhat complicated by the fact that their appearance, as far as the theme goes, is hardly necessary. They do serve the symbolic purpose of reinforcing Tirian's faith, and they physically release him, but they are in fact subsidiary to the main action rather than occupying their usual central position.

Though used less often than in many of the previous books, the descriptive passages should not be underrated when we assess the impact of the book as a whole. For various reasons, Lewis played down the description of Narnia in decay. He relies on images of cold, dark, west, and autumn to give the impression that all is not what it was. The absence of descriptions of the beauty of Narnia is effective, in a negative way, when we have the memory of earlier parts of the *Chronicles*, in setting the tone of decay and nostalgia. Symbolically the appearance of Puzzle as Aslan is to the true Aslan, as we are led to feel, Narnia under Calormen rule would be to the Narnia we find on the other side of the stable door.

Thus Lewis seems purposely to reduce description in the first half of the book, giving us little but the Tower and then the Stable. The central position of the stable, with action swirling about it, gives dramatic intensity and focus to the novel, and Lewis uses light, dark, and shadows effectively and symbolically—what appears in firelight is not always truth. It is not until we pass through the door that Lewis gives full scope to his descriptive power. Dramatically this technique is most effective since we cannot see through the door and can only guess, with the characters, the nature of what is on the other side.

Lewis uses several descriptive devices; one is the firsthand narration of Emeth, who later recounts his experiences and sensations in stilted and courtly Calormen fashion. More effective is the contrast between what is described and what the Dwarfs remain stubbornly unwilling to see. Most effective is Lewis's direct description. The supreme example in all his work is the extended description of Narnia's destruction followed by our entrance into the real Narnia. "Night falls on Narnia" contains the most condensed and evocative of Lewis's descriptions.

The bonfire had gone out. On the earth all was blackness: in fact you could not have told that you were looking into a wood, if you had not been where the dark shapes of the trees ended and the stars began (p. 149).

The descent of the stars, the judgment, the telescoping of time, are finally followed by:

A widespread noise broke the silence: first a murmur, then a rumble, then a roar. And now they could see what it was that was coming, and how fast it came. It was a foaming wall of water. The sea was rising. In that treeless world you could see it very well (p. 155).

And out there it began to grow light. A streak of dreary and disastrous dawn spread along the horizon, and widened and grew brighter, till in the end they hardly noticed the light of the stars who stood behind them (p. 156).

The giant threw his horn into the sea. Then he stretched out one arm—very black it looked, and thousands of miles long—across the sky till his hand reached the Sun. He took the Sun and squeezed it in his hand as you would squeeze an orange. And instantly there was total darkness (p. 157).

Lewis never encompassed more evocatively the utter absence of all he called Joy. With condensation and poetic force, he captures in these simple pictures, the great modern fear of the void, and though it is a description of negation, it has all the power of that companion piece, the creation of Narnia in *The Magician's Nephew*. The sentences are crisp and direct, the verbs and adjectives, clear and forceful, and the movement almost scientifically precise as the world grinds to a halt.

Unfortunately the description of the new Narnia further up and in is no match for this in power and economy. Perhaps because it is a copy of what Lewis has often shown us before, he could offer little more beyond the suggestion that the true Narnia is the original of that reflected one we knew.

The new one was a deeper country: every rock and flower and blade of grass looked as if it meant more. I can't describe it any better than that: if you ever get there, you will know what I mean (p. 171).

We are hardly satisfied by being foisted off this way and can, with some reason, accuse Lewis of telling us about what it was like rather than following the advice he so often gave others to make the reader *feel* what is being described. Apart from the happy reunion and sense of liberation and recognition which we feel in entering this deeper country, Lewis's description somehow fails at the last to raise us to the height of Joy. Perhaps that is asking too much, having, in fact, brought us so far.

The book is a singular achievement, none the less, awarded the Carnegie Medal in 1956, partially on its own merits and as the capstone of the *Chronicles*. It is more, in my estimation, as a part of the *Chronicles* than as a single work that the book deserves to be praised. Alone, it has less meaning and point than any of the other books because it relies so heavily on an accumulated experience which no amount of cleverly inserted recapitulation can provide, though Lewis makes a fine attempt. It is, I have pointed out, essentially a strong book in its portrait of a society in degradation, and the final apocalypse and glory can only be truly understood and savored when we know how much we have lost and what we have gained in place of that apparent loss. The characters, the plot, even the significant and stirring action, are not presented with the attention to detail and organic unity which each of the other books displays. This is a rounding-off and tying-up book, as *The Magician's Nephew* is the opening one, but *The Last Battle* lacks the self-contained coherence of the former story.

What it offers us, whether we wish to read it as a separate work or as a part of the larger whole, is the embodiment of Lewis's belief that this sort of fiction is the appropriate mode for expressing his theme. No one will deny with any real conviction that *The Last Battle* does draw us up and into Lewis's ideal Joy justified by faith. The book compels us to experience the sadness of loss occasioned by the end of Narnia and the joy of discovery that "The dream is ended: this is the morning" (p. 183). The book in its own way presents us with a powerful symbolism. Like the children, we must come to understand that our excursions into the land of heart's desire are limited, but we learn too that the land of fantasy is only a reflection of deeper or more eternal forms, and that in a sense it is only by losing that fantasy, poignant as the loss may be, that we can gain the real world of which it is only an image. On the level of spiritual meaning, we are clearly learning to die in order that we may live eternally. On the level of art, which may ultimately be the least significant for Lewis and for us, we are dealing with the idea that there comes a point beyond which the artist may not pass in attempting to describe that which has called his art into being. "But for them it was only the beginning of the real story. All their life in this world and all their adventures in Narnia had only been the cover and the title page: now at last they were beginning Chapter One of the Great Story, which no one on earth has read" (p. 184). Lewis, like Poe and Coleridge, has passed as far along the road to ultimate truth as one genre can take him. There is no form which can express for Lewis what lies beyond.

9. *TILL WE HAVE FACES* 1956

The biographers have given us a definitive look at the composition of this last novel by Lewis so that it is not necessary to do more than refer the reader to that account for the history of its composition (*Biography*, pp. 260-266). Lewis's preface indicates that we have his reinterpretation of a story that had pestered him since his undergraduate days. Suddenly the form came to him, and the book came into focus.[1] There are some other facets of Lewis's attitude toward the book recorded in his correspondence which bear study.

I've given up the Phoenix story for the present. An old, 25 year old, idea having just started into imperative life! My version of Cupid, Psyche. Apuleius got it all wrong. The older sister (I reduce her to one) couldn't *see* Psyche's palace when she visited her. She saw only rock, heather. When P. said she was giving her noble wine, her poor sister saw and tasted only spring water. Hence her dreadful problem: "is P mad or am I blind?" As you see, tho, I didn't start from that, it is the story of every nice affectionate agnostic whose dearest one suddenly "gets religion," or even every luke warm Christian whose dearest gets a vocation. Never, I think, treated sympathetically by a Christian writer before. I do it all thru' the mouth of the elder sister. In a word, I'm much "with book"....[2]

Lewis's intentions are undisguised. Unlike the early poetic treatment of the story "a masque or play of Psyche and Caspian," and the later

Psyche and Jardis fragment, Lewis seems intent in his final treatment on revealing the effect of a vocation upon those who surround the one who has the vocation. He is treating the effect of Christian vocation upon the "affectionate agnostic." More intensely than in any earlier work of fiction, his gaze is directed here at the personality of his characters, at their responses to their human situation, at their relationship with others. As he pointed out in his retrospective letter to Clyde Kilby, the point of the book centers on the "case" of Orual, human affection and its possessiveness in the face of the possession of its object of affection by a higher power.

It was to Mrs. Farrer that he would later write concerning the difficulty of dialogue between Orual and Psyche. Earlier he had indicated the problem to her in a general comment. "I think dialogue is frightfully tricky: partly because it is so hard to stop writing it (characters *will* talk: at least so I find) and partly because so much that wd. be alright in real conversation looks different when it gets into print."[3] With specific reference to her criticism of the dialogue of *Till We Have Faces*, he wrote,

The criticism of the dialogue style of the two sisters is an eye-opener, and that defect, if you are right (and I expect you are) w. have been fatal. Every correction I made in those passages was leading me further into this schoolgirlish gush! I was lured on by the desire to avoid what Owen Barfield calls "the expository demon," my native tendency to be too argumentative and make people talk like a Platonic dialogue. But, clearly I have fallen into Scylla while shunning Charybdis. About Psyche herself your *diagnosis* is wrong, but that only shows I have failed to get across what I intended. Pin-up girls, nothing! The attempt was precisely to show the biddable ideal daughter, Maia's little pet (the ideal object for a devouring maternal love, the live doll) turning into the, sometimes terrifying, sometimes maternal Goddess. I'll try to mend it, but not, I think in the direction you suggest. I think she must have the same deep voice as Orual for "you also are Psyche." The whole thing is v. tricky, though. The numinous breaking through the childish mustn't be made just like the mature breaking thru the juvenile; the traits of eternal *youth* have to come in. [4]

It is the "numinous breaking through" which characterizes the best of Lewis's fiction, and here in the final work of fiction Lewis has brought the numinous and the real closest together without the mediation of science fiction or fairy tale. He has, in the words of his letter to Father Peter Milward, achieved his own "good myth," a story which gives different meanings for different readers. Allegory gives only one meaning. Into an allegory man can put only what he knows already—in a myth he puts what he does not yet know and couldn't come to know any other way.[5] Lewis began his career as a writer of fiction with an allegory, *The Pilgrim's Regress*, and no one disputes its limitations. Though it would be unfair to neglect the natural growth and maturing of Lewis's creative ability over the years which intervene before the publication of *Till We Have Faces*, a study of the last work reveals how far Lewis had come in actively developing his skills as a writer. His control of characterization and dialogue, his sense of timing and plot movement, his choice of the dramatic episode, and his grasp of the psychological states of his characters, all indicate the high level of achievement which has ironically been undervalued by his most dedicated admirers.

I am so glad you [Joan Lancaster] liked *Till We Have Faces*, because so few people do. It is my biggest "flop" for years, and so of course, *I* think it my best book.[6]

Owen Barfield has indicated to me that he finds this novel most interesting among Lewis's fictional work, although in speculating about which works by Lewis will last, he feels that it will be the *Chronicles of Narnia* rather than *Till We Have Faces*.[7]

We do not have to dig deep to discover the meaning of the story. Written in two parts, it is an almost classic example of an attack upon the gods—"I say the gods deal very unrightly with us. For they will neither (which would be best of all) go away and leave us to live our own short days to ourselves, nor will they show themselves openly and tell us what they would have us do" (p. 249).[8] "I saw well why the gods do not speak to us openly, nor let us answer. Till that word can be dug out of us, why should they hear the babble that we think we mean? How can they meet us face to face till we have faces?" (p. 294). The theme is the single one which moves through nearly the whole body of Lewis's fiction, from *The Pilgrim's Regress* to this final work where it finds its most subtle and dramatic presentation. It is the theme of the search for meaning, for the Joy which Psyche experiences in her union with Cupid and which Orual mistakenly clutches at in her possessive hold on Psyche, the Fox, and Bardia. It is that impulse toward self-transcendence which is represented in concrete form in the longing of John for the distant Island in *The Pilgrim's Regress*, by the harsh reality of the shining paradise in *The Great Divorce*, the real pleasure which cannot be duplicated by Screwtape, the gardens of Meldilorn and the Holy Mountain of *Perelandra*, the sanctity of St. Anne's, and the two Narnias one within the other.

For the first time, however, Lewis has placed the quest and journey within the structure of a traditional myth and has given the center of the stage to an unwilling searcher, one who is searching for the source of Joy in an object which she thinks she can possess, mistaking her selfish pride for selfless devotion. Orual thus becomes the only example in Lewis's work of the unwilling convert. Eustace, perhaps Jill and Rilian, even Edmund and Jane and Mark Studdock may approach the qualities which we find in Orual, but in each case they are at the periphery of the central action, and they are searching, however, misguidedly, in the right direction. With Orual, Lewis would attempt to show the extreme case, the pre-Christian agnostic, whose complex search for Love draws her through these stages: from maternal affection in her early love for Psyche, to friendship in her admiration for the rationalism of the Fox and the courage of Bardia (both of whom she successfully emulates in ruling Glome), to erotic love expressed in her possessive lust for Psyche, and to a final end in the charity which marks the revelation of her coinherence with Psyche and her common bond with humanity, and that all-encompassing union with Him who is coming (cf. *The Four Loves*). "I loved her as I would once have thought it impossible to love, would have died any death for her. And yet, it was not, not now, she that really counted. Or if she counted (and oh, gloriously she did) it was for another's sake.... And he was coming" (p. 307). Her recantation ends on the word "might" which in its double significance of possibility and power suggests the end to which Lewis brings the book and Orual's quest. From the negation of her hatred, we come to the acceptance of her new face.

The theme, centering as it does on the search for Joy through the attainment of human happiness, gives Lewis the opportunity to study human relationships and reactions more closely than he had in any previous work of fiction. In earlier works the reader's view had always been outer-directed, drawn away, sometimes from the very first moments of the story, into a symbolic and actual journey up and out of the mundane reality that represented the earthly condition. John's journey to the East, Ransom's celestial voyages, the bus ride of *The Great Divorce*, and the journeys into Narnia and within Narnia, all are adventures in which the protagonists seek the excitement of new lands or an escape from some unpleasant situation. They move inevitably outward and usually upward, always to the mountains, the heights, where they will meet their desire, in whatever unexpected form it may take, e.g., Augray, the Oyarsi, or Aslan. Only in *The Screwtape Letters* does Lewis depart from the traditional structures and movement of his other works to give us an inversion of his usual journey to Joy. Even here, once the inversion is understood, we have, in fact, a similar quest, which by its very nature throws it into sharp contrast with that of the seeker after Joy and connects it with *Till We Have Faces*. The infernal joy is absorption of other souls. The merger desired is one in which the stronger soul eats the weaker. Lewis makes clear that this act is a parody of the divine union of the soul with God in which there is equality and yet hierarchy: freedom and adoration, free will and obedience.

As *The Screwtape Letters* is told in the first person using the epistolary form, so *Till We Have Faces* turns to the personal record, the indictment of the gods, a first-person document presumably written from mature convictions and with a selective eye. It is not entirely correct to state as the biographers do that this book hides Lewis's style, outlook, and mode of argument under his assumption of the character of Orual. They suggest that for them, at least, this change puts them off.[9] The fact is that so much of Lewis is to be found in this work precisely in style, argument, and outlook, and the major accomplishment of the book is that he has molded his materials through a fine and mature craftsmanship into the convincing portrait of his commanding central figure, Orual. And although he may have succeeded in becoming Orual for a time, and though much which we find in Orual's story may describe experiences in the life of Joy Davidman and reflect her influence on Lewis, the major impact of the book rests on its artistic achievement as a fictional vehicle for the continued examination by Lewis of the pervading theme of the journey to Joy.

It is not my intention to make an exhaustive study of the theological implications or the possible allegorical and symbolic meaning which may be derived from a study of the book. Much critical energy has been expended in this task already. What I want to do is follow the method which I have used to this point, establishing first the general meaning of the book and then examining the techniques used and assessing the suitability of the form for conveying the themes presented.

In choosing to reinterpret a myth, here through the eyes of one of the minor actors in the story—the sisters have no names in the Apuleius version—Lewis has plunged boldly into the matter. His comments and the recorded grip of the myth on his imagination, from early maturity onward, show that it contained for him significant meaning. Undoubtedly like so much of his imaginative life, the significance of his response shifted in meaning with his conversion to belief so that built into his very understanding of these myths and stories was the transformation which deeper knowledge and faith can effect in the imaginative perception. We cannot know what

Caspian and Psyche or Jardis and Psyche might have come to if
Lewis had completed their stories and if he had not undergone the
conversion which prefaced his fictional works. We do know that
myth became for him the literary expression of the deepest meaning,
and that he would have sought no higher praise as a literary artist
than to have it said of him that he had become a mythmaker. Perhaps
that is why he disliked being called an allegorist, for to him allegory
was the lesser art.

The myth here is not of his making. His use of it was undoubtedly
to add significance to the action, to give it historical perspective
and allusiveness, to place it in a remote and mysterious antiquity.
But given the theme of Orual's complaint and her capitulation, we
can imagine that Lewis saw this myth as a particularly apt example
of unselfish belief and devotion, as he draws it, which contrasts
with the grasping possessiveness of the protagonist. Psyche's temptation, fall, and trial leading to her reunion with Cupid in bliss and
immortality are a pagan prefiguration of central Christian themes,
and Lewis's elaboration of the myth leads to the highlighting of
these prefigurations. Psyche is charity incarnate; her beauty is
divine, her touch heals, and she gives herself willingly as a sacrifice.
Her translation is reflected to the uncomprehending Orual in her
radiant well-being and joy as well as in her commanding physical
strength and will. The god and his motives are pushed into the
background, and it is solely Orual's malicious distortion of love
as a tool of her own desire that brings about Psyche's unmerited
fall. "'And even now,' said Psyche, 'I know what I do. I know that
I am betraying the best of lovers and that perhaps, before sunrise,
my happiness may be destroyed forever. This is the price you have
put upon your life. Well, I must pay it.... Go. You have saved your
life; go and live it as you can'" (pp. 166-167). Once Psyche has
fled into the wilderness, her tasks and trials, as we later discover,
are subsumed in those of Orual. From this point onward, the myth
operates upon Orual not as a direct force in the action of the story
but as the counter current to the flow of her life and history from
this turning point to her moment of epiphany.

There are in fact two myths in operation; one is that of the
submissive victim led to a fate which is the miraculous opposite of
that anticipated. Behind this myth lurks the uneasy remembrance
for those who know the Apuleius rendition of the story with its
erotic elements, sexual jealousy, the greed and vanity and injured
pride of both the earthly and Olympian characters. The other myth,
the one on which Lewis places central interest, is that of the unwilling victim, sport of the God, dragged protesting her fate to the

throne of judgment, wretch and ingrate, who, contrary to her own expectation and deserts, is granted Joy and transformed from beast to beauty. By using a parallel structure, Lewis is able to counterpoint the two myths and thus reinforce the particular meaning which he goes to some pains to give us.

The themes are, as I indicated, consistent with all that Lewis has shown us in his fiction before this story. Faith alone will bring us through the perils of life to truth, though it may be a dangerous journey requiring courage and may present seemingly insurmountable obstacles. Reason unaided by faith, and human love without the knowledge of its source (cf. Ansit and Orual's love for Bardia or Orual's love for Psyche), can only lead to the destruction of the love object. Courage without faith and wisdom is noble but cannot lead to Joy, cf., Bardia's career. Orual mistakes her selfish desires for love and mistakes Psyche's love and faith for selfishness. Her will blinds her to the simple truth that she is mistaking the object of Joy for the Joy itself, and she sees only the reflection of beauty and love, mistaking that for truth. Her complaint is, as she says, its own answer. "To have heard myself making it was to be answered" (p. 294).

When Lewis shows us, so far in advance of the end, the inexorable movement of Orual toward her unveiling to eternal truth, he must exercise considerable skill to keep us concerned with the continuing movement and action of the book. There are the contrasts of the two stories, but by mid-book, Chapter 15, Psyche's story is over except as a myth which lurks in Orual's conscience, haunting her with cries and dreams of tasks she cannot accomplish. There is the irony of Orual's success as warrior and stateswoman, following the disaster of her temptation of Psyche. Lewis projects this last half of the book as the rise of the Queen and the fall of Orual. Four chapters are devoted to the establishment of her rule and two more to the consolidation of her power and the end of her reign. We may wonder why Lewis has drawn out the story at such length.

Lewis is giving us, for the first and last time, a full scale characterization, a life. He might in one sense have been said to have attempted this scope of characterization before in John's life in *The Pilgrim's Regress*, but John is hardly a character in the sense that he comes to life. He remains an abstraction. Even Ransom, and certainly Jane and Mark, and the children of the Narnia stories suffer from Lewis's consciousness of what role they must play. His artist's eye is on them in their roles, and they rarely act without our feeling his premeditation. His triumph with Orual is that she is a person before she has a chance to become an abstraction. Only one other of Lewis's characters comes to such full life and that is Aslan, who though compelling, lacks the common humanity that draws our empathy and belief to this ugly, veiled woman. It is further to Lewis's credit that as unsympathetic as he seems, on the surface at least, to feminine characteristics, he has succeeded in giving us such a strong and convincing portrait of a woman. In a letter to Kathleen Raine (October 5, 1956) Lewis wrote:

I think what makes Orual different from the 'warrior maiden' archetype is that she is *ugly*, represents virginity not its high poetic state but as a mere misfortune, and of course, masculine activities as the *pis aller*, the thing she is driven into because nothing else is left her. (A bit of ambivalence too. Bardia's attempt to treat her as a man is agony, yet also to be as much of a man as possible and share his masculine activities is the only thing that links her with him at all and, in that way, precious to her.) Even so, she does feel on killing her first man that she has somehow been debauched.[10]

The immediate rejoinder, of course, is that she is a masculine character; however, that hardly convinces us that Lewis has simply put skirts on a male. We might accept such a description of Fairy Hardcastle but not of Orual. And even with Fairy, Lewis is clearly manipulating her "masculinity" for certain effects in the novel.

The method of presenting this life is direct and plain, like the quality of the life itself and its setting in Glome. The country is remote, uncivilized, and grim: Trom, Glome, Shennit, the names themselves suggest the guttural speech of an uncouth country. The atmosphere is captured in the description of the House of Ungit, the pagan fertility goddess, the black and unsightly Aphrodite, suggesting the dark, fecund power of blood. "She is a black stone without head or hands or face, and a very strong goddess" (p. 4). She is a faceless power whose external influence on Psyche's life, as in the sacrifice to the Shadowbrute, reflects the brutal force of Orual's destructive love for Psyche. Later when she attends the seasonal birth rites of Ungit, she describes Ungit in more detail.

The story was that at the very beginning she had pushed her way up out of the earth—a foretaste of, or an ambassador from, whatever things may live and work down there one below the other all the way down under the dark and weight and heat. I have said she had no face; but that meant she had a thousand faces.... She was now more rugged than ever because of all the blood they had poured over her in the night. In the little clots and chains of it I made out a face; a fancy at one moment, but then, once you had seen it, not to be evaded. A face such as you might see in a loaf, swollen, brooding, infinitely female (p. 270).

It is this face which she recognizes as her own when, in her dream, her father makes her confront herself: "that all-devouring woman-like, yet barren, thing" (p. 276).

Into this land, ruled by brute force and superstition, first comes death (Orual's mother), then reason (the Fox), and finally beauty (Psyche). The Fox's stoic rationality counsels acceptance of all that nature brings, and nature in Glome brings little to gladden the heart. But Psyche transforms nature. "She made beauty all around her. When she trod on the mud, the mud was beautiful; when she ran in the rain, the rain was silver. When she picked up a toad—she had the strangest and, I thought, unchanciest love for all manner of brutes—the toad became beautiful" (p. 22). The action becomes rapidly more complex. From the healer she becomes the accursed, and then the Great Offering to the Brute. Thus Lewis suggests that the course of Beauty is always toward sacrifice to the claims of materialistic expediency. The dialogue of the King and the Priest, the dramatic encounter between earthly and spiritual power, shows Lewis's care in developing suspense and in revealing the King's relief that he is not the chosen sacrifice.

From this point until the sacrifice, the narrative centers on Psyche's relationship with Orual and the desperate attempts made by Orual to find a way out of what becomes increasingly a fated situation. Psyche's own protestation of her longing for death, though unconvincing to Orual and the reader, lends that sense of inevitability which tests the rationalism of the Fox and gives the first hints of Psyche's election to a higher reality which will be borne out by her later appearances to Orual. "'Do you remember? The colour and the smell, and looking across at the Grey Mountain the distance? And because it was so beautiful, it set me longing, always longing. Somewhere else there must be more of it. Everything seemed to be saying, Psyche come!'" (p. 74).

Orual's jealousy, anger, and despair at her loss of Psyche, and her own misery reflected in her sickness, form a lull in the action preceding the quest which begins as a duty to seek out and bury Psyche's remains. Lewis handles this journey with skill by understating the significance of the journey itself and of the momentousness of the discovery of Psyche alive on the other side of the stream. Orual first feels the lifting of the spirits which approach to the mountains brings. "The sight of the huge world put mad ideas into me, as if I could wander away, wander forever, see strange and beautiful things, one after the other to the world's end" (p. 96). The irony of the revelation is that Orual can see only part, not all; she sees the object of her desire but not the mystery of incarnation which now mantles Psyche.

It is in this central section that Lewis's control of dialogue is particularly apparent. He gives Psyche new command of herself and her speech, and the dialogue moves from a narrative of Psyche's trial and redemption to a loving debate between the believing and nonbelieving sisters. Lewis had shown us a similar debate in *The Great Divorce* between the Lady and the Tragedian, but here the debate slowly unfolds the essential selfishness of Orual and Psyche's unshaken trust in truth. "'Orual, don't look so sad. All will be well; all will be better than you can dream of'" (p. 128-129). Playing on Orual's sexual fears and jealousies, Lewis can give scope to the great divide between a woman's experiences: virgin and wife, possessor and possessed, seeker and initiate. "'This shame has nothing to do with He or She. It's the being mortal—being, how shall I say it? ....insufficient'" (p. 114).

One of the most arresting descriptions and one of the most effective that Lewis ever drew verbally is the vision which Orual has of Psyche's palace. It is this premonition of the truth which will plague her rational belief until finally she accepts. In the misty, grey, coldness of twilight

... when I lifted my head and looked once more into the mist across the water, I saw that which brought my heart into my throat. There stood the palace, grey—as all things were grey in that hour and place—but solid and motionless, wall within wall, pillar and arch and architrave, acres of it, a labyrinthine beauty....unbelievably tall and slender, pointed and prickly as if stone were shooting out into branch and flower (p. 132).

This description is effective because of its suggestiveness. Unlike Narnia or Perelandra which are demonstrably other worlds, this is a vision in the here and now, the cold, windy reality of the mountains. It is as real and as tantalizing to us as it is to Orual, and its very brevity and simplicity give that sense of momentary insight Lewis is trying to achieve.

On the second quest, now hardened and prepared to use every means to force Psyche's return, even blackmail through love, Orual extends her debate to another level. The Fox has described her as being "'transported beyond all reason and nature. Do you know what it is? There's one part love in your heart, and five parts anger, and seven parts pride'" (p. 148). This journey in rain and wet is an inversion of the first. Orual, in her jealousy and possessiveness, reveals to Psyche the depth of her degradation so that the unveiling is really Orual's.

"You are indeed teaching me about kinds of love I did not know. It is like looking into a deep pit. I am not sure whether I like your kind better than hatred. Oh, Orual—to take my love for you, because you know it goes down to my very roots and cannot be diminished by any other newer love, and then to make of it a tool, a weapon, a thing of policy and mastery, an instrument of torture—I begin to think I never knew you. Whatever comes after, something that was between us dies here" (p. 165).

Out of the fierce light of revelation "the look of lightning, pale, dazzling, without warmth or comfort, showing each smallest thing with fierce distinctness...." (p. 172) speaks the unmistakable voice of a god and comes the symbolic devastation of the holy valley. "It was all bare rock, raw earth, and foul water...." (p. 175), and Psyche's weeping is all that remains to Orual.

The final half of the book represents a third quest. Orual has been told that she also is Psyche, and she must determine what that message means. Her external aim was "to build up more and more that strength, hard and joyless, which had come to me when I heard the god's sentence; by learning, fighting, and laboring, to drive all the woman out of me" (p. 184). But her rule is just, her commands fair, her bravery tested in battle against the coward Argan. Her trials are not unlike those of Psyche. She offers herself, cynically, as a sacrifice for her country. Though she succeeds brilliantly as queen, she cannot subdue the woman Orual, and the poignance of her response to hearing the cry, and her reaction to the banquet, a moment of great external glory, show the growing inner depths of her soul. Separated from Psyche, the Fox, and now Bardia—she, a woman in a world of men's pleasures, "the gobbling, snatching, belching, hiccuping, the greasiness of it all...." (p. 224)—she plays the role Weston designs for the Green Lady. "I was a great, sad queen in a song. I did not check the big tears that rose in my eyes. I enjoyed them. To say all, I was drunk; I played the fool" (p. 224).

The fourth quest, ostensibly a royal progress, ends where the first quest began, with the knowledge that her motives in loving Psyche had been, as she claimed, misinterpreted. Thus she confronts the gods, and they return the answer which serves as the climax of the book.

The final quest is an internal one, made up of dreams and visions. A casual encounter with Redival's first love reveals to Orual the loneliness of her sister. The dream of Psyche sorting seeds, the sorting of the complex motives which make up Orual's quest and love, gives way to the brilliant dialogue of the two women who love Bardia.

Descending through the recognition of her possessive love for Bardia in the dream of herself as Ungit, as a swollen spider, filled with men's lives, an image reminiscent of Tolkien's Shelob, she attempts suicide.

Unveiled at last, she faces the truth. This section of the book is its weakest. Though Lewis is not as explicit as he might have been, he does not resist the temptation to make his meaning absolutely clear when a little veiled mystery might give a better conclusion. The surrealistic trial provides a moment of high intensity, but we come down to be lectured by the Fox and led through the moving story of Psyche now seen through Orual's corrected vision. The happy ending, bringing a vision of beauty to Orual is pleasant but distracting, and we feel that Lewis would have achieved a more dramatic effect if he had not pursued Orual quite so far into the vision of Paradise which ends the novel. Like so much of Lewis's fiction, once the quest is over, there is a tendency to linger long and to attempt a description of the state of transcendent being, of being in Joy. That never succeeds in rounding the quest out because it is the struggle to reach the goal, not the goal itself, which occupies the thrust of the action.

The major achievement in this final work is the fitting of Lewis's traditional themes into a structure which was rather foreign to his own experience as a writer of fiction and somewhat hostile to the purpose he would put it to. The novel, and I would call this book a novel, is rarely used in modern days as a vehicle for spiritual revelation. Par Lagerkvist has experimented with this technique, but generally speaking the novel of this sort has been neither wholly successful nor popular. Lewis's novel cannot be said to be popular, but his success in using the techniques of the modern novel is readily apparent. The predominance of dialogue, the swift movement of the action, the simple and often earthy language all contribute to the sense of realism which pervades his descriptions of Glome and his account of the life and times of Orual. The novel would not be properly called a modern one because its subject is historical or at least archaic. So it is perhaps unjust to suggest that Lewis, at the end of his career as a fiction writer, was a successful modern novelist; but it would be appropriate to point to the evidence at the end of his career, of a high degree of technical skill in characterization, dialogue, plot movement, and tension. Technically it is one of the most polished of his works, and there is no evidence that he spent any time in extensive revision.

We may wonder why he called it a "flop." The answer to that is neither simple nor easy, but it must lie in the way we read the book. As Lewis suggested, a good book compels a good reading which consists of the control over our emotional and intellectual response exerted by the book. When the structure and theme work together in an organic fashion, the result is an unmistakable elevation of our response to what Lewis calls the level of best reading, where the meaning is sanctified by the expression of it. That response is felt in some of the *Chronicles* and in *Perelandra* but not in *Till We Have Faces*. Perhaps the method of self-analysis which Lewis employs in presenting this story is antipathetic to this response. We are too often on guard, with Orual, to see what trick the gods will play next.

The atmosphere is too stern and cold to be conducive to lulling our disbelief into the acceptance of impossibilities as probabilities. Perhaps it requires the tinge of *faerie* which Lewis admired in other writers and understood so well how to manipulate himself. The very theme, based on the question of belief, may work against the organic sanctity of meaning which I have described earlier as Lewis's highest achievement. We admire the accomplishment of this book, but we do not feel it keenly, and though the quest for belief in Joy draws us on to grasp the theme intellectually, we still prefer compulsion to persuasion.

Conclusion

When we survey the work of C. S. Lewis, we might pause to look at the role we have played as readers and critics and assess whether or not we have become the good readers Lewis wished for and the disinterested critics he described in *An Experiment in Criticism*.

Lewis has clearly distinguished his reader from his critic. The good reader is what most of those who have come this far in this book are: open, receptive to all that the works have to offer, ready to look, listen, and receive. I would like to think I have been that kind of reader, too. Unlike the evaluative critics, we are content to look at what Lewis has created for us and test it according to the yardstick of how much it compels our participation, how far it enlarges our being, and what sort of window on the world it opens and invites us to look through.

Judged by these standards, I would say that Lewis measures up very well. We have seen the steady growth of his work from *The Pilgrim's Regress*, where he begins to develop the basic theme and form of his work, the *Logos* and *Poiema*: what he calls these essential and interrelated aspects of literature. The good reader feels the theme more than the form, or at least more potently and quickly. It takes the critic in us to take a closer look at form and that look will deepen and broaden our appreciation of what Lewis meant to say to us.

Lewis had essentially one message: the search for truth begins with a longing to recapture an impression which has tantalized our senses and our minds. We look and long to find that truth and search through life in books and music, in paintings, in nature, and in other people, and ultimately we discover that we have mistaken the earthly experience for a spiritual one. We have accepted the reflection of the truth for its reality. Our corrected vision shows us that we must move further in and higher up to achieve the satisfaction of that longing, to come to what Lewis calls Joy.

The road to such an understanding takes us down many side paths through allegory and science fiction, by fairy tales and satire, and finally through myth itself. Lewis began his journey, like his pilgrim, John, by trying to comprehend how the seeker after truth, longing for another vision of his island, could find his way through a world of choices among reason, relativism, aestheticism, eroticism, broad and sensible churchmanship, and all the snares which confront John in *The Pilgrim's Regress*. For John, Lewis, and the good reader, the first attempt to find the path is not further in, but a regress back from a false goal. Lewis shows us that we essentially cannot get ahead until we clear the path of the obstacles and distractions which a conventional, cluttered, contemporary life surrounds each of us with and smothers us in each day. He probably had to fight his way through this slough of despond as a newly converted journeyer on the way to truth just as we wade through his allegorical presentation.

With the space trilogy, we begin to ascend both a literary landscape and an imaginative terrain which open our eyes as good readers to new sights. Allegory is old and somewhat musty. Science fiction brings a new whiff of the unknown. So we begin with Ransom, walking our way into an adventure, unexpected, unsolicited, and even unwanted. For both Ransom and us there comes the revelation that we are weak, small, failed creatures in a universe so brilliant and mighty that our pride is reduced to utter insignificance. We appreciate Ransom in a way we could not even find to empathize with John. We are Ransom, discovering that it takes the human imagination to perceive that Deep Heaven is there not to be conquered and exploited by men like Weston and Devine, but as the real home of man, the center of meaning of the quality called *hnau*, where all creatures have a place under the watchful guidance of Maleldil.

With *Perelandra*, we come into even closer contact with Ransom who is now our emissary to a new world. We long to be there with him, experiencing the delights and the anguish of his unique situation. We watch and listen as he makes his way around the new paradise, and we wait to see if he will be able to rise to the demands placed on him. More than in the earlier two works, we empathize with the protagonist and become involved in his decisions and his fate. Lewis has invited us and now compels us to feel Ransom's disorientation when he enters the new, watery, and unanchored world of the Green Lady. We are almost physically present when Ransom eats the berries and steps into the bubble trees. We sense his awe of the Green Lady, his reverence for her beauty and her majesty. We quail at the appearance of Weston and are as frustrated and enraged as Ransom when he begins to lose the debate. The final decision to "do his best" comes to us with all the imaginative power of a similar turning point in our own spiritual careers.

Perelandra offers more imaginative food than either of the two previous works. As readers, we applaud Lewis's achievement in moving us to such a compelling other world and successfully coupling this sensuous experience with a theme which touches us more deeply and intimately than he had achieved before. We come away changed, transformed for a time by the knowledge that we are Ransom and must perform the tasks set for us or else run the risk of failing not only ourselves but all human kind.

The last book of the trilogy takes us yet further in, if not further up, on the road of meaning and creative achievement. Jane and Mark Studdock are more approachable than Ransom is now, and we see in them Lewis's reduction of his vision to our daily life with its selfishness and petty ambitions. A less pleasant book than *Perelandra, That Hideous Strength* is nonetheless gripping in its psychological truth and its insistence upon the force of evil as it operates through willing subjects like Frost and Wither. There is a coldness about the book that grips and holds us like walking out of an Indian summer sun into the chilling shade of a late November afternoon. We are gripped by Lewis's conviction that only a clear and selfless examination of our own motives and goals can lead us to know what way we should pursue in achieving the good and our salvation.

We are both Jane and Mark, lost in the coils of self-love and intellectual pride, and as they become absorbed and then submerged in the ever larger world of forces that vie for their souls, we come to see our own littleness. Yet we find that they and we are important; each of us must choose. From the least important to the most, each character in this work chooses and reaps the rewards of that choice. There is no way to escape the pursuit of the strength which invests Ransom and Merlin and all of St. Anne's. As readers, we are swept along at an almost breathless pace as Lewis unfolds episode after episode, firing our imaginations by allusions and often by violent action. The book is apocalyptic, and we leave Jane and Mark in their self-transcendent state, smaller and more human, more lovable and loving than ever. Ransom, at the other extreme, symbolizes the final goal, the journey to the world beyond worlds and beyond description.

Now we come to a plateau on the road. *The Screwtape Letters* and *The Great Divorce* serve to reinforce what we have felt to be the themes of the earlier works. Lewis has been instructing us by means of imaginative and pleasurable forms, using allegory and science fiction techniques to steal past our defenses and to open intellectual and spiritual windows by enchanting our disbelief. We accept the stories and loosen our hold on many cherished prejudices just long enough to break from the confines of our shell of rationalism, skepticism, and sophistication to become infected by the romantic longing which started us on this journey in the first place.

The Screwtape Letters is an earthbound book. Lewis does not hide our mortality, pride, greed, sloth, and pettiness from us here. In fact, by showing how easily we are manipulated, he makes us painfully aware of just who we are, not as in the three earlier books where he hinted at who we may in fact become. The reader's view is not up, but down and in, toward a rigorous self-examination. The humor and ironic inversion help us to take the bitter dose, and a bitter picture we have of what we find when we stray too far from the path. Never before or again did Lewis draw such an utterly convincing and realistic portrait of evil incarnate—and Screwtape is only a minor devil, at that.

The Great Divorce continues this direction and gives us once more instruction on what we might do to achieve the growth which will take us further on. We do not see far ahead on that road, only a shortsighted view of a longer vista. Our concern here is for lessons which may be hard to apply to ourselves. Rather than admitting that we are Ransom and Jane and Mark, we may find ourselves rejecting the Big Ghost or the Dwarf and his Tragedian because Lewis is not creating that imaginative reality that compels us to enter this book. Some readers may prefer this less romantic and more intellectually orderly approach. I would rather be lulled and charmed and then caught in the net of Lewis's meaning.

Now comes a dramatic climb on the road of Lewis's meaning. In a single bound, we find ourselves in higher country surrounded by talking animals, witches, Marshwiggles, and Aslan. The imaginative and creative leap here is enormous. The Narnia books are more than simply *in* another world; they create and establish that world as the proving ground for obedience, belief, sacrifice, redemption, and so many more self-transcendent messages that we cannot record all of them or all of the levels at which they affect us as readers: as children, then as adults, as nonbelievers and believers. All readers seem to agree, even if they agree about nothing else to do with Lewis, that here he made his most influential and lasting mark on literature and on his readers.

As he said himself, it is the Lion who draws them all together and brings us up and into his country. We find it easy to become a child again, if we need to in order to enter this world; we slough off our old skin of prejudices and preoccupations and have our vision cleared and renewed for the make-believe we are offered. We weep with Digory and Jill, we lie with Edmund and complain with Eustace. We laugh with Lucy and share both her shame at overhearing her friends and her rapture when she reads the story of refreshment. We feel the pain of Aslan's death and the joy of his return. We move about in Narnia and Calormen and over the ocean to the uttermost East. We become more than we were by letting go of the security of our little, realistic lives and by trying the back of the wardrobe to see if there just might really be another world beyond.

We can safely look back down the road and see how far Lewis has brought us on the journey toward the truth. From this distance, *The Pilgrim's Regress* looks, with its allegorical stereotypes and headlines, like those pale ghosts who hobble over the hard realities of Paradise. The great achievement of the Narnia stories is that they have brought us such a distance with such effortlessness. Lewis learned steadily by writing just how to make each reading better for his reader and at the same time easier.

The last climb is to myth. I suppose that the natural conclusion of my analogy of the road would make *Till We Have Faces* Lewis's destination. On the contrary, Lewis never arrived, at least in this life, at his destination, literary or spiritual. He was still growing; and so the end of our journey is only a stop at a shrine by the wayside where we now, as pilgrims of the way, pause to do homage to the enshrinement of Lewis's last enchantment. Lewis had been making for this spot from the beginning of his career when he told us that myth is the most perfect literary embodiment of truth. He worked his way, step by step, up to the point where he could take a myth and show its truth by turning a new light upon its many-faceted meaning and thus make it shine for his readers. The story of Cupid and Psyche now comes alive for us as the ultimate revelation of belief to the most recalcitrant of unbelievers. We may see ourselves in Ransom and Jane, Lucy and Eustace, but Orual is as far beyond us as Psyche is beyond Orual. The story and characters move away into a mythic distance as we reach out to draw them closer. So we are drawn beyond ourselves to see the one central story that we have followed so long displayed in all its grandeur.

Lewis did not have to walk back along the route John took when he came back to find that his Island was really right where he had first seen it, at home. Lewis never left home. He invited the reader to enter his familiar world of struggling humanity and observe the human journey to understanding and salvation. He makes us so at home and comfortable that we slip into his worlds and accept his message with ease, delight, and gratitude.

Lewis's critic might want a word or two before the end. His duty as outlined by Lewis is to establish an inner silence within which he can receive the literary work without letting his own feelings and desires get in the way. I hope I have in some measure been Lewis's critic, as each reader of Lewis should also attempt to be. It is much harder to be such a critic than to be the good reader. Good readers tend to become enthusiasts and sometimes fanatics about their subject. That is why Lewis wanted critics to keep us on the road and out of the ditch. As critics, we look at what Lewis has done, and if it is good, we try to multiply, safeguard, or prolong those good moments for future readers.

We look at Lewis's *Poiema* and find there a studied and disciplined and intelligent grasp of the art of enchantment. Lewis clearly knew how to give a reader a good read. He began with himself and studied his own reaction, discovering that it was when the moments of sensuous intensity were supported by an underlying and often undiscerned meaning that they affected him most keenly. As he studied works which he admired, not necessarily those critics told him to admire, he came to believe that the way to move readers was to draw them, by highly imaginative structures like fairy tales or satires or science fiction, out of their protective and secure literary shells and entice them into a new world where highly charged experiences offered the author the opportunity of depositing a message. It was not until he had a message worth expending his creative imagination on that he turned to the work which forms the basis of this study.

As critics we look at *The Pilgrim's Regress* and see many moments that are not worth preserving. The structure and the theme work in unison by the traditional method of the allegory determining each step of John's progress in belief. We can nearly always predict what will happen next. There is too much information and too little feeling. Lewis seems to be teaching us rather than leading us to understand that we may find the vision we long to recapture in the least likely place, right in front of our eyes, if we only have the simple clear vision to see it and the common sense to look. There is little enchantment here and much to be studied and pondered over.

Lewis learned how to become a better enchanter. In *Out of the Silent Planet*, we critics notice a definite shift to a more imaginative form. Characters begin to spring to real life. We care about Ransom's fright and come to detest Weston and Devine. We empathize with Hyoi and look with interest at the *harandra* and with growing awe at the brilliance of Deep Heaven. Now we are freer to hear and touch and feel a new world that comes increasingly to matter to us as Ransom's journey draws him closer to Meldilorn. There are bad moments when Lewis lets Augray discourse and Weston rant, but as critics we agree that the form begins to suit the theme, reinforcing meaning and underlining truth.

In *Perelandra* we are overwhelmed by the sensuous beauty of this new world. We ask where Lewis found the talent for the incredible creation of this planet. We swim and float with Ransom, and gradually, carefully guided by Lewis's craftsmanship, we gain a sense of orientation and learn our way and discover our task and become, before we are aware, a living part of an adventure which holds deep meaning. Color, movement, characterization, and the subtle orchestration of debate all converge to meld the meaning and structure into one—not perfectly seamless, but organic unity where we feel and think simultaneously. Lewis makes us actively care that Ransom chooses wisely. We are involved in the outcome of this tale because we have been drawn up and into an action on a grand scale. Subtly Lewis has made us at home with Ransom and then shown us that as Ransom is more than we supposed, so too are we.

That Hideous Strength surprises our critical judgment because it shifts the creative ground we have been standing on from heaven to earth and causes us to reconsider Lewis's method. He can construct an earthly environment for his message as skillfully as a cosmic one. We approve of the inversion of vision from high to low, the reduction of the macrocosm to the microcosm, the diminishment of the action to humbler figures like Jane and Mark. The dialogue in college, the mystery of Merlin, the diabolical last supper are only a few of the moments worth preserving. The humble entry of Jane into St. Anne's, the moment when Mark says "no," and the arraying of the nuptial chamber all show us Lewis's new skill in using little touches.

The Screwtape Letters and *The Great Divorce* are masterful pieces but not of the sort we have just passed through. Wit and irony are the tools of *Screwtape* and pointed *exempla* in a dreamvision style those of *The Great Divorce*. We would be poor critics if we failed to acknowledge Lewis's very real achievement in these two short works. He manages by direct, frontal attack, to prove that evil exists, that it can kill souls, that it destroys by stealth, and that our major protection against it is laughter. He states also that we may be offered salvation but unless we actively seek to accept it, we will probably remain in the lonely isolation of the shadowy land.

Our chief delight, the moments we would most like to share and save, to safeguard and multiply, are those in the Narnia books. We will probably not agree about all those we would use to show how profoundly Lewis had achieved an art that enchants, but we know that he worked to make his stories simple, his characters accessible, his message oblique, and his plots engaging. Tolkien suggests that there is an elvish craft involved in writing the fairy tale. Lewis never claims that for himself, but we sense as critics that he was a conscious artist as he created these works. We have watched him move from story to story, building the land of Narnia in our imaginations, with its creatures and landscapes, its lands and customs, its dynasties and finally its decline and destruction. The moments which we would preserve are those I have earlier called moments where the style unites organically with the meaning to sanctify that meaning. One example will do for all: when Lucy looks into the book of spells in *The Voyage of the 'Dawn Treader,'* we know that she has seen God, and we feel through her that we have, too, even though neither she nor we actually see anything concrete in Lewis's description of the scene. We feel the truth in his description of her action because the structure of the scene with its magic incantations and book of spells underlines and reinforces the spell which Lucy falls under. From a simple act of *faerie* we get the beatific vision.

We look at the last work and wonder. Lewis liked this book, and he put much of his finest effort as a novelist into its construction. He lavished thought and skill on the creation of Orual, even on Trom and Redival and Ansit. He probed deeper here into the psychology of his characters and constructed a country and culture in which Orual could play out her tortured quest for the truth. He used a myth and created through it another myth of love and sacrifice which leads to the ultimate truth. We critics point to Lewis's mastery of fiction in this complex and disturbing, almost modern book, and lay before those who have not yet met Lewis his final artistic achievement.

As critics we have spent more time analyzing what Lewis did as a writer than as readers we did in responding to what he was writing about. Indeed, we are foolish to attempt to separate the form and meaning even this long. Lewis's significance cannot be measured in parts, only as a whole. It cannot be measured separately by reader or by critic. To approach Lewis as he would perhaps have done himself, we must put reader and critic aside and open the door to a new adventure prepared by our desire to receive what lies beyond the cover, waiting to draw us in to further mystery, back to remembered Joy, and up into meanings which will enrich the rest of our lives.

Endnotes

Chapter I

1. Greeves-Lewis correspondence. MSFAC, Bodleian, b. 49, item #20, dated "early 1915?". The originals are housed in the Lewis collection of Wheaton College, Wheaton, Illinois. MSFAC refers to copies of these originals. Bodleian refers to original letters housed in the Bodleian Library Lewis Collection, Oxford University. These originals are catalogued and housed by box, (b.) and item (#). Hereafter cited simply as "Greeves" or in the case of other correspondents, the correspondent's name, and then the box, item, and date. The Greeves correspondence is now published under the title, *They Stand Together*, ed. Father Walter Hooper, New York: Macmillan. Parentheses around dates indicate uncertainty in dating. Hereinafter cited as *Together*. *Together* p. 62 [Nov. 17, 1914].
2. Greeves, b. 49, #33, dated ("spring 1916?"). *Together* p. 70 [May 4, 1915].
3. Greeves, b. 50, #131, October 6, 1929. *Together* p. 312. (Of Siegried Sassoon he wrote—"a horrid man.") *See* b. 50, #15 (late Sept. 1918), *Together* p. 232.
4. Greeves, b. 49, #131 (early 1917 May). *Together* p. 197 [August 4, 1917].
5. *Letters of C. S. Lewis*, ed. W. H. Lewis (London: Geoffrey Bles, 1966), p. 28. To Arthur Greeves (undated). Hereafter cited as *Letters. Together* p. 95.
6. *Letters*, p. 29. To Arthur Greeves (undated). *Together* pp. 109-110.
7. *Letters*, p. 30. To Arthur Greeves, 27 September 1916. *Together* p. 112.
8. Greeves, b. 49, #215 (June) 1918. *Together* p. 217 [May 29, 1918].
9. C. S. Lewis, *Surprised by Joy* (New York: Harcourt Brace, 1955), p. 4.
10. Greeves, b. 49, #215, 225 (June) 1918. *Together* pp. 218, 219, 221 [May 29, 1918, June 3, 1918].
11. Greeves, b. 50, #29 (1918) reference to "Ask, King Mark and Tristram," *Together* p. 239; b. 50, #56 (Easter Vac. 1919), reference to "Merlin and Nimue," *Together* p. 254; b. 50, #60 (May 7, 1919), *Together* p. 251, reference to "Venus"; b. 50, #69 (*circa* July 14, 1919), reference to "Medea," *Together* pp. 167, 256.
12. Greeves, b. 50, #29 (1918). *Together* pp. 238-39.

13. Greeves, b. 50, #31, New Year's eve 1918. *Together* p. 205.
14. Greeves, b. 50, #40 (Feb. 1919). *Together* p. 245.
15. Greeves, b. 50, #69 (*circa* July 1919). *Together* p. 256.
16. Greeves, b. 50, #78 (March 1920). *Together* p. 266.
17. English Literature Manuscripts, Bodleian Library: c/220/4, #39 (April 1920). These manuscripts are letters to other correspondents and hereafter will be cited by Bod. with the call number, e.g., c/220/4, and the date and name of correspondent if not included in the text.
18. Bod., c/220/4, #43, Sept. (1) 1920.
19. Bod., c/220/4, #61, July, 1921: Leo Kingsley Baker.
20. Bod., c/220/4, #17, November 4 (1925).
21. Greeves, b. 50, #89 (June 1920). *Together* p. 281.
22. Greeves, b. 50, #94 (Sept. 1920). *Together* p. 261.
23. Greeves, b. 50, #100 (Autumn 1920). *Together* p. 263.
24. Greeves, b. 50, #47, March 2, 1919, Sunday. *Together* p. 250.
25. *Letters*, p. 91. From his journal, 9-16 July 1924.
26. Bod., c/220/4, #125 (1928).
27. Greeves, b. 50, #139, Thursday, October 17 (1929). *Together* p. 316.
28. "The Problem of C. S. Lewis." *See*: David Holbrook, "The Problem of C. S. Lewis," *Children's Literature in Education*, No. 10 (March 1973), pp. 3-25.
29. Greeves, b. 50, #159 (Jan. 1930). *Together* p. 328.
30. Greeves, b. 50, #202. *Together* pp. 363-64.
31. Greeves, b. 50, #206, June 31, 1930. *Together* p. 366.
32. Greeves, b. 50, #208, July 31, 1930. *Together* p. 368 [July 8, 1930].
33. Greeves, b. 50, #225, August 18, 1930. *See also*: Roger Lancelyn Green and Walter Hooper, *C. S. Lewis: A Biography* (London: Collins, p. 110, hereafter cited as *Biography*). *Together* pp. 378-79.
34. Greeves, b. 50, #247, September 15, 1930. *Together* p. 392.
35. Greeves, b. 51, #15, February 1, 1931. *Together* p. 405
36. Greeves, b. 51, #21, March 29, 1931. *Together* p. 410.
37. Greeves, b. 51, #21, March 29, 1931. *Together* p. 410.
38. Greeves, b. 50, #243, August 31, 1930. *Together* pp. 388-89.
39. Greeves, b. 51, #42, September 22, 1931. *Together* p. 422.
40. Greeves, b. 51, #51, October 18, 1931. *Together* p. 427.
41. *Surprised by Joy*, pp. 219-220.
42. *Letters*, p. 228, 23 April 1951, to Dom Bede Griffiths.
43. *Letters*, pp. 147-148, 17 January 1932, to his brother.
44. Greeves, b. 51, #53, November 8, 1931. *Together* p. 430.
45. Greeves, b. 51, #67, Easter Sunday, 1932. *Together* p. 442.
46. Greeves, b. 51, #76, February 4, 1933. *Together* p. 449.
47. Greeves, b. 51, #80, March 25, 1933. *Together* pp. 451-52.
48. Greeves, b. 51, #92, September 1, 1933. *Together* pp. 460-61.
49. MSFAC, c/53, #15, September 2, 1937, to Owen Barfield.
50. MSFAC, c/47, #7, January 8, 1936, to Dom Bede Griffiths.
51. Greeves, b. 51, #121, December 9, 1935. *Together* p. 476.
52. Bod., c/220/4, #129, January 11, 1939, to A. K. Hamilton Jenkin.

53. Bod., c/220/1, #8, July 9, 1939, to Sister Penelope.

54. Bod., c/220/1, #5, November 4, 1940, to Sister Penelope.

55. *Letters*, pp. 182-183, to Dom Bede Griffiths.

56. *Letters*, p. 182.

57. Bod., c/220/4, #147, August 13, 1941, to Miss Jacob.

58. *Letters*, p. 194, October 9, 1941.

59. *Letters*, p. 195, November 9, 1941.

60. Bod., c/220/1, #24, August 22, 1942, to Sister Penelope.

61. *Letters*, p. 203-204.

62. Bod., c/220/1, #28, March 25, 1943, to Sister Penelope.

63. Bod., c/220/2, #30, undated, to E. R. Eddison.

64. Bod., c/220/2, #39, undated, to E. R. Eddison. "Sir yd you knowe ought of the nuptiall practices and amorous carriages of beares, fayle not to let me knowe for I have brought in a beare in the book I now write and it shall to bedde at the end with the other."

65. Bod., c/220/2, #41-42, to E. R. Eddison.

66. Bod., c/220/2, #46, February 5, 1943, to E. R. Eddison.

67. Bod., c/220/2, #60, April 25, 1943, Easter Day, E. R. Eddison to Lewis.

68. Bod., c/220/2, #64, April 29, 1943, to E. R. Eddison.

69. *Ibid.*

70. Bod., c/220/2, #69, 10/ VIII/43, E. R. Eddison to Lewis.

71. Bod., c/220/2, #204, April 29, 1946, to Hamilton. In a letter to an admirer of Eddison's, Lewis described his own reactions to Eddison's work. "Eddison is among the most startling literary experiences I have ever had. All modern prose looks *thin* after it. (There are of course thin beauties, and by *thin* I don't mean bad. But it is the opaque blaze in Eddison wh. is so wonderful, the enamel). I don't think Eliot cd. ever like it. It's as if you offered smoking venison and a great port to a man who wanted thin bread and butter. But I know one *youngster* who admires him: so there's hope."

72. MSFAC, c/47, #48, December 20, 1946, to Dom Bede Griffiths.

73. *Letters*, p. 205.

74. Greeves, b. 51, #112, December 26, 1934. *Together* p. 470.

75. Bod., c/220/3, #33, January 4, 1947, to Ruth Pitter.

76. Bod., c/220/3, #20, July 24, 1946, to Ruth Pitter.

77. *Ibid.*

78. Bod., c/220/3, #66, August 10, 1946, to Ruth Pitter.

79. *Ibid.*

80. Bod., c/220/3, #63, appended to letter, 29/9/48, to Ruth Pitter.

81. *Ibid.*

82. Bod., c/220/1, #35, 31/8/48, to Sister Penelope.

83. *Letters*, p. 222, undated, 1949.

84. MSFAC, c/53, #199, 30/5/49, to Owen Barfield.

85. Bod., c/220/2, #154, December 23, 1950, to Sheldon Van Auken.

86. Bod., c/220/1, #181, 28/3/53, to W. L. Kinter.

87. Bod., c/220/4, #234, March 24, 1954, to Miss Rhona Bodle.

88. Bod., c/220/4, #188, November 16, 1956, to C. A. Brady.

89. MSFAC, c/53, #73, February 5, 1960, to Susan Salzberg.

90. Bod., c/220/4, #188, November 16, 1956, to C. A. Brady.
91. MSFAC, c/48, #113, 28/9/55, to Mr. Henry.
92. MSFAC, c/48, #123, August 18, 1953, to Allen C. Emery, Jr.
93. Bod., c/220/1, #185, July 30, 1954, to W. L. Kinter.
94. Bod., c/220/3, #153, April 15, 1954, to Joan Lancaster.
95. MSFAC, c/48, #63, July 4, 1955, to Father Peter Milward. "In my own view *Perelandra* is worth 20 *Screwtapes*." MSFAC, c/48, #163, April 28, 1958, to Martin (Kilmer). Regarding *Perelandra*: "I enjoyed that imaginary world so much myself that I'm glad to find anyone who has been there and liked it as much as I did."
96. Bod., c/220/2, #120, March 14, 1954, to Harry Blamires.
97. *Biography*, p. 241.
98. *Letters*, p. 271. The original letter reads "come by" for "know."
99. Bod., c/220/4, #167, December 4, 1953, to Mrs. Katherine Farrer.
100. Bod., c/220/1, #140, June 27, 1953, to Dr. Warfield Firor.
101. Bod., c/220/3, #120, December 21, 1953, to Ruth Pitter.
102. Bod., c/220/4, #19, December 22, 1953, to Joy Gresham.
103. Bod., c/220/4, #23, January 20, 1956, to A. C. Clarke.
104. MSFAC, c/48, #143, December 28, 1954. This is a facsimile of a copy of the letter. *See: Letters*, p. 260.
105. *Letters*, p. 261, to a Lady, February 2, 1955. Also Bod., c/220/3, #204, April 2, 1955, to Katherine (Mrs. Katherine Farrer).
106. Bod., c/220/3, #204, April 2, 1955, and #205, July 9, 1955, to Katherine Farrer.
107. Bod., c/220/2, #83, October 5, 1956, to Kathleen Raine. *See also*: MSFAC, c/48, #163, August 7, 1957, to Anne and Martin (Kilmer).
108. Bod., c/220/3, #182, April 20, 1959, to Joan Lancaster. "I am glad you liked *Till We Have Faces*, because so few people do. It is my biggest 'flop' for years, and so of course *I* think it is my best book."
109. *Letters*, pp. 278-279. September 2, 1957.
110. Bod., c/220/3, #166, June 26, 1956, to Joan Lancaster. *See also: Letters*, p. 270.
111. Bod., c/220/3, #180, August 31, 1958, to Joan Lancaster.
112. MSFAC, c/48, #166, September 29, 1958, to Martin (Kilmer).
113. Bod., c/220/3, #135, January 31, 1956, to Ruth Pitter.
114. Bod., c/220/3, #147, August 20, 1962, to Ruth Pitter.
115. MSFAC, c/53, #63, June 3, 1956, to Mr. Keith Masson.
116. Bod., c/220/1, #122, October 15, 1949, to Dr. Warfield Firor.
117. *Letters*, p. 307, September 17, 1963.
118. MSFAC, c/53, #5, December 10, 1952, to Mrs. Sandeman.

Chapter II

1. *An Experiment in Criticism* (Cambridge: Cambridge University Press, 1961), p. 141. Hereafter cited as *Experiment*.
2. *Experiment*, p. 136.

3. *Experiment*, p. 132.

4. W. W. Robson, "C. S. Lewis," *Cambridge Quarterly* (Summer, 1966), pp. 252-272 and *Critical Essays* (London: Routledge and Kegan Paul, 1966), pp. 56-75. References are to *Critical Essays*, p. 65.

5. Robson, p. 67.

6. Robson, pp. 73, 65 respectively.

7. Robson, p. 74.

8. *See* Chapter I, note 33. Greeves, b. 50, #225, August 18, 1930. Also note 100, Letter to the Milton Society of America, December 28, 1954.

9. Robson, p. 171.

10. Robson, pp. 58, 65.

11. *Experiment*, p. 115.

12. *Experiment*, p. 116.

13. *Experiment*, pp. 137-138.

14. *Experiment*, p. 139.

15. *Experiment*, p. 85.

16. *Experiment*, p. 132.

17. *Experiment*, p. 19.

18. *Experiment*, pp. 82-91.

19. *Experiment*, pp. 91-92.

20. *Experiment*, pp. 33-34.

21. *Experiment*, p. 21.

22. *Experiment*, p. 112.

23. Robson, p. 65.

24. *Experiment*, p. 92.

25. *Experiment*, p. 92.

26. Experiment, p. 120. This quotation comes from Matthew Arnold, *Pagan and Medieval Religious Sentiment.*

27. *Experiment*, p. 120.

28. *Experiment*, p. 120.

29. *Experiment*, p. 121.

30. C. S. Lewis, *Of Other Worlds* (New York: Harcourt Brace Jovanovich, 1975), p. 10. Hereafter cited as *Worlds*.

31. *Worlds*, "On Stories," p. 17.

32. "On Stories," p. 17.

33. "On Stories," p. 10.

34. "On Stories," p. 12.

35. "On Stories," p. 15.

36. "On Stories," p. 20.

37. "On Stories," p. 21.

38. "On Stories," p. 18.

39. *Worlds*, "On Three Ways of Writing for Children," p. 23.

40. *Worlds*, p. 29.

41. *Worlds*, "Sometimes Fairy Stories May Say Best What is to be Said," p. 38.

42. *Worlds*, p. 36.

43. *Worlds*, p. 37.

44. *Worlds*, "On Science Fiction," p. 70.
45. *Worlds*, pp. 65, 69.
46. C. S. Lewis, *Selected Literary Essays*, ed. Walter Hooper (Cambridge: Cambridge University Press, 1969), p. 286. "Psycho-Analysis and Literary Criticism." Hereafter cited as *Essays*.
47. *Essays*, p. 287.
48. *Essays*, p. 288.
49. *Essays*, p. 290.
50. *Experiment*, "On Myth," pp. 43-44.
51. Robson, p. 69.
52. *Worlds*, "On Criticism," p. 44.
53. *Worlds*, p. 46.
54. *Worlds*, p. 50.
55. *Worlds*, p. 52.
56. *Worlds*, p. 51.
57. *English and Medieval Studies Presented to J. R. R. Tolkien on the Occasion of his Seventieth Birthday*, ed. Norman Davis and C. L. Wrenn (London: George Allen and Unwin, 1962), p. 303.
58. *Worlds*, "On Criticism," p. 56.
59. *Worlds*, p. 57.
60. *Experiment*, pp. 75-76.

Chapter III

The Fiction

1. Robson, p. 58.
2. Robson, pp. 57-58.
3. Clyde S. Kilby, *The Christian World of C. S. Lewis*. William L. White, *The Image of Man in C. S. Lewis*. Gunnar Urang, *Shadows of Heaven*. Dame Helen Gardner, *C. S. Lewis*. Charles S. Moorman, *Precincts of Felicity*. Chad Walsh, *The Literary Legacy of C. S. Lewis*. Jocelyn Gibb, ed., *Light on C. S. Lewis*, and numerous unpublished dissertations, especially: Albert F. Reddy, *The Else Unspeakable: An Introduction to the Fiction of C. S. Lewis*. University of Massachusetts, 1972, Ph.D. Dissertation, *DAI*, 2949-A.
4. Robson, pp. 67-68.

The Pilgrim's Regress

1. C. S. Lewis, *The Pilgrim's Regress* (Grand Rapids, Michigan: Wm. B. Eerdmans, 1973). Hereafter cited as *Regress*.
2. Greeves, b. 50, #206, June 31, 1930. *Together* p. 366.
3. Greeves, b. 50, #206, June 31, 1930. *Together* p. 366.
4. Greeves, b. 51, #73, December 4, 1932. *Together* p. 445. *See: Biography*,

p. 128. The book was written during a fortnight holiday in Ireland.

5. Greeves, b. 51, #119, December 9, 1935. *Together* p. 474.
6. *Letters*, pp. 248-249, 19 January 1953, to Mrs. Edward A. Allen.
7. *Regress*, p. 10.
8. For a comprehensive plot analysis *see* Clyde S. Kilby, *The Christian World of C. S. Lewis* (Abingdon: Marcham, 1965), pp. 25-36.
9. *Regress*, pp. 26-27.
10. *Regress*, p. 86.
11. *Regress*, p. 24.
12. *Regress*, p. 38.
13. *Regress*, p. 120.
14. *Regress*, p. 176.
15. *Regress*, p. 14.
16. *Regress*, p. 13.

Out of the Silent Planet

1. *Surprised by Joy*, pp. 6, 13.
2. *Surprised by Joy*, p. 15, note 1. *See also Worlds*, "Preface" by Walter Hooper, vi, "Boxen is empty of poetry and romance."
3. *See* Corbin Carnell, *Bright Images of Reality*.
4. Greeves, b. 49, #20 (early 1915); #56 (October 1916); #151 (May) 1917; and b.50, #41 (February, 1919); #100 (Autumn 1920); #123 (1929).
5. *Surprised by Joy*, pp. 15-17.
6. Greeves, b. 50, #123, April 22 (1929), regarding *Bleheris,* a work of Lewis's. *Together* p. 302.
7. Greeves, b. 50, #60 (February, 1919). *Together* p. 251.
8. Greeves, b. 50, #159 (January 1930), *Together* p. 328; #206, June 31, 1930, *Together* p. 366; #219, same date, *Together* p. 375.
9. Greeves, b. 51, #25, February 1, 1931. *Together* p. 405.
10. *Ibid. Together* p. 405.
11. Bod., c/220/3, #33, January 4, 1947, to Ruth Pitter.
12. *Letters*, p. 205. October 29, 1944, to Charles A. Brady.
13. Bod., c/220/1, #181, March 28, 1953, to W. L. Kinter.
14. Bod., c/220/3, #33, to Ruth Pitter; c/220/3, #197, July 11, 1963, to Joan Lancaster. Bod., c/220/3, #201, January 31, 1960, to Alan Hindle.
15. J. P. Pick, Colin Wilson, E. H. Visiak, *The Strange Genius of David Lindsay* (London: John Baker, 1970), pp. 46, 85, 109.
16. *Ibid.*, p. 98.
17. *Ibid.*, p. 115.
18. Bod., c/220/4, #11, December 7, 1943, to A. C. Clarke.
19. *Ibid.*
20. W. Olaf Stapledon, *Last and First Men* (London, 1930), p. 240.
21. Stapledon, pp. 332, 339.
22. Stapledon, p. 63 ff.

23. Stapledon, pp. 219-220. *See also*: Angele B. Samaan, "C. S. Lewis, the Utopist, and his Critics," *Cairo Studies in English* (1963-66), pp. 137-166, ed. Magdi Wahba. Published by The Anglo-Egyptian Bookshop, 165 Mohamed Farid Street, Cairo, U.A.R. Samaan suggests that Alcasan is a parody of this section of Stapledon's book and that Stapledon is the person on whom Weston is based. *See* especially p. 158.
24. *Worlds*, "A Reply to Professor Haldane," p. 78.
25. MSFAC, c48, #63, July 4, 1955, to Father Peter Milward.
26. *Letters*, p. 167, to Sister Penelope, July 9, 1939.
27. Milward, July 4, 1955.
28. *Letters*, p. 166.
29. Bod., c/220/1, #172, November 27, 1951, to W. L. Kinter.
30. Bod., c/220/1, #167, January 14, 1951, to W. L. Kinter.
31. Bod., c/220/2, #64, April 29, 1943, to E. R. Eddison.
32. *Worlds*, "A Reply to Professor Haldane," p. 77.
33. *Worlds*, p. 77.
34. *Worlds*, "Unreal Estates," p. 88.
35. Bod., c/220/1, #172; #64, to E. R. Eddison.
36. Bod., c/220/4, #141, July 3 (1941), to Miss Jacob.
37. Robson, p. 60.
38. C. S. Lewis, *Out of the Silent Planet* (New York: Macmillan, 1972), p. 55. Hereafter cited as *Planet*.
39. Bod., c/220/2, #26, September 2, 1957, to Jane Gaskell. *See also: Letters*, p. 278.
40. *Ibid*.
41. *Worlds*, "On Stories, " p. 10.
42. *Worlds*, p. 15.
43. *Worlds*, p. 12.
44. Robson, p. 60.
45. *Planet*, p. 31.

The Dark Tower

1. *Planet*, p. 160.
2. *The Dark Tower*, ed. Walter Hooper (New York: Harcourt Brace and Jovanovich, 1976), p. 19. Hereafter cited as *Tower*.
3. *Tower*, p. 48.
4. *Tower*, p. 49.
5. *Tower*, p. 68.
6. *Tower*, p. 76.
7. *See* "A Note on *The Dark Tower*," by Walter Hooper, pp. 92-98 in *Tower*. Hooper arrives at many of the same conclusions.
8. *Tower*, p. 78.
9. *Tower*, p. 87.
10. David Lindsay, *A Voyage to Arcturus* (London: Ballentine, 1972).

Perelandra

1. *Letters*, p. 195, November 9, 1941, to Sister Penelope.
2. *Letters*, p. 200, May 11, 1942, to Sister Penelope.
3. Bod., c/220/1, #11, November 8, 1939, to Sister Penelope.
4. *Letters*, p. 167.
5. *Ibid.*
6. Bod., c/220/1, #4, October 4, 1940, to Sister Penelope.
7. Bod., c/220/1, #5, May 4, 1940, to Sister Penelope.
8. Bod., c/220/1, #9, November 9, 1941, to Sister Penelope.
9. *Letters*, p. 188, July 20, 1940, to his brother regarding *Screwtape*.
10. Bod., c/220/4, #147, August 13, 1941, to Miss Jacob.
11. *Letters*, p. 182, April 16, 1940. *See also: Letters*, p. 195, November 19, 1941, to Sister Penelope.
12. *Letters*, p. 195, November 9, 1941, to Sister Penelope. *See also: Biography*, p. 170.
13. MSFAC, c/54, #28, n.d.
14. MSFAC, c/54, #8, n.d.
15. *Letters*, p. 160, Letter to the Milton Society of America, December 28, 1954.
16. Bod., c/220/3, #33, January 4, 1947, to Ruth Pitter.
17. *Ibid.*
18. *Planet*, p. 91. Note spelling with an "e."
19. For a pictorial representation of the scene, *see: Horizon*, May 1959, pp. 64-69. Painting is by James Lewicki.
20. C. S. Lewis, *Perelandra* (New York: Macmillan, 1968), p. 35.
21. *Perelandra*, p. 50.

That Hideous Strength

1. Bod., c/220/2, #39, to E. R. Eddison, received by Eddison on December 20, 1942.
2. Bod., c/220/2, #64, to E. R. Eddison.
3. Greeves, b. 51, #153. *Together* pp. 499-500.
4. Bod., c/220/1, #22, September 24, 1943, to Sister Penelope.
5. Bod., c/220/1, #25, #27, to Sister Penelope.
6. Bod., c/220/1, #28, to Sister Penelope. *The Great Divorce* also mentioned as likely to appear in August 1945, actually was published in 1946.
7. Bod., c/220/1, August 22, 1942, to Sister Penelope.
8. Bod., c/220/1, #18, February 20, 1943, to Sister Penelope. *See also: Letters*, p. 203.
9. *Ibid.*
10. Bod., c/220/1, #19, March 25, 1943, to Sister Penelope.
11. *Letters*, p. 203, February 20, 1943, to Sister Penelope.
12. Bod., c/220/1, #20, August 10, 1943; #22, September 24, 1943; #23,

October 5, 1943, to Sister Penelope.

13. Bod., c/220/2, #28, November 16, 1942. The bracketed section was deleted from a draft but appears in the original: "Of which I have right good exaumple by a foolish book (on the *novello*) that came late to my hands, made by some poore seely wench that [seeketh a B. Litt or a D. Phil,] when God knows shad a better bestowed her tyme [makynge sporte for som good man in his bed and bearing children for the stablishment of this reaulme] or else to be at her beads in a religyous house."

14. *Letters*, p. 184, April 18, 1940, to a Lady.

15. Bod., c/47, #179, October 31, 1949, to Vera Mathews. Lewis mentions the deer in the Magdalen grove, "(rather like my Bragdon Wood, only not as large)" and any visitor will clearly be reminded of his description of Bragdon's mystery and peace on looking in on the Magdalen Deer Park.

16. MSFAC, c/53, #95, Whitsunday, May 27, 1928, to Owen Barfield.

17. Bod., c/220/2, #163, February 26, 1955, to Sheldon Van Auken.

18. Bod., c/220/1, #185, July 30, 1954, to W. L. Kinter.

19. "Psycho-Analysis and Literary Criticism" and "The Anthropological Approach," in *Selected Literary Essays*.

20. *Letters*, p. 211, undated: 1947, to Mrs. Frank J. Jones.

21. *Letters*, pp. 179-180, March 26, 1940, to a Lady.

22. C. S. Lewis, *That Hideous Strength* (New York: Macmillan, 1968), pp. 70-71. Hereafter cited as *Strength*.

23. MSFAC, c/48, #63, July 4, 1955, to Father Peter Milward.

24. Robson, p. 60.

25. *Worlds*, "Unreal Estates," p. 88.

26. *Letters*, p. 207, September 26, 1945, to I. O. Evans.

27. *Strength*, p. 89.

28. Robson, p. 60.

29. *Strength*, p. 50.

30. *Strength*, p. 361.

31. *Strength*, p. 291.

32. Bod., c/220/2, #233, December 21, 1959, to Martin Skinner. Lewis, reacting to a poem of Skinner's which presents Merlin, gives his own analysis of what Merlin should speak like, an accurate assessment of his own accomplishment with Merlin in his dialogues with Ransom.

   "But what you haven't so far got is a style in which great or wise and almost numinous persons can speak. Thus all the good dialogue goes to the enemies.... Merlin must speak like one whose father was an aerial daemon, and A. [Arthur?] like one who has been in Avalon."

33. Robson, p. 60.

34. *Worlds*, part 3.

The Screwtape Letters

1. Bod., c/220/1, #59, June 18, 1956, to Sister Penelope. Later she would ask for and be given his permission to sell the *ms.* in order to raise money

for a project the Sisterhood had underway.

2. Bod., c/220/3, #33, January 4, 1947, to Ruth Pitter. The Preface, though written later, covers these matters fairly thoroughly.
3. Bod., c/220/2, #120, to Harry Blamires.
4. MSFAC, c/47, #48, December 20, 1946, to Dom Bede Griffiths.
5. C. S. Lewis, *The Screwtape Letters* (New York: Macmillan, 1971), p. ix. Hereafter cited as *Screwtape*.
6. *Screwtape*, "Preface," p. ix.
7. *Screwtape*, p. xiii.
8. *Screwtape*, p. 36.
9. *Screwtape*, p. 50.
10. *Screwtape*, p. 164.

The Great Divorce

1. *Biography*, p. 220.
2. Bod., c/220/1, #27, January 3, 1945, to Sister Penelope.
3. Bod., c/220/1, #28, May 28, 1945, to Sister Penelope.
4. *Letters*, p. 259, December 22, 1954.
5. Bod., c/220/1, #185, July 30, 1954, to W. L. Kinter.
6. C. S. Lewis, *The Great Divorce* (New York: Macmillan, 1971), p. 29. Hereafter cited as *Divorce*.
7. *Divorce*, p. 128.
8. John D. Haigh, *The Fiction of C. S. Lewis*. Unpublished dissertation. University of Leeds, 1962, p. 95.
9. *Biography*, p. 221.
10. Haigh, pp. 95, 103.

The Chronicles of Narnia

1. *See also*: Walter Hooper, "Narnia: The Author, The Critics, and the Tale," *Children's Literature*, 111 (1974), pp. 12-22.
2. Haigh, p. 109.
3. Bod., c/220/1, #181, March, 28, 1953, to W. L. Kinter.
4. Robson, p. 68.
5. MSFAC, c/48, #113, September 28, 1955, to Mr. Henry.
6. MSFAC, c/48, #123, August 18, 1953, to Allen C. Emery, Jr.
7. *Letters*, p. 260.
8. *Worlds*, p. 42.
9. *Biography*, p. 239 and Bod., c/220/4, #188, November 16, 1956, to C. A. Brady. "It might amuse you that the whole thing took its rise from nightmares about lions which I suddenly started having."
10. *Biography*, p. 240.
11. Walter Hooper, "Past Watchful Dragons," in *Imagination and Spirit* (Grand Rapids: Eerdmans, 1971), pp. 306-307.
12. *Biography*, p. 248.

13. *Worlds*, pp. 12, 15.
14. *Worlds*, p. 15. *See also: Letters*, p. 283, to Mrs. Hook. Also: MSFAC, c/4, #145, December 29, 1958. This letter indicates that the "as if" in Aslan as Christ is not allegory. The point Lewis makes in the letter and in the essays is that we are, in fact, in another world, not just this world with a few changes. This is a crucial point because it is the "otherworldi-ness" which attracts us, seduces us, and gets us past the dragons. Narnia is not England anymore than the Shire is. One of Lewis's greatest achieve-ments, parallel to Tolkien's in *The Lord of the Rings*, is his creation of a world. Certainly the only other fiction in which he approaches this success is *Perelandra*, and there I have pointed to the dichotomy and opposition between the world and what takes place in it. In Narnia there is no disunity of description and meaning.
15. *Worlds*, pp. 28, 36. *See also: Letters*, p. 307, December 2, 1962, to an Enquirer, on the restrictions imposed by this form of fiction.
16. *Worlds*, p. 27.
17. Father Walter Hooper suggested that Lewis may be known for these stories because they are classics in children's fiction.

The Lion, the Witch and the Wardrobe

1. *Letters*, p. 203, February 20, 1943, to Sister Penelope.
2. Haigh, pp. 250, 255.
3. Haigh, Chapter IV, "The Children's Fantasy."
4. C. S. Lewis, *The Lion, the Witch and the Wardrobe* (New York: Macmil-lan, 1974). All references to the *Chronicles* in the text are to Macmillan editions.
5. *Letters*, p. 279, September 2, 1957, to Jane Gaskell. Lewis counsels her to do nothing which would wake the reader or bring him back with a 'bump' to the common reality.

The Voyage of the 'Dawn Treader'

1. *Biography*, p. 243.
2. *See: The Tolkien Reader*, "On Fairy Tales," for Tolkien's definition of the "escape of the prisoner" as opposed to the "flight of the deserter."

The Horse and His Boy

1. *Biography*, pp. 244-245. Dedicated to his stepsons to be, David and Douglas Gresham, there are certain interesting parallels between the doubles Cor and Corin and these two boys. But since Lewis did not yet know them well, pushing the possible connections would hardly be reasonable or sensible.

2. *Biography*, p. 245.
3. *Biography*, p. 244.

The Magician's Nephew

1. *Biography*, p. 242.
2. *Biography*, pp. 247-248.
3. *Biography*, p. 248.
4. A letter to Greeves, dated (probably October 1916) MSFAC, b. 49, #56, refers to this name: "...perhaps they are caught like Wan Jadis in the Gray Marish on the way to the country of the past." *See* Chad Walsh, *The Literary Legacy of C. S. Lewis* (New York: Harcourt Brace and Jovanovich), p. 128. Wan Jadis is a knight who appears in *Bleheris*.
5. MSFAC, c/47, #50 to Dom Bede Griffiths.
6. Bod., c/220/1, #185.

The Last Battle

1. Bod., c/220/3, #153.
2. Bod., c/220/3, #154, May 7, 1954.
3. Bod., c/220/1, #7, May 15, 1941, to Sister Penelope. *See also: Letters*, pp. 193-194.
4. One might suspect Lewis of an indirect criticism of British socialism in Shift's promises.

Till We Have Faces

1. *Biography*, p. 261.
2. Bod., c/220/3, #204, April 2, 1955, to Katherine Farrer.
3. Bod., c/220/4, #166, June 10, 1952, to Katherine Farrer.
4. Bod., c/220/3, #205, July 9, 1955, to Katherine Farrer.
5. *Letters*, p. 271, September 22, 1956.
6. Bod., c/220/3, #182, April 20, 1959, to Joan Lancaster.
7. Interview with Owen Barfield, July 16, 1974, London.
8. C. S. Lewis, *Till We Have Faces* (Grand Rapids, Michigan: Wm. B. Eerdmans, 1972).
9. *Biography*, p. 265.
10. Bod., c/220/2, #83, October 5, 1956.

Index